LIGHTS
OUT!

LIGHTS OUT!

TEN MYTHS ABOUT (AND REAL SOLUTIONS TO)
AMERICA'S ENERGY CRISIS

SPENCER ABRAHAM

WITH WILLIAM TUCKER

ST. MARTIN'S PRESS NEW YORK

www.stmartins.com

Library of Congress Cataloging-in-Publication Data

Abraham, Spencer.
    Lights out! : ten myths about (and real solutions to) America's energy crisis /
Spencer Abraham.—1st ed.
        p. cm.
    ISBN 978-0-312-57021-7
    1. Power resources—United States.   2. Energy conservation—United
States.   3. Energy policy—United States.   I. Title.
    TJ163.25.U6A267 2010
    333.790973—dc22   2009047032

First Edition: July 2010

10 9 8 7 6 5 4 3 2 1

With love and affection to my children
Betsy, Julie, and Spencer

CONTENTS

ACKNOWLEDGMENTS

Attempting to properly acknowledge all the important people who have contributed to a book of this nature is in many ways an impossible task. I would like to thank all my colleagues at the Department of Energy; in particular, I want to acknowledge Kyle McSlarrow, who provided insight and advice as I worked on this book, and I am grateful for his help and his friendship.

Since leaving public office I have worked with an outstanding group of individuals in a consulting business that we began in 2005. I am deeply grateful to my two partners, Joe McMonigle and Majida Mourad, for their contributions to this book.

A number of other people who work or worked in our firm have helped with this project. Jason Van Buren worked with me at the Department of Energy and is a very able, hardworking energy advisor at our firm. Special thanks go to Jenny Stein, who worked as an associate at our firm when I began this project and helped me during its early stages. Thanks also to Carly Swanberg, who also assisted in early development efforts. Perhaps the toughest assignments as the book moved through its various development stages were handled by Brittany Curley, who had the unenviable tasks of attempting to interpret my editing efforts and pulling together the various disparate pieces of the manuscript into one coherent draft. Finally, I had the benefit of having several talented interns assist with various research assignments. Andrew Kane was a great help in the early stages of this effort and I am very appreciative of his work, as I am of Kathleen Hsu's work in the later part of the process. James McAleese took on the lion's share of the fact-checking work on the book and proved outstanding in this assignment.

The actual process of launching this effort began some two years ago when I had the good fortune to meet my collaborator, William Tucker, an outstanding energy analyst and policy expert. I met Bill through my literary agents, Lynn Chu and Glen Hartley. It was really Glen and Lynn who first encouraged me to consider writing a book on energy and I am grateful for their support as well as Lynn's hard work in helping find a publisher interested in presenting a book of this kind. I want to thank St. Martin's Press, a great company whose support through this process has been outstanding. In particular, I want to thank my editor, Phil Revzin, who had faith in this work from day one and who was willing to put his institution behind a first-time writer like me.

I have enjoyed a very successful professional career and have been able to do so because I have been blessed with a family that provided encouragement for my efforts throughout my life. No one could have had a more supportive set of parents than I. The rest of my family, from sisters, to cousins, to in-laws, has also provided unceasing support to me and I will forever be in their debt for all they have done.

My three children, Betsy, Julie, and Spencer, have been involved in nearly all of my professional activities whenever it was possible. They mean everything to me. Finally, I want to acknowledge with love and affection my wife, Jane. It was my great fortune that this wonderful woman came into my life and we have enjoyed a fantastic life together ever since. None of my achievements, including this book, would have been possible without her.

For weeks I had been quietly lobbying to land a seat in the cabinet of newly elected president George W. Bush. I hailed from Michigan, one of the nation's biggest labor states, and had served on the Commerce, Science and Transportation Committee in the U.S. Senate, so my name was being mentioned as a candidate for secretary of Labor or Transportation.

Still, people in the know considered me a long shot. I did, too. Now, at 5:00 P.M. on New Year's Eve 2000, I would finally get the word. A White House operator on the line informed me that Andy Card, the president-elect's chief of staff designate, wanted to talk to me.

Must be a no, I figured. Wouldn't George Bush be on the line if I were being offered a job? After a brief exchange of season's greetings, Andy got down to business. "I am calling to see if you would be interested in serving as secretary of . . ."

"Yes," I interrupted, the words jumping out of my mouth.

"Energy."

Energy? Not labor or transportation? Euphoria jostled with concern. I was happy to be given the chance to serve in the cabinet, a longtime professional goal of mine. Moreover, as I quickly thought it over, energy was a much more exciting portfolio. It was an area in which both the president-elect and vice president-elect had worked for years and thus would likely be a priority in the

new administration. Plus it was a rising area of international challenge, even though it had been simmering on the back burner in
recent years. There was only one problem. As a member of the Senate, I had cosponsored a bill to abolish the Department of Energy!

"There's one little thing that might become an issue," I told
Card sheepishly. "I'm sure it's only minor, but in the interest of full
disclosure . . ."

I think he expected me to say something about drug addiction
or a mental disorder. I told him the truth.

"Oh, that's all right," he said with a sigh of relief. "I'll get back to
you as soon as I convey all this to Governor Bush."

For more than an hour I sat staring at the telephone. Finally the
call came back. "The president-elect is comfortable so long as you
still don't want to abolish the department you're being asked to
head." I told him I was on board all the way. "All right, be in Aus-
tin tomorrow for a formal interview."

Less than forty-eight hours later, I was standing beside the pres-
ident- and vice president–elect hearing my name announced as
the next secretary of energy.

A few weeks later, my former colleagues in the Senate were having quite a bit of fun at my expense. "Do you still favor abolishing
the Department of Energy?" was the first question at my confirma-
tion hearing—from a friend and fellow Republican. Needless to
say, I was prepared with an answer.

"I changed my mind," I explained, "after Congress passed legislation in 2000 reorganizing the department. I now believe it is
much better organized and will be easier to manage in an intelligent fashion." Amid grins and winks from friends on both sides of
the aisle—all of whom had changed their positions on issues at various times over the years—we moved on to other topics.

The rest of the hearing was uneventful—actually quite boring.
It got so mind numbing that a friend sitting behind me in the
hearing room actually fell asleep during one of my more long-
winded answers. As he dozed off, his image was captured by the
TV media and the footage became the only part of my hearing to

make the network news. It seemed to underscore the noncontroversial nature of my nomination. The committee approved me unanimously.

Finally, on January 20, 2001, a few hours after President Bush was sworn into office, the full Senate formally confirmed my nomination. I learned the news in the middle of the inaugural parade when a military aide tapped my wife and me on the shoulder and asked us to follow him to be sworn in. We soon found ourselves standing with Colin Powell, Donald Rumsfeld, Paul O'Neill, Don Evans, and Anne Veneman and their families in a theater-like room in the Old Executive Office Building next door to the White House. After a long wait, a door opened and in walked a fairly nondescript fellow who announced he was clerk of the White House Office of Administrative Services. He would be swearing us in.

Everyone was mildly astonished. "Shouldn't the president be performing this ceremony?" someone piped up.

"No," he told us, "the president doesn't have the authority to swear in federal officials." So much for the president's broad constitutional powers! "As president of the Senate, the vice president does have the authority," he went on, "but unfortunately the vice president is not available. He's still watching the parade."

So, with a few shrugs, things got started. Colin Powell, his wife Alma, and their children mounted a small stage, and soon America had its first black secretary of state. A few minutes later, it also had its first Lebanese-American secretary of energy.

And so began my journey into the exciting, enormously important world of energy. Along the way I gained something akin to a doctoral degree in energy economics and a masters degree in energy technology. I found myself traveling the world in pursuit of new energy alliances—and traveling up to Capitol Hill to try to develop alliances with my former colleagues as well. I learned that much of the conventional wisdom and rhetoric concerning energy is nothing more than a set of myths propagated by advocates at both ends of the political spectrum to advance their causes. And I learned the real facts about our energy challenges—a set of facts that demand far more attention than we have been willing to devote to them.

Perhaps most important, I determined that because the politics of energy and the environment have come to so dominate all serious discussion, that we have refused to do what is necessary to protect our economic security and national interest, leaving our nation at grave risk on a variety of fronts.

Just how much politics interferes with energy policy making became painfully apparent to me almost the moment I was sworn into office. While my cabinet colleagues were enjoying a brief honeymoon in their new jobs, I was suddenly plunged into the deep end by the ongoing electricity blackouts that were strangling California. Within hours of the inaugural ball, I was on the phone with California governor Gray Davis, trying to find out what Washington could do to help.

His answer was simple. Just before leaving office, my predecessor, Energy Secretary Bill Richardson, had used the emergency powers of the executive branch to require power-generating companies to sell power to California's nearly bankrupt utilities—for five days. The order was about to expire on day three of the new administration. Governor Davis told me the California legislature was about to pass a law allowing the state to stand behind the utilities' future power purchases, but it would take two weeks to get that accomplished. Meanwhile, the people of California needed electricity. In short, he needed an immediate extension of Richardson's order.

The following morning, a Monday, the first business day of the Bush administration, I found myself at the White House briefing the president's senior aides on the California situation. To my amazement, there was a wide divergence of opinion at 1600 Pennsylvania Avenue about extending the order. Some people felt requiring power companies to sell to the unsecured and potentially bankrupt utilities was wrong. Others seemed less than enthusiastic about helping the home state of the left-wing Hollywood elite, who they felt had created the crisis themselves by refusing to build new power plants.

"But we can't just stand by while the lights go out on thirty-six million people," I argued. Finally, the recommendation went up to the president to extend the emergency order for two weeks. Later that day the White House called to express further concerns about this interventionist approach. I gave them a sober assessment of the situation. Not extending the order threatened widespread blackouts that would result in stupendous economic losses, widespread crime, and threats to the physical safety of millions of people.

I was informed that same day that the recommendation had been accepted. A day later I was told this was just the beginning. The president had decided to put together a multiagency task force chaired by Vice President Richard Cheney that would develop an energy plan to guide the country. Already, energy was emerging as a central concern of the new administration.

The National Energy Policy Development Group operated for four months. In the end, we produced a report of over a hundred pages containing dozens of crucial recommendations. Almost nobody ever read it. Instead, all the attention focused on the makeup of the committee and how we operated. Democrats, still angry over the demise of Hillary Clinton's Health Care Task Force in the early 1990s, were looking for payback. Environmentalists and the mainstream media joined the charge.

Most of our recommendations focused on the environment, renewable energy, energy conservation, and developing better relations with our international trade partners. In the press, however, the plan was said to be all about drilling and environmental degradation. The vice president made things worse when he gave a speech just prior to the plan's release in which he said, "Conservation may be a sign of personal virtue, but it is not a sufficient basis all by itself for a sound, comprehensive energy policy." While a perfectly accurate statement, critics began

repeating the statement but omitting the qualifier, "all by itself."
Overnight, we became the "Anti-Conservation Task Force." And
so it went.

The Clinton task force had gotten into trouble because it had
included outsiders, such as Ira Magaziner, who were given quasi-
official status even though they did not have government positions. We decided to avoid this problem by including only cabinet
members and agency administrators. It was your classic inter-
agency policy group. Nonetheless, the press scurried around trying to uncover "secret" members or meetings and challenging the
White House's assertions of executive privilege. Even though we did
everything by the book, it ended up seeming like a clandestine operation.

What we recommended was not much different from what the
president had campaigned on without controversy during the
election. The only significant additions were a few proenviron-
ment, conservation, and alternate-energy proposals. As secretary
of energy, I was dispatched to Capitol Hill to defend it. Within a
short time it became clear to me that virtually no one in Congress
or the press had actually read the plan. Both defenders and critics
alike were just reciting their standard lines on energy policy. The
rhetoric on all sides was almost totally devoid of seriousness, ex-
treme, and often silly. The cumulative results were catastrophic in
terms of addressing our critical energy challenges.

Congress spent four years debating our legislative proposals
and in the end could only pass a compromise bill that was defi-
cient in many ways. Meanwhile, our energy and environmental
problems only worsened, presenting serious threats to our economic and national security. It was a hard lesson in how difficult it
is to get anything done on these issues in Washington due to political factors.

This pattern of dealing with energy problems began long before
George W. Bush took office and continues today. Our failure to act
responsibly on these problems has intensified them without resolution. We have a very short time left in which to act.

The purpose of this book is to put these threats into perspective and to illuminate the hard choices we have to make as a nation. My goal is to state in stark terms the extent to which we have failed, so far, to meet these challenges and the consequences of this continuing failure. Finally, I hope to outline a realistic agenda of what needs to be done if we truly wish to address our challenges before it becomes too late.

Introduction

For decades American politicians have debated energy and environmental policy. Virtually every significant interest group has weighed in on these issues, and energy has been a front-burner media story throughout this period as well.

Unfortunately, much of this discussion has taken place against the backdrop of myth and misinformation. Far too often the real facts about energy have been obscured and public policy debates have, as a result, been generally unproductive.

Thus, despite the very serious energy threats facing America and the rest of the world, we are still confronting extremely large challenges as we enter the second decade of the century.

The purpose of this book is to help us focus on the real threats to the energy marketplace and to outline some of the hard decisions that need to be made soon if we are going to address them effectively. Along the way, we will puncture some of the long-standing myths about energy that have undermined our ability to capably deal with our problems. We will also provide the reader with some of the most important facts about energy that must be understood if we are to honestly address our challenges.

Through this analysis the reader will gain a better sense of why we have been so ineffective in dealing with our energy threats to date and come to recognize that mistakes have been made on all sides when it comes to formulating energy policy. Finally, this book will provide a blueprint for addressing our toughest energy challenges. To get there, though, it is important to begin with a better fundamental understanding of the world of energy.

BOOK 1

Energy Myths and Facts

CHAPTER 1

Ten Myths About Energy

1. We Can Achieve Energy Independence.

2. If Gas Prices Rise Abruptly, It Must Be Due to an Oil Company Conspiracy.

3. Global Warming Is a Complete Hoax.

4. Nuclear Plants Are Just as Unsafe as They Were at Three Mile Island.

5. Renewable Energy Is Universally Popular and Completely Safe for the Environment.

6. We Are Entering an Age of Natural Gas That Will Follow the Ages of Coal and Oil, and It Will Largely Solve Our Energy Problems.

7. Raising CAFE Standards 30% Will Produce a 30% Reduction in Oil Consumption.

8. Electrical Transmission Lines Cause Cancer.

9. All the Government Has to Do Is Choose the Right Energy Technology and Subsidize It.

10. All We Need Is a New Manhattan Project to Solve Our Energy Problems.

As secretary of energy, I found that energy is a very complicated topic—both from a scientific and a political point of view. For instance, someone might suggest that to save energy it makes sense to launch a national campaign to get everyone to turn off their computers when they're not using them. Sounds easy. But is it? For instance, how do we know turning off computers is going to save electricity? Some people say computers use more electricity because there's a big burst of electrical consumption when they are turned on. Well, maybe we should design a computer that doesn't have that burst. Is that possible? No, wait a minute, maybe the best strategy is a sleep mode where the computer draws very little energy when not being used. Hasn't someone already invented that? Yes, they have, and it works well. But maybe we should be doing the same thing for DVD players. You see how things can get complicated.

It gets even more complicated because the process of decision making is constantly distorted by politics. Some individual or group is always certain they have the *only* solution to the energy problem. Senators from coal states are morally certain the answer is coal. Various pundits are certain that global warming is a hoax and that human beings cannot possibly do anything so harmful to the environment. Environmental groups believe with their heart and soul that drilling in the Arctic National Wildlife Refuge will mean desecrating the crown jewels of America's natural heritage, while the senator from Alaska says drilling is the way to wean us off foreign oil.

All this is part of the deliberative process. That's what democracy is about. But while I was perfectly willing to accept input from advocacy groups and congressional representatives, I soon learned that there are certain energy arguments and assertions that just aren't true. It is often said, "It's not the things people don't know that get them into trouble but the things they know that just ain't so." From my perspective, it became clear that the first step in understanding our energy problems is to recognize that much of the accepted wisdom about energy simply isn't true, and that the propagation of these myths has proved fatal to the development of good energy policy. For that reason, I'm going to start this book by briefly outlining ten myths about energy that we have to clear away before we begin the real business of trying to figure out how to solve our energy problems. In part these myths have been responsible for the failure of our energy policy efforts to date, as will be discussed in later chapters. Thus, an examination of energy mythology is in order. So here we go.

Myth 1. We Can Achieve Energy Independence.

As late as the 2008 presidential campaign, candidates were still running around suggesting that America can achieve energy independence. This is a myth that must be put to rest once and for all. We aren't ever going to be able to provide ourselves with all our energy. We live in an interdependent world and we might as well get used to it. The key consideration is that America's oil production peaked in 1970. At that point in high-demand periods we were producing 10 million barrels a day and consuming around 14 million. Today we import over 60% of our oil.

We may be able to cut down on some of that dependency or shift it to nations we aren't so worried about. But we're never again going to produce all of our own oil, and we're not going to be replacing that oil with any other fuel or technology in the foreseeable future.

Congressmen on both sides of the aisle seem to have a hard time accepting that. Free-market enthusiasts promise that high prices will automatically call forth new production. Technology enthusiasts say we can come up with some new discovery that will solve the problem at a stroke. Environmentalists say all we have to do is mandate greater conservation and start phasing in renewable energy.

There is some potential in all these approaches, but together they don't add up. There is only so much oil in the ground. Some older wells in Texas are now pumping almost all water. Enhanced recovery methods may force out a little more of this oil, but domestic production will never supply the nation the way it did in the 1950s. Likewise, mandated standards may give cars greater gas mileage but they cannot guarantee that people will *buy* these cars or, when they do, that they won't just drive them more and use the same amount of fuel. Conservation and efficiency measures can slow the rate at which our energy consumption *increases* year to year, but they can rarely, if ever, produce an overall decline in energy use. Population increases and growing affluence cancel them out.

In the long, long run gasoline-powered cars may be replaced by some completely new fleet running on electricity or hydrogen, but these vehicles would require building a whole new infrastructure to deliver the fuels to consumers. That construction is a long way off, and may never happen. For the present we had best face facts. We are dependent on the rest of the world for much of our oil and will be for a long time to come.

Myth 2. If Gas Prices Rise Abruptly, It Must Be Due to an Oil Company Conspiracy.

Every time the price of gasoline spiked while I was secretary, as certain as the dawn follows the night, the phones rang off the hook at the Department of Energy, particularly at my desk, asking why I wasn't doing something about it. With each run-up in price, congressmen and senators of both parties would call demanding I take action. The suggested actions were usually absurd.

Republicans, supposedly the party of business, often wanted investigations into the energy companies for price gouging. Democrats, supposedly the party of conservation, wanted to slash the federal gas tax or open up the Strategic Petroleum Reserve (SPR) so that people could go on consuming at their accustomed level. I especially appreciated the calls from members of Congress who opposed drilling offshore and in Alaska. Now they wanted those oil companies to start producing oil—pronto! They never understood there might be a connection.

Having served in the Senate for six years, I understand the need to posture during a crisis in order to create the impression that you are doing something for the folks back home. But these guys were always over the top. They couldn't even admit in private that you can't just summon resources out of thin air.

The simple fact is that the price of gasoline is only now catching up to the overall rate of inflation over the last quarter century. As I like to say to audiences, "Name one other liquid that sells for less than three dollars a gallon!" Even milk doesn't sell that cheaply in a lot of places. Americans will pay more for boutique water and gourmet coffee, for liquid plumber, for just about any other fluid you can mention, without complaint. Somehow, though, we have come to believe that the price of gasoline is constitutionally guaranteed to remain below $3 a gallon no matter what happens in other corners of the world.

Think what it takes to provide you with a gallon of gasoline. First somebody has to go out and discover oil through the always chancy process of exploration. Then there is the cost of extracting it from a mile or two beneath the ground in some remote corner of the globe or even under the ocean floor. Then the product has to travel by pipeline to be loaded onto a vessel and carried often thousands of miles across the ocean to a U.S. port or via miles of pipeline. After off-loading, the oil then moves to a refinery where it is blended to some very high specification of gasoline mandated by federal or state law. All along the route here, each player is collecting a piece of the action. Finally the end product is trucked to your part of the world and sold by some guy in your neighborhood who is also trying to scrape out a living. Tack on the 18.4¢ per gallon in federal taxes plus an average of 28.6¢ in state taxes and it seems a miracle that we're paying less than $3 a gallon. But if it jumps above $3 because of a refinery fire, pipeline explosion, or outbreak of a civil war somewhere, it's time to call in the FBI to investigate oil companies or gas station owners.

Conspiracy theories don't get us anywhere. The way to bring down energy prices is to increase our production or decrease our consumption, or—better yet—do both.

Myth 3. Global Warming Is a Complete Hoax.

While we're on the subject of conspiracy theories, let's look at climate change. The myth in some quarters is that it's all a hoax dreamed up by environmentalists who want us to go back to living in the Stone Age. Sure, there has been some exaggeration and the "Climategate" revelations of apparent collusion between some climate researchers to exaggerate their data in late 2009 has further muddied the waters. While there are still doubts about the seriousness of the consequences, the thesis that burning fossil fuels will have an effect on our climate has to be factored into any energy equation.

First, it's unrealistic to think that we can ever know *with absolute certainty* that global warming is really happening. The standards for scientific proof are very strict. You need an experimental object and a "control," which is identical in all ways. Then you subject the two to different conditions. If a difference in outcome occurs, then you have a measurable effect. Think about it. Where are we going to get a "control" to compare what is currently happening on the earth? You'd need another identical planet, wouldn't you? You'd also have to have precise control over the levels of carbon dioxide in the atmosphere in order to predict what would happen on earth in eighty or so years. Obviously, that's not going to happen.

Instead, scientists have tried to predict what will happen by creating computer models. These models are limited and are always going to be in dispute. We will always be working with partial knowledge. No one questions that burning fossil fuels is raising the level of carbon dioxide in the earth's atmosphere. Nor is there any resonable argument over whether the earth's temperature has risen over the past three decades. The question is: Are the two *related*?

Given this uncertainty, the issue is whether we should try to do anything about it. I think the answer is yes. There are plenty of reasons to think that burning fossil fuels may eventually affect the earth's climate and plenty of reasons to be reducing our consumption of fossil fuels anyway. Conventional coal power causes an estimated 24,000 lung-disease deaths a year through its particulate matter and sulfur dioxides. It's worth doing something about them. Furthermore, any effort to control carbon emissions will nudge us toward other technologies and reduce our imports. Our oil supplies are always going to be at risk, so there's plenty of reason to explore electric or hydrogen cars. All these factors come as a bonus to any effort to control greenhouse gases.

Some global warming advocates may be overstating their case, some may be over the top, and some may be attempting to use warming as an excuse to advance a political agenda. But the notion that *all* the scientific evidence suggesting the potential seriousness of CO_2 emissions is a hoax is untenable.

Myth 4. Nuclear Plants Are Just as Unsafe as They Were at Three Mile Island.

Probably nothing had a more chilling impact on nuclear power in America than the events that took place in 1979. On March 16, Hollywood released the movie *The China Syndrome,* starring Jane Fonda, Jack Lemmon, and Michael Douglas, which depicted the near meltdown of a nuclear reactor. On March 28, in a "life imitates art" moment, Unit 2 of Pennsylvania's Three Mile Island nuclear facility experienced a partial core meltdown that constituted the worst nuclear accident in U.S. history. Thirty years later critics still cite Three Mile Island to fight new nuclear plant builds.

That a great deal has changed since 1979 goes without saying as a contemporary viewing of *The China Syndrome* reveals. Fonda plays a TV reporter relegated to covering silly human interest stories by her L.A. station. In her first appearance on screen we see her doing a feature piece in which she unveils an exciting new cultural phenomenon: the singing telegram. That's just the start. Later we see ads for a brand new household product—the microwave oven. Meanwhile, Fonda's camera crew uses reel-to-reel tape recorders and movie film to do its work. No one has a cell phone and the characters use pay phones, which are in abundant supply. Importantly, when Fonda sits down at her desk in the newsroom, she writes her script on a manual typewriter because newsrooms didn't have PCs or word processors in those days. In 1979 correcting IBM Selectric typewriters were replacing "white-out" as the hottest new type of information technology. Just as 1979 newsrooms weren't very high tech in comparison to their counterparts today, neither were nuclear power facilities.

We've come a long way since 1979 in learning how to build and operate nuclear reactors. Although few people realize it, half our fleet of 104 reactors was not completed until after Three Mile Island. Safety features improved a lot over that period. Then in the 1990s a group of new "merchant" energy companies emerged that began buying up reactors and running them better. They've made tremendous improvements in performance and safety records—and learned to run them very profitably at the same time. That's why they want to build more. Added to that is the experience gained in France and Japan, which never stopped building. In fact, three of the world's four largest nuclear companies are foreign owned, and America's only entry, General Electric, now does virtually all its nuclear work in partnership with the Japanese firm Hitachi. Much of the experience in building and operating nuclear reactors is now coming from abroad.

The nuclear landscape has changed drastically since 1979, yet both in Congress and the media, critics of nuclear energy talk as if nothing has changed. This would be like having a discussion about long-distance telephone calls without taking into account telephone deregulation, cell phones, satellites, wireless communication, fiber optics, the Internet, and all the other things that have happened in the last thirty years. We would never consider having an outdated discussion on any other subject. Yet with nuclear power it is somehow routine.

At the time of Three Mile Island, many people who had trained to be plant managers had little more than a high school education. The assumption was that the engineers who designed the reactors were such geniuses that they could build them so nothing could go wrong. This turned out to be a big mistake. Although research had proved it by then, somehow the nuclear industry hadn't gotten the message that *human error* is the main cause of most industrial accidents. Thus, when a small valve got stuck in the Three Mile Island reactor, the automatic safety systems worked fine. The problem was that because the poorly prepared operators were working in a poorly designed control room, they *overrode* the safety mechanisms and caused a meltdown.

The professionalism that goes into running reactors today is light-years ahead. The whole industry is structured completely differently. Now an operator has to study the technology intensively for two years before he can even touch the controls in a nuclear operating room. Before the Three Mile Island incident different utilities owning and operating nuclear reactors barely talked to each other. The valve that failed at Three Mile Island had failed *nine times* before at other reactors, yet the manufacturer had hushed things up. Today the nuclear industry shares so much information it must constantly make sure it is not violating antitrust laws. If the smallest glitch occurs in a reactor somewhere, the entire industry knows about it within a matter of hours. Special emergency teams are ready to be dispatched anywhere in the country at a moment's notice to deal with malfunctions.

That's why the nuclear industry now sets records every year for safety and reliability. In the old days, generating stations were up and running about 60% of the time and some ran less because they were constantly having safety problems. Today the nation's fleet of 104 reactors is operating *90%* of the time. Reactors now run for almost two years straight without shutting down. From 1978 to 1987 there were twenty-three reactor shutdowns of over a year because of equipment and safety problems. From 1988 to 1997 there were twenty-six. Since 1997 there has been only one. The transformation of the nuclear industry is one of the great untold stories of the past decade.

For all these reasons, I don't have any hesitation in saying it's time we should build more nuclear plants.

Myth 5: Renewable Energy Is Universally Popular and Completely Safe for the Environment.

At the U.S. Department of Energy, most announcements tend to be unpopular. As secretary, for example, I had the dubious distinction of releasing the weekly information on the average price of gasoline in the United States. Since prices were usually on the upswing, I was generally in the media telling Americans how much more they were going to pay for gas. It's not the best way to enhance one's popularity. I also had to issue reports on security failures at our nuclear weapons labs, increases in the amount of our oil imports, and a wide variety of other rather negative news.

One day, though, we had a good news story. We were going to increase the expenditures for wind energy research. I figured this was perhaps the only action we might take that would be universally well received. How wrong I was! The very next night, at a charity dinner, I found myself cornered by a lobbyist for one of the animal rights organizations. His group was deeply concerned that birds and bats have a tendency to fly into large windmill blades. Animal rights groups felt our budget increase would add to the slaughter. It turned out renewable sources aren't without their detractors as well.

Like almost every other form of energy generation, renewable sources are perfectly all right as long as they're in someone else's backyard. Offshore winds are extremely strong, for example. Therefore it makes sense to build wind farms off the coast. But the coastline is where many wealthy people have their homes. The prospect of having even a tiny portion of their view disrupted by a forest of wind towers is usually not popular with them. In large measure for that reason, we still haven't managed to build any offshore wind farms despite years of trying.

Not that wind farms are any more popular inland. The truth is that a lot of people don't enjoy living near them. Windmills give off a low-decibel droning sound that some people say drives them almost crazy. There is even a psychological condition describing it called "wind-turbine syndrome." Also, when you're living in a picturesque rural landscape, the sight of a fifty-story tower hovering nearby, always in motion, can be disconcerting. So why not put them where no one lives? Well, wind actually works best on top of mountain ridges, where the wind blows the strongest. But some people consider mountain ridges to be *scenery*. Covering them with giant industrial structures is not everybody's idea of enhancing the landscape.

Solar energy has its detractors as well. In the desert solar collectors will take up a huge amount of land—dozens, perhaps hundreds of square miles. All the land beneath them will be deprived of sunlight, which means whole ecosystems will collapse. On suburban rooftops, people often complain that they make a family home look like an industrial installation and degrade property values. Happily, greater focus on the aesthetics of solar has taken place in recent years, but the stereotype is hard to overcome.

Then there's hydropower, which to some people is "solar energy"; to others the word summons images of "giant dams that drown hundreds of square miles of historic landscape." Polls show that most Americans still think that most of our electricity comes from hydro when it is really only about 6%. It's not likely we'll have any more giant dams anyway because most of the good sites have already been developed. Even then, hydroelectricity, like every other form of energy, has its opponents. Even damming small rivers can interfere with fish migrations. Animal-rights groups, along with the fishing industry, have long opposed hydro because of its impact on fish populations.

Indeed, the federal government regularly pays hundreds of millions of dollars in damages to offset the impact of dams on fish catches. The Bonneville and Grand Coulee dams in the Northwest are particularly expensive. I remember learning this while putting together my first budget as energy secretary. The dams had been called on for particularly large output the previous year, and fish damage payments were so high we had to cut other programs to make them.

People have somehow gotten the impression that renewable energy is a vast bounty of free energy we can tap with almost no environmental impact. Nothing could be further from the truth. In the December 2007 issue of *Scientific American,* three scientists outlined a plan to power the entire nation on solar energy by 2050. All we'd need to do is put up solar panels in the southwestern deserts and pump it off to the rest of the country. The land required would amount to 45,000 square miles—one-third of New Mexico's area. Don't you suppose that might have an environmental impact! I'm a fan of renewable sources, but the notion that expanding their use will be uncontroversial is another myth that we must be prepared to address.

Myth 6: We Are Entering an Age of Natural Gas That Will Follow the Ages of Coal and Oil, and It Will Largely Solve Our Energy Problems.

At some point in my term as secretary, a nice, four-color circular came across my desk. It was illustrated with three separate graphs—coal, oil, and natural gas. Coal, it showed, first mined in the eighteenth century, had peaked toward the middle of the twentieth. It would eventually decline (although not too soon, since we still use it for half our electricity). Oil, first discovered in 1859, really took off with the development of the automobile and was the world's most important source of energy in the last half of the twentieth century. But oil supplies are finite, and it, too, will soon fade.

What comes next is natural gas. Gas was originally regarded as a waste and was flared off in the fields. Not until the pipeline construction of the 1920s did it become a commercial product. Then federal price controls were imposed and production was suppressed for several decades. By 1990, however, the price controls had been removed and production began to soar. Environmentalists became enamored with the idea of substituting natural gas for coal in generating electricity—which had been illegal up to that point—and since then 90% of our new power generation facilities have been gas plants.

All this hit a wall in 2000 when domestic output leveled and prices took a sixfold climb—a steeper run-up than during the Arab oil boycott. This was one factor that contributed to the California electrical crisis. During the Bush administration we spent much of our time trying to open up offshore and federal lands for drilling, hasten the construction of an Alaskan pipeline, and clear the way for natural gas (LNG) imports. In each of these efforts we met with strong opposition from environmental groups—even though many of the same people were simultaneously touting natural gas as the natural replacement of coal. Domestic production remained flat through my entire term and imports from Canada and Mexico crept up to 15%. For some time, it seemed that the notion of gas as a superfuel was over.

As usually happens in America, however, the problem was solved outside of Washington. For decades people in the oil industry had known there were huge reserves of gas in the "tight" rock of shale formations. After 2000, engineers, geologists, and drilling experts finally went to work on the Barnett Shale formation in

Texas. They found that by cracking the rock with water and then employing new horizontal drilling techniques, they could free huge quantities of gas that were formerly inaccessible.

Our gas reserves have since increased nearly 50%. There are shale formations underlying most of the Mississippi watershed, including the huge Marcellus formation that extends all the way into upper New York State. By some current calculations, we may now have enough gas to last us more than 125 years.

But let's be careful. As we saw a decade ago, there are no guarantees. I've seen bubbles occur like this with other resources, only to prove overrated. Already there are some reports that shale wells tend to go into steep decline much earlier than conventional wells, although this is still very much in dispute. Moreover, shale gas is more expensive because of the technology needed to produce it, and prices will have to stay high to recover those costs. Recovery also requires the injection of huge amounts of water, and there are concerns that extensive drilling may affect aquifers. The point is, we are still in the early stages of the shale gas boom and should not get too far ahead of ourselves.

Most important, we should not immediately deploy all these gas supplies to producing electricity while ignoring other options. Generating electricity is probably not the most valuable use of this resource. Gas is arguably much more valuable for home heating and as a feedstock for the chemical and plastics industries. During the high-price years from 2000 to 2006 we saw more than 100,000 manufacturing jobs move overseas, in part because we were using gas to generate 20% of our electricity, and much higher natural gas prices were the result. California, which has banned both coal and nuclear as fuels, now generates 40% of its electricity with natural gas, which is a high-risk and costly strategy.

In short, it is best not to count on a utopian age of natural gas to solve our energy problems. At best, these new discoveries have given us time to get our house in order. But to squander natural gas while ignoring other energy resources would only be setting ourselves up for a bigger fall.

Myth 7. Raising CAFE Standards 30% Will Produce a 30% Reduction in Oil Consumption.

If only it were that easy. The solution always offered for our oil problems is to mandate that the auto companies produce more efficient cars. The Clean Energy Act of 2007 raised mileage standards from 27.2 miles per gallon to 35 by 2020, with SUVs included this time. Congressional representatives confidently predicted that this 32% increase would produce a comparable reduction in oil consumption.

But it never works that way. The experience with conservation mandates has typically been that, while we may save energy over some projected future level of consumption, we never *reduce* our energy consumption below today's level. One way or another, energy consumption stays abreast of the times and usually keeps going up.

In 1974, the U.S. auto fleet averaged 15.8 miles per gallon. Then in 1978, Congress adopted the Corporate Average Fuel Economy (CAFE) program, which mandated that passenger vehicles improve their fuel efficiency to 27.5 miles per gallon by 1985. In fact, we have reached that goal, which is a very impressive achievement. Yet since 1974 our national oil consumption has *increased* by 33%, from 15 million barrels per day to 20 million barrels per day. What happened? We may have consumed less than we would have without CAFE standards, but consumption did not decline. The main reason is that people travel more. Since 1970, total passenger mileage has more than doubled, from 1 trillion to 2.5 trillion miles per year. Greater fuel efficiency may have actually *encouraged* some of this increase. When cars consume less gas, the owners are tempted to travel more.

I don't know anybody who wakes up on New Year's Day and says, "I think I'm going to drive ten thousand miles in my car this year." However, a lot of people I know design a family budget and put down an amount to be spent for gasoline. If their fuel-sipping car takes them farther on that amount, so much the better. What they are doing is trading fuel savings for greater consumption. The same thing will likely happen if we improve the mileage on SUVs. If they become more fuel-efficient, people may start trading up from smaller cars. Although we may be able to consume at a slower rate, oil consumption is likely to go on increasing.

Myth 8. Electrical Transmission Lines Cause Cancer.

I'll bet I heard this story more than a dozen times while I was in office. It pops up every time someone tries to build a new transmission line. The myth was widely circulated in the 1980s and 1990s and played a big role in blocking the expansion of our electrical grid.

In fact, building transmission lines has probably become even more difficult than siting new power plants. The reason is what's called the NIMBY syndrome. People want access to energy but when it comes to bearing the consequences, they say, "Not in my backyard." (This is opposed to the more severe BANANA syndrome, which says, "Build absolutely nothing anywhere near anything.") Whenever anyone wants to build a transmission line, opponents quickly announce that it will go right through—or at least very near to—a schoolyard, a church, a nursing home, a quiet residential neighborhood, a scenic rural landscape, an important historical landmark, or any of the other normal things that can be found anywhere. There is always some better option somewhere else. Of course, the person near that "better option" is already raising his or her own objections, and so nothing ever gets done. NIMBY is a universal currency. It works everywhere.

As a consequence, we now have what the electrical engineers are calling a "third-world grid." There are still enough remote areas around the country where power plants can be sited without opposition—and where local residents may even welcome them because they deliver jobs and taxes. The problem is always getting the electricity to where it's needed. Moving it will become especially important as we develop renewable sources, since the plants will probably be sited in remote areas where wind or sunshine is strongest. Although renewable sources may "distribute" electrical generation, we will likely become even more reliant on long-distance transmission.

The more frail and outdated our transmission system becomes, the more likely it is that the whole thing will come crashing down. The Great Northeast Blackout of 2003 occurred because a utility in Ohio didn't keep up with trimming the trees beneath its power lines. When power lines become overloaded, they heat and sag, and they can touch trees and short out. The resulting power losses can cascade through the system for hundreds of miles. Those sagging lines in Ohio triggered a blackout all across the Northeast and Canada and left fifty million people without electricity.

We don't need any more myths about how power lines are harmful to people's health. We need more lines. By refusing to upgrade our energy infrastructure, we are leaving a lot of people at enormous risk.

Myth 9: All the Government Has to Do Is Choose the Right Energy Technology and Subsidize It.

How many times have we heard advocates tell us that the answer to our energy problems is waiting in the wings if only the government would give it a little help? The claim is often made that there's some vast conspiracy of business or the sluggishness of the market that's preventing this technological solution from happening. All the government has to do is to subsidize or *mandate* some new energy technology and everything will be solved.

Except it isn't that easy. Look at what happened with ethanol. The ethanol boom kicked off in the 1970s when we thought we were running out of oil. Somebody came up with the idea that harvesting and burning crops for fuel would be a good way to reduce our foreign dependence on oil. Farmers, of course, were delighted at having a new market, so a bill to subsidize ethanol passed with a great deal of support. Before anyone had given it much thought, Congress had exempted corn ethanol from federal gasoline taxes plus a large number of state taxes—amounting altogether to a tax break of 40+ cents per gallon. We were on our way to "energy independence."

It hasn't worked out at all. First, nobody ever took the time to find out whether ethanol *saves* energy. A lot of energy goes into growing crops and distilling corn. If ordinary price mechanisms were allowed to work, all these costs would be taken into account, since energy costs should be factored into any price equation. But this component has been overridden by the federal subsidy. As a result, we now find ourselves, years later, burning almost one quarter of our corn crop, with little or no gain in energy independence. Many farmers have stopped growing other crops in order to take advantage of the tax subsidies, and land that probably should be left fallow is being farmed. What do consumers get out of it? Ethanol replaces less than 3% of our oil consumption.

That's not the end of the bad effects. The diversion of crops to ethanol production has driven up food prices. Corn is used to feed dairy cattle, of course, so its use for ethanol has increased the price of milk. Beef prices are also up. Outside the United States, it's even worse. Tropical farmers have started switching crops and burning down rain forests in order to ship so-called biodiesel to Europe and America. World food prices have soared. There have been food riots in Mexico and protests in other countries. The government of Haiti fell over food issues. The United Nations Food and Agriculture Organization calls the production of biofuels "a crime against humanity."

And it isn't just ethanol. For every silver-bullet solution there are multiple other considerations and dozens of hidden costs. You never know where hidden costs or unforeseen consequences are going to emerge. The problem with government subsidies is that they tend to override these warnings.

There are no easy answers. We can't just substitute our own judgment for the market's decision because the market is telling us how much value we're getting out of any technology. As Fred Krupp, president of the Environmental Defense Fund, states, in *Earth: The Sequel*, "In essence, renewable standards, subsidies, and other mandates assume that the government has all the answers, rather than letting the market figure out the best way to produce clean energy at the lowest cost" (p. 57). The idea that government can rush us into a bright energy future by mandating or subsidizing untested technologies is a myth. We have to listen to the feedback of the market to know how much these technologies are really worth.

Myth 10. All We Need Is a New Manhattan Project to Solve Our Energy Problems.

This is my favorite. We don't need to build old-fashioned power plants and transmission lines, dig for oil and gas, develop clean coal, or reconcile ourselves to the fact that nuclear power isn't as scary as we imagine. All we have to do is identify the great scientific minds of the era, put them in a room, and wait for them to come up with a new solution. Another version of this story is that we just have to turn loose a few hundred Silicon Valley entrepreneurs and inventors in their garages or basements and they'll solve our problems. Just as Silicon Valley gave the world computers, so it can give us the answer to our energy problems. I hate to say it, but it isn't going to happen.

The first thing to recognize is that there is a very big difference between a Manhattan or Apollo project and the search for a safe new form of energy. In the case of Manhattan and Apollo, we were focused on a single task—building an atom bomb or sending a man to the moon. Most of the theoretical work had been accomplished. We knew there were vast stores of energy in the nucleus of the atom. We just had to unlock it. That was an engineering problem. We knew the ballistics of propelling a rocket to the moon. Building a space capsule and rocket was an engineering problem.

Today we don't even have a *theory* that suggests where to look for some new source of energy we haven't yet tried. There is no Manhattan Project–style easy fix in the future. So we're pretty much limited to improving what we have. More on this a little later.

So there they are, my ten favorite myths about energy. Dispensing with them may not accomplish too much but it does one important thing. It makes us realize how difficult it is going to be to face our energy challenges. There will be no easy solutions, no painless formulas, no magical breakthroughs or astounding technological accomplishments that will make the whole issue go away. We still face hard choices. To begin to gauge how hard they are, it now makes sense to replace our energy myths with a few energy facts. Once we gain a better grasp of the reality, we can start exploring the substantive challenges we face and begin to formulate a plan for addressing them.

CHAPTER 2

Energy Realities

This book is not about boring statistics. Readers won't need a magnifying glass to decipher integers set in minute type. Nor will anyone have to turn the book broadside in order to read a complex chart too wide to fit on the page.

However, I have learned in Washington that a war of data can be fought over just about every issue America faces. Hence, someone making a case without using numbers is bound to be critiqued for not knowing the facts or assaulted by critics from some think tank who did a regression analysis that calls into question what one asserts.

Faced with the choice of a boring book or risking the ire of various know-it-all data crunchers, I have settled on a compromise. In this single short chapter I intend to present a few energy-related numbers that help illustrate what we are up against. Bear with me. I promise this lesson will be over quickly.

The Numbers

This chart has the important numbers you need to know. As you can see, there aren't any numbers above 500 and there are none of those confusing decimal points or minus signs. I haven't labeled the rows or columns to create suspense, but for those of you with Type A personalities, we will be examining them row by row. Here we go.

1	20	36	46	63
2	11	21	18	0
3	1	3	6	20
4	0	0	3	0
5	38	22	77	47
6	380	280	387	460

Row 1: Oil Imports

1960	1973	1995	2009
20%	36%	46%	63%

The first row of numbers shows the percentage of oil the United States has imported in four selected years. Before 1960 we were importing less than 20% of our oil. After that, imports began to rise as U.S. production slowed. By 1973, during the first Arab oil embargo—which nearly derailed the entire economy—we were importing 36%. By 1995 that number had swollen to 46%. Today we are importing 63%.

This increase in imports is staggering in its implications for U.S. energy security. Imagine an economy as oil-intensive as ours dependent on foreign sources for 60% or more of our supply. Just think about what it means in terms of trade. In 2009 oil averaged over $60 a barrel, and we imported more than eleven million barrels a day. That means on average in excess of $650 million dollars headed offshore every twenty-four hours just to buy oil. The trade and economic consequences of this are a substantial and growing concern, and this first row of numbers strongly underscores the urgent need to address our energy problems.

Row 2: Nuclear Power Production

1980	Today	2020	2050
11%	21%	18%	0%

The numbers 11, 21, 18, and 0 again reflect percentages, in this case the percentage of America's electricity we generate from nuclear power. Back in 1980 nuclear accounted for 11% of our power production. That number rose to 20% in 2001 as the last reactors came on line and their owners learned to operate them more efficiently. But the figure is going to begin declining because nothing is being added to the U.S. nuclear capability. If no new nuclear plants are built by 2020, nuclear will drop to only about 18% of supply and continue its decline thereafter.

Nuclear plants have experienced tremendous increases in efficiency in the past decade. But it will be next to impossible to wring any more capacity out of them. As the need for electricity keeps growing, nuclear plants will supply an ever smaller portion of our power, even as they operate at full tilt. Moreover, nuclear plants cannot last forever. Slowly but surely our existing facilities will begin to reach their maximum life expectancy. When they do, they will be shut down and decommissioned. The best current estimate is that the last one will close around 2050. When it does, nuclear energy's contribution will be zero without new plants.

The implications of nuclear power's decline are gigantic. Finding a substitute for over 20% of our power supply is a daunting challenge by itself. But nuclear power plants do not emit pollutants or carbon. Therefore, if the percentage of power from nuclear declines, greenhouse gas emissions will rise precipitously unless every last megawatt of nuclear production is replaced by a megawatt of energy from some nonemitting source.

As we will later discuss, there is reason for optimism that, in the future, renewable energy sources can carry a much higher level of our power load. However, even if we drive non-hydro renewable sources up to 12% by 2020—the low end goal of the proposed federal "renewable portfolio" law—the combination of renewable sources and nuclear in that year will be only slightly higher than they are at today unless we build new nuclear plants. Similarly, if we are able to increase renewable sources to an extremely impressive 25% by 2050, the combined percentages will remain identical to today's numbers without new nuclear plants.

Row 3: Renewable Energy Production

1980	TODAY	2020—EIA'S CURRENT ESTIMATE	2020— PROPOSED FEDERAL REQUIREMENTS
1%	3%	6%	20%

Now we really get down to basics. The numbers 1, 3, 6, and 20 reflect the 1980 level, current level, optimistic prediction, and proposed federal legislative requirement for the role of nonhydro renewable energy in producing our electricity. Only a short time ago, the best estimates were that we might reach 6% from renewable sources in another decade. Now the "renewable portfolio" in the proposed federal energy legislation *mandates* that we get to 20% by then.

The categories that Congress has approved for its renewable definition are: (1) solar power, as in the direct translation of the sun's rays into a photovoltaic power generation process; (2) wind energy; (3) biomass, meaning the burning of wood, waste, vegetation, and so on; (4) geothermal energy, meaning energy harnessed from the earth's deep subterranean sources; and (5) tidal energy, meaning anything derived from ocean waves, currents, or tides.

When you hear environmentalists and media folks discuss the potential of renewable sources, it is important to remember where we are today. The numbers 1 and 3 reflect our recent and present positions. Back around 1980 America derived less than 1% of its energy from non-hydro renewable sources. Since then, thanks to some very generous federal tax subsidies, we've tripled the amount of energy from wind, solar, geothermal, and biomass. Unfortunately, that means that, as of 2010, despite all the effort, we are only generating about 3% of our electricity from these renewable sources.

I don't mean to downgrade renewable sources. I only want the reader to understand how far we have to go to meet the ambitious goal the federal renewable energy legislation proposed by Congress represents. In 2009, the Energy Information Administration made what seemed like an optimistic projection and said we might be able to reach 6% from renewable sources by 2020. When the Obama administration came to power in 2009, it threw aside these numbers and began projecting much higher figures. The federal renewable energy bill passed by the House sets a standard of 20% by 2020, although 5% of this can be reached through improvements in energy conservation. Another 3% can be canceled by governors for their states.

I remember when I first saw the data on the current use of renewable sources. It was 2%. I was staggered. I had assumed—as I suspect many other reasonably informed people would—that renewable sources were a much bigger part of our current power generation. I had just driven from Los Angeles to Palm Springs and seen whole hillsides filled with windmills. (By the way, I am convinced this constitutes the entire renewable exposure of many Americans.) I knew that the Department of Energy had an entire laboratory in Colorado devoted to research in this area. I had watched TV ads from traditional energy companies bragging about their newfound devotion to renewable energy.

That 2% (this was 2001, remember) hit me right between the eyes. Wow! At first I concluded that the thing I was missing was how much power was derived from hydro sources. Once again, I was surprised. It turns out that hydro peaked at around 33% of our electricity supply in the early 1940s. After World War II hydroelectric sites began to grow scarce, and we went back to building coal plants. Hydro gradually declined, to around 6% today. It's never going to go any higher. Still, it constitutes around 67% of our renewable electricity. Even with hydro, renewable sources make up less than 10% of our electrical generation.

As for the proposed legislative mandates, it is important to be realistic. If 5% of the 20% renewable requirement by 2020 can be achieved through energy conservation, and 3% waived by governors, then a mandate of 12% for the whole country, by that date, may be attainable. California, for example, already gets 11% of its electricity from nonhydro renewable sources, although this is possible because the state has ample geothermal resources that most states do not have. (California currently has its own mandate to expand renewable sources, to 20% by 2010, a goal it will almost certainly not achieve.) Nevertheless, meeting a goal like this on a national level poses a serious challenge.

Row 4: New Facilities

New nuclear licenses issued since 1980	New refineries built since 1980	New LNG terminals 1980–2009	Impact of 2005 and 2007 energy bills on such infrastructure
0	0	3	0

For those intimidated by big numbers, here's a chart for you: 0, 0, 3, and 0. These goose eggs put into perspective our failure to meet our energy challenges in recent years.

The first zero represents the number of new nuclear energy plants licensed in America since 1980. That zero has huge implications. Without new nuclear plants we have had to build a lot of

natural gas and coal plants in the last thirty years. That has trans-
lated into more carbon emissions and an increasing percentage
of imported energy. We will examine later the many reasons why
America ceased building nuclear plants. Suffice it to note, however, that that decision has had serious consequences.

The second zero represents the number of new oil refineries
built in this country since 1980. This lack of new refineries has a
great deal to do with the price of gasoline. The primary reason we
haven't seen a new refinery is that it is nearly impossible for an
operating company to secure all of the required environmental
and zoning permits from federal, state, and local agencies. Few
companies even bother trying anymore. Instead, they have expanded existing refineries. But the absence of new construction
has left the nation very little margin for error. Whenever there is a
work stoppage, fire, or mechanical problem at a refinery somewhere in the country, gasoline prices respond almost immediately.
Such disruptions can occur frequently.

One of the outcomes of the Clean Air Act of 1990 was that the
EPA has established varying air quality standards for different
areas of the country. This means refineries have to produce highly
specific gasoline blends for each region. Usually these are mandated for summer months. This means that at least twice a year
refineries have to shut down in order to retool their operations, a
time-consuming and expensive task. Every time this happens, especially in the late spring, gasoline supply falls and prices are
pushed upward. This is why prices usually rise at the beginning
of summer. Simply put, unless we create some spare capacity in
our refinery infrastructure, we will continue to experience the
kinds of price spikes that anger consumers and undermine the
economy.

The 3 represents the number of new liquefied natural gas receiving terminals built in the United States since 1982. Not surprisingly, they are all in the Gulf of Mexico (two in Louisiana and
one in Texas), since building LNG terminals has proved almost
impossible on the East and West Coasts. Opposition has largely

been based on the predictable Not in My Backyard syndrome, usually related to safety.

Over the years there have been a handful of accidents at LNG terminals that have made a big impression on the public. In Cleveland
in 1944, the first LNG terminal ever built in this country sprang a
leak and emitted gas, which ran down into sewers and then into
people's homes. A series of explosions killed 130 people and de-
stroyed a one-square-mile area. The incident precluded any new
LNG construction around the country for many years. Then, in
1973, an empty storage tank on Staten Island exploded while being
refurbished, killing thirty-seven construction workers. Though
overall the industry's safety record has improved greatly, there are
still a small number of accidental deaths from gas leaks around the
country each year.

Since September 11, the question has also arisen as to whether
an LNG terminal might be the target of a terrorist attack. To try to
respond to these concerns, I asked the Sandia National Laboratory
to conduct an in-depth study of LNG safety. The lab produced an
important study entitled "Guidance on Risk Analysis and Safety
Implications of a Large Liquified Natural Gas (LNG) Spill Over
Water." In it, researchers determined that most of the safety threats
from an accidental or intentional breach of LNG would be confined to an area within less than 500 meters from the site of the
breach. It also suggested that almost all of the risk would be contained within approximately 1,600 meters of the breach. The study
strongly suggests that a very high degree of safety can be achieved
if LNG activities are carried out in more isolated settings.

Unfortunately, critics were undeterred, and continue to assail
proposed LNG facilities almost regardless of the safety steps and
precautions taken to protect them. Consequently, we have found
ourselves caught between calls for building more LNG terminals
out of economic necessity on the one hand, and fierce Not In My
Backyard opposition to them on the other.

This tension was vividly reflected in a pair of news stories written about natural gas a few years back. They appeared in *The Washington Post* within four days of each other in March 2004 while I was trying to promote the construction of new LNG terminals. One piece, which appeared on page one of the *Post*'s business section, outlined the problems a wide variety of U.S. industries that use natural gas as a feedstock—such as the chemical sector—were having with the soaring price of natural gas. The thrust was that high prices were driving businesses and jobs offshore. We'll look at these problems in more depth later.

The other piece appeared on page three of the *Post*'s A section. It was a story lionizing a small port community, Harpswell, Maine, that had thwarted the efforts of ConocoPhillips to build an LNG receiving terminal within its boundaries. As portrayed by the *Post*, the small-town Davids had prevented the big, bad oil-and-gas-company Goliath from constructing a dangerous plant in their neighborhood and ruining the environment. Of course, it was exactly this type of behavior that was driving up the price of gas and undermining the economy as alluded to in the other story.

The Maine experience is not unique. On both the East and West Coasts, extensive speculation about the building of new LNG terminals ended up with nothing being accomplished. Despite the advantages of siting an LNG facility near California's huge market, energy companies decided that the risk wasn't worth taking. Instead Sempra, a San Diego–based utility, decided to build its new LNG terminal in Baja California. That's in Mexico. Now we have the prospect of seeing the jobs and economic advantages associated with a new LNG terminal migrating to Mexico. Meanwhile, Californians will pay more for natural gas and electricity.

This may be fine for now, but what happens if tensions over illegal immigration or drug wars turn relations sour between the two countries? Is it possible Mexico could retaliate by threatening to nationalize these plants or charge a huge tariff for sending gas or power across the border? After growing so dependent on im-ported oil, you'd think we'd have enough sense not to increase our imports of other key energy resources unless we absolutely have to.

The final zero reflects the number of provisions in recent energy bills that have been enacted *and* effectively implemented to help launch the construction of new refineries, new LNG terminals, and new nuclear power plants.

On new refineries, these energy acts were essentially silent. Despite the dearth of new construction over the past thirty years, the bills failed to include any provisions to help the country move in that direction.

With respect to nuclear plants, the 2005 legislation included a few important provisions, but Washington has failed to implement them effectively. As we will later explore, the single greatest im-pediment to the licensing and construction of the first new nuclear plants in thirty years is the financial risk associated with launch-ing one of these very expensive projects. Utilities fear that if the political winds blow in a new direction that stymies construction, hundreds of millions of dollars will have been lost. To address this, the 2005 Energy Bill included loan guarantees and production tax credits for the first new plants. Yet, notwithstanding President Bush's strong commitment to a nuclear renaissance, no loan guar-antees were awarded during his presidency, and DOE did not get around to making preliminary selections until 2009.

As for LNG terminals, the 2005 energy bill included one impor-tant provision, a section that placed the Federal Energy Regulatory Commission (FERC) in charge of approving the siting of new LNG facilities. This provision allows FERC to supersede any state and local siting processes being used to stop LNG projects. But while the bill took siting out of the hands of local politicians, it still in-cluded nothing in terms of initiating new LNG projects. A host of federal permits must still be secured, and opposition groups can challenge these at every turn.

Row 5: Projected Energy Demand Increases: 2005–30

Global Energy Demand	Oil	Electricity	Natural Gas
38%	22%	77%	47%

The numbers 38, 22, 77 and 47 here speak to projected increases in energy demand over the period 2005–30.

The first figure, 38%, is the increase in overall global energy demand. It is a staggering number. Much of the increase will come from the developing world, especially China and India. In these countries, hundreds of millions of people are moving out of poverty into a rudimentary prosperity. As they ascend the economic ladder, they will become consumers of electrified homes, gasoline-powered vehicles, personal computers, electronic appliances, and a variety of other products that people naturally desire. In almost every case, this new consumption will mean a rising demand for energy.

The 22% indicates the projected growth in worldwide oil demand by 2030. Meeting this will be extremely difficult. Failure to keep pace, however, will mean an upward price spiral due to market scarcity. Just imagine the implications of a world in which the daily production of oil is several million barrels less than demand.

Electrical demand will also skyrocket between 2005 and 2030. Current estimates are for a 77% increase in worldwide demand, with an even higher increase in developing countries. Keep in mind, we are talking about a near 80% increase in demand at precisely the time we are also trying to reduce carbon emissions. No matter what we do in America, we will have a difficult time achieving emission cuts given these trends. Unless developing nations are prepared to shelve their ambitions for growth—or assume a very active role in carbon mitigation—this projected

77% increase in electricity will make it very difficult to achieve any meaningful reduction in carbon emissions, or demand, for various fuels.

The final number, 47%, represents the consequences of the huge increase in electrical demand we have just discussed. It represents the projected increase in natural gas demand over the same period—another big number. Meeting this demand will require not only a vast effort in exploration and development but also a huge expansion of global infrastructure. Pipelines, LNG liquefaction and re-gasifying facilities, and a much bigger fleet of LNG tankers will have to be built. Failure to build will produce very tight markets and drive prices through the roof.

Row 6: Greenhouse Gas (GHG) Emissions

650,000 years ago	1850	Today	2050
380 ppm	280 ppm	387 ppm	460 ppm

The final chart—380, 280, 387, 460—indicates the amount of carbon dioxide in our atmosphere in parts per million. At the beginning of the industrial era, it was 280 ppm. Today it has risen to 387 ppm. The last time it was this high, according to samples taken from the Greenland ice cap, was 650,000 years ago, at a time when the earth was a much warmer place. The last column is the projected level for 2050 if we continue putting 10 billion new tons of carbon dioxide into the atmosphere each year. In terms of previous levels in the earth's history, it is off the charts. No one can be sure what will happen if CO_2 reaches this level, since it hasn't happened in millions and millions of years.

Summary Table

OIL IMPORTS

1960	1973	1995	2009
20%	36%	46%	63%

NUCLEAR POWER PRODUCTION

1980	Today	2020	2050
11%	21%	18%	0%

RENEWABLE ENERGY PRODUCTION

1980	Today	2020—EIA's Current Estimate	2020— Proposed Federal Requirements
1%	3%	6%	20%

NEW ENERGY FACILITIES

New nuclear licences issued since 1980	New refineries built since 1980	New LNG terminals, 1980–2009	Impact of 2005 and 2007 energy acts on such infrastructure
0	0	3	0

PROJECTED ENERGY DEMAND INCREASES, 2005–30

Global Energy Demand	Oil	Electricity	Natural Gas
38%	22%	77%	47%

GREENHOUSE GAS (GHG) EMISSIONS

650,000 Years Ago	1850	Today	2050
380 ppm	280 ppm	387 ppm	460 ppm

Facts, as they say, are stubborn things. Understanding the facts I have outlined here is indispensable if we are going to tackle the issues of energy and the environment seriously. As promised, I have tried to make the information as brief and comprehensible as possible. Nevertheless, I believe these statistics provide a compelling case for decisive action by our country. In the following sections, I will use them to discuss the serious threats facing America and our planet.

BOOK 2

Threats to Our Energy and Environmental Security

CHAPTER 3

Threats to the Energy Marketplace: It's Supply and Demand, Stupid

Perhaps the most significant threat facing our energy marketplace is the simple law of supply and demand. In recent years, growing energy consumption has resulted in tight markets and an upward pressure on prices. The economic slowdown of 2009 has dampened worldwide demand temporarily, but no one should think this signifies any new trend in energy consumption. As we will see in this chapter, the long-term outlook for energy is dim: Demand will increase continually and supply will have a very hard time keeping up.

According to the Energy Information Administration's *International Energy Outlook,* global energy demand is projected to increase 44% between 2010 and 2030. That's a staggering number. It is hard to imagine that the world is capable of increasing energy output more than 40% over this short period of time.

The challenge ahead becomes even more daunting when we examine the various components of the energy mix. For example, by 2030 the projected growth in oil consumption is approximately 20–25 million net barrels per day. Right now we consume 85 million barrels per day. By 2030, experts expect this to rise to 105–110 million. Producing this amount will be even harder to achieve because many existing sources of production will be depleting over the next two decades. Thus, new production will likely have to add up to something over 40 million barrels per day in order to meet demand. That's a near 50% rise in capacity!

The magnitude of this challenge is almost beyond belief. At a time when much of the least expensive and most accessible oil has already been tapped, the world is facing a gigantic increase in demand. I have queried numerous oil experts about where this new production is going to come from. I haven't yet found one who can tell me. Optimists say the Canadian tar sands can give us 5 million new barrels per day over the next twenty years. Saudi Arabia and the other Middle Eastern countries are believed to be able to increase their production by 6 million during that time frame, and Russia by around 3 million. Even if these three large supply sources should meet projections, we are still less than halfway to filling the needed growth. I'm not saying it's impossible, but it won't be easy, even in a highly favorable environment. And, of course, oil isn't the only challenge.

The International Energy Agency, which also conducts credible forecasting, estimates that by 2030 worldwide demand for electricity will also skyrocket, with global demand increasing by 77%. In the developing countries the increase will be higher. What will fuel this massive increase in electricity production? According to the IEA, natural gas will pick up a large portion of it, with demand increasing 47%. This growth projection may be nearly as difficult to meet as the demand for oil.

Why is all this happening? As has occurred throughout history, economic growth is inextricably linked to an affordable energy supply. As the citizens of developing countries achieve a semblance of middle-class life, their demand for energy inevitably increases. This growth is not limited to China and India. We are also seeing it in countries such as Egypt, Brazil, and Indonesia and in many of the smaller nations of Asia, the Middle East, and Latin America. But it's not just developing countries that are driving this demand. Our own electrical consumption is expected to grow by at least 26% in the two decades ahead as well.

And that means we've got other challenges. According to the

North American Electric Reliability Council (NAERC), the growing demand for electricity will place an enormous burden on the U.S. transmission grid. As we will later explore, grid reliability will be a serious challenge, especially if we're going to be bringing large quantities of renewable energy from faraway places to demand centers.

Now that we've examined the energy demand curve, let's look at production. Regrettably, the supply side is a different story. A variety of factors have combined to make it nearly impossible for energy supply to grow at the same pace as demand. The first factor is that most of the easy resources have already been discovered. The days when Jed Clampett of *The Beverly Hillbillies* could find oil by shooting his rifle into the ground in his backyard are long gone. From the Permian Basin in Texas to the deserts of the Arabian Peninsula, the low-hanging fruit has already been plucked. There is still a lot of oil left in these traditional areas, but much of it has already been accounted for.

As a result, nontraditional sources will now have to shoulder a much larger burden, and that won't be cheap. Offshore oil is an example of high-cost product. No one knows exactly how much oil and gas can be found in the deeper parts of the Gulf of Mexico and other bodies of water around the world, but it is expensive to drill deep. Nevertheless, market demand is making it profitable. The Alberta tar sands are becoming a rapidly expanding source of energy, and are currently producing more than 1 million barrels a day, but this is not so easy as drilling for oil in West Texas. Huge layers of overburden—dirt and rock—must be removed to reach it and the tar must then be boiled out of the sands. It is a very thick, sulfur-heavy product that needs extensive refining. Not surprisingly, the cost is a lot more than for conventional oil. As traditional sources are depleted, however, this more expensive oil will become increasingly competitive, and it will exert upward pressure on prices per barrel and at the pump.

Just how much of the world's oil reserves we have already used is another subject of intense debate. One of the most intriguing theories in the world of energy is the concept of "peak oil." Peak oil is the point at which we will have exhausted half the world's resources. From that point on, production will inevitably go down. (See Matthew R. Simmons, *Twilight in the Desert: The Coming Saudi Oil Shock and the World Economy,* also Kenneth S. Deffeyes, *Hubbert's Peak: The Impending World Oil Shortage.*) This has actually already happened in the Lower 48, where oil production peaked in 1970. It was this peak in output, matched against demand that kept right on going upward, that helped precipitate the oil shortage of the 1970s. We recovered for a while with the opening of Alaska's Prudhoe Bay and other new sources, but, overall, our production has continued to decline, which is why we import 60% of our oil.

The question now arises, "Can the same thing happen at a world level?" Some of the trends are not hopeful. The discovery of oil worldwide actually peaked in the 1960s. This is supposed to precede the peaking of production by about thirty-seven years. Since the early part of this decade many of the leading pessimists, such as Colin Campbell, a veteran Scottish geologist, have been saying world production will peak at any moment. Production from conventional sources does seem to have peaked in 2006, but the difference was quickly made up by unconventional sources such as the Athabasca tar sands in Alberta. In contrast to people like Campbell, free-market advocates argue that higher prices will always bring forth new supplies; so the idea of peak oil is mistaken. Who's right? I think it's a matter of definition. I am not persuaded that we've reached worldwide peak oil, but I do feel we have probably reached the limits of cheap oil at the levels to which we've become accustomed. In short, costs are going to go up, and energy is going to get more expensive.

In addition to fundamental supply challenges, there are other impediments as well. One of the most troublesome is the NIMBY syndrome, "Not in My Backyard." The simple fact is that people want affordable energy without experiencing the consequences. They love using energy but don't want to have anything to do with its production or distribution.

Usually, NIMBY opposition is a local matter. Anyone will object if someone wants to build an energy installation in their immediate vicinity, but often the imposition is very slight, and sometimes it just becomes a matter of principle. The Cape Wind Project off the coast of Nantucket Island and Martha's Vineyard has been delayed for years and may never be built largely because the windmills would be visible from the high-priced real estate on the shoreline. Although opponents have tried to characterize their objections as environment-based, the fact that many of Cape Wind's opponents are prominent, influential, and well-funded has been pivotal. (See Robert Whitcomb and Wendy Williams, *Cape Wind: Money, Celebrity, Energy, Class Politics, and the Battle for Our Energy Future*.)

The opposition from the citizens of Nevada to the Yucca Mountain Nuclear Waste Repository is something entirely different. The site is ninety miles north of Las Vegas in the middle of an old air force bombing range and nuclear testing site. But people resented the idea that their state was going to become "the nation's nuclear waste dump." In response to this political pressure the Obama administration derailed the project in its first six weeks in office. The simple fact is that nobody wants to be associated with the heavy lifting of producing energy. The easiest thing to do is to export the hard work to other countries, which is what we are doing with LNG terminals, oil refineries, and offshore drilling. Is it any wonder that we end up dependent on other countries for our energy?

Environmental regulations, however meritorious, have, in general, put a big crimp in energy production. For example, the 1990 Clean Air Act required every new coal plant in the country to have the latest pollution equipment, regardless of the cost. As a result, utilities kept running their old coal boilers instead of building new ones. To overcome this effect the EPA adopted something called New Source Review. Every time a coal plant made some major repair, such as installing a new turbine, it would be regarded as a "new source" and would therefore require the installation of expensive baghouses and scrubbers. To evade these associated costs the utilities started skimping on major repairs. Hence, we are now operating dilapidated older coal plants instead of modernizing them, and that has reduced the efficiency, and therefore the output, of these facilities.

Environmental concerns have likewise played a significant role in limiting the scope of offshore energy production in the United States. We have basically forbidden offshore drilling on the Atlantic and Pacific Coasts for fear of oil spills. Meanwhile, other countries are not handicapping themselves in the same way. Cuba is now talking about drilling for oil in places that extend into our offshore territory. If it does so, we would get the same environmental risks and none of the oil. The biggest environmental battle of all is likely to occur when the question arises about extracting shale oil in the Rockies. The Green River deposit in western Colorado has the largest concentration of hydrocarbons in the world, but it will be even messier to extract than the Alberta tar sands.

Of course, the most famous example of environmental concerns blocking significant energy production has occurred with respect to the Arctic National Wildlife Refuge, or ANWR. For decades, environmental advocates have employed ANWR as the prime example of a fragile ecosystem too important to be used for energy production, despite U.S. Geological Survey estimates, that as many as 16 billion barrels of oil exist there.

Against this backdrop, advocates for greater U.S. energy independence have called for opening up a small portion of ANWR for production. Environmentalists have, however, always been able to prevent development in ANWR, either because they were close to the White House or had enough votes in Congress to prevent development from moving forward.

In one of my first speeches as energy secretary I called for opening up ANWR. I pointed out that the portion of ANWR where drilling might occur was roughly the size of the state of South Carolina, but that the footprint needed to extract oil and gas from that huge area was only about the size of a major city airport, such as Dulles International Airport, near Washington, D.C. Despite this very modest footprint, opposition continues to prevent this project from moving forward.

Not surprisingly, when energy prices are low the public supports the environmentalists. But when gasoline prices skyrocket, as they did in the summer of 2008, a majority of the public switched to a pro-drilling viewpoint. Nevertheless, congressional Democrats were able to stall any action and the new Obama Administration has taken a fairly dim view of domestic energy development thus far.

The harsh reality is that the absence of oil from ANWR is hurting the United States. If there was ever an example of a situation in which pragmatism is required, it is here. The notion that the costs, caused by this tiny development footprint in an area as big as a geographically large state, outweigh the benefits is very difficult to defend. And the fact that we haven't tapped this resource is one reason why oil markets tighten so much during periods of high demand.

While existing environmental rules and politics have already impacted energy production, the adoption by the United States of an enforceable carbon framework will even more dramatically change the energy production outlook. Under any form of modestly rigorous carbon rules, the likelihood that any new coal-fired power plants will be built is dim. A carbon framework would also put a new set of constraints on the production and use of oil and natural gas. While new regulations might be justified in terms of trying to limit carbon emissions, there is no question that such a regime, like previous environmental regulations, will make it even more difficult to produce enough energy to keep up with demand.

Failure to invest in infrastructure is also creating roadblocks and bottlenecks. During my first days in office, California was suffering from rolling blackouts because it didn't have enough electricity. The worst problems were in the northern part of the state around San Francisco. As it turned out, Southern California had surplus electricity. Unfortunately, an expansion of Path 15, a transmission corridor designed to carry power between north and south, had long been delayed by NIMBY and environmental objections, as well as opposition to power lines in general. California had been aware of the danger for many years but had failed to act.

Over the years the urban legend has grown that the California electrical shortage was somehow *caused* by Enron and a few other companies pulling various tricks to circumvent the price controls the state had put on wholesale electricity. Enron, for example, sold electricity out of state and then brought it back in again in order to avoid the price controls. The actions of Enron and others were deplorable, as will be discussed later, but the California electrical shortage primarily occurred because the state stopped building major power plants from 1980 to 2000 and tried to substitute renewable and "distributed" energy in its place. When natural gas prices spiked and hydroelectricity from the north ran short, the state was stuck without sufficient power. Only the construction of 13,000 MW of new natural gas plants over the next three years ameliorated the problem.

Even now, California state auditors say the Golden State may be headed for another power shortage because of its refusal to build conventional power plants. Rebecca Smith, writing in *The Wall Street Journal*, July 3, 2009, in "State's Renewable Energy Focus Risks Power Shortage," begins:

> *California officials are beginning to worry that the state's focus on transitioning to renewable-energy sources could lead to power shortages in the near term.*
>
> *The state has been so keen to develop renewables that relatively few conventional power generators, such as gas-fired plants, have been built lately. That risks a possible energy shortfall in certain places if the economy rebounds any time soon.*
>
> *California's utilities are barreling ahead to try to meet a state mandate to garner 33% of their power from renewable sources by 2020, and some officials are concerned the effort might push up electricity prices and crimp supplies.*

Once the initial blackout crisis was resolved, I empowered our department's Western Area Power Administration to address this problem. Ultimately, we were able to put together both the financing and expertise to expand Path 15. The project to widen and increase the corridor was completed on time and under budget in December 2004. I regard it as one of the victories of my term in office.

Other infrastructure has also been neglected. As previously noted, we haven't built a refinery in the United States since the 1970s. Without these important assets, it is no surprise that demand should be outstripping supply. The refinery situation is a good illustration of how NIMBY policies, tough environmental requirements, and the general attitude that bringing supplies to market is someone else's problem, combine to frustrate the public and make energy more expensive.

As previously noted, every spring most refineries must shut down for a while to change their operations in order to comply with Clean Air Act requirements. Hence, during my tenure as secretary, I would annually start getting congressional calls around the middle of May, after gasoline prices had jumped. People in a congressman's district were complaining, and what was I going to do about it? How about tapping the Strategic Petroleum Reserve? I would explain patiently that oil supplies were not the problem. The bottleneck was refinery capacity. We hadn't built a new oil refinery in this country in thirty years. Perhaps the congressman would like to encourage the building of one in his district? By this time the member had usually stopped listening. He probably voted for the Clean Air Act requirements but didn't recognize the connection.

I believe we have entered an era in which energy supplies are going to be challenged increasingly to keep up with demand. Meeting demand is going to require difficult choices. There are too many impediments to supply and too much potential for demand growth. Inevitably, this will place upward pressure on energy prices.

Worse still, our tight energy markets are going to be very susceptible to disruption. Any infrastructure breakdown, any natural disaster, any geopolitical crisis, is likely to have a profound impact on our energy economy.

CHAPTER 4

Geopolitical Threats to Energy Markets

In recent years we have come to recognize that our energy supplies are vulnerable to international events. With every new terrorist attack, with every new case of civil unrest in a producing nation, with every hostile pronouncement by the leader of a major energy exporter, we are compelled to realize that our energy and economic stability are strongly affected by geopolitical factors.

For most Americans, the dominant issue is oil imports. Almost every American is dismayed to see the vast amounts of money we send to foreign countries in payment for our imported oil. Because many of these export countries benefit from U.S. aid and security, American citizens then ask, Why are we providing support to countries that charge us so much for oil? That many of the 9/11 terrorists came from Saudi Arabia, our chief source of oil in the Middle East, only heightens the frustration. As we will discuss in this chapter, however, dependence on the Middle East for oil supplies is only one of the geopolitical challenges we face.

One place to begin this discussion is by asking: Does the amount of energy we import really matter? And does it matter from whom we import it? Economists argue that the world's oil supply is "one big bathtub" and that it doesn't matter where the oil comes from or where it goes. The amount we pay for oil, they say, will simply depend on overall supply and demand. Other people argue that it's good to import oil because we are conserving domestic resources. To try to limit our oil imports would be to "drain America first."

Let's think about it.

During the 1973 oil embargo it took virtually all of the Arab oil-producing countries working together to deny the energy marketplace enough oil to create serious supply disruptions and so raise the price to a level that created serious consequences. Back then we were only importing 35% of our oil, and the world was awash in the product; there was substantial spare capacity for the United States to fall back on. But now we import more than 60% of our needs, and the world's spare capacity is more limited. This has logical consequences.

Regardless of who we buy our oil from, the fact that we purchase over 11 million barrels a day is very consequential. When oil eclipsed $100 a barrel in 2008, we were exporting more than $1 billion a day, and over $30 billion a month. If the percentage of oil we import were to grow, or if prices were to continue to remain high or to climb, the impact would be even greater. Importing this much energy does put us at risk both economically and politically. I think most Americans recognize this. Our growing dependence has real implications and, as most people realize, the simple fact is there are many political issues connected to those countries that are the most significant sources of exported energy. For that reason, the Persian Gulf War of 1991 was supported by a majority of the American people.

I was working as a senior White House aide in 1991 and remember clearly the night President George H. W. Bush announced that we were going to lead an international coalition to force Saddam Hussein out of Kuwait. It had not been an easy decision. There wasn't overwhelming congressional support, and no one knew what kind of resistance we would meet. But most Americans appreciated the potential leverage Saddam Hussein would have over energy-importing countries if he controlled both his own reserves of oil and those of Kuwait. A secondary fear was that he would look for other areas of conquest if he were allowed to seize Kuwait without opposition.

So the American people get it. They know we would be at high risk if too much control of the international supply of oil fell into the hands of virulently anti-American despots. Unfortunately, despite all the talk about energy independence, we aren't going to be domestically producing even half the oil we need any time in the foreseeable future. And so we face serious challenges made more complex by various geopolitical factors. Here are a few examples.

In recent years we have seen a variety of destabilizing events take place in far corners of the world. In Nigeria, for instance, local political unrest and civil disorder constantly undermine oil production. Each time the country shuts down, world prices head north. Speculators have no idea whether the disruption will last for days, weeks, or months, so they bid up the price dramatically. Even though prices decline once the trouble subsides, over time this uncertainty adds another increment to the price of oil.

Meanwhile, Iran's efforts to enrich uranium have also been a source of destabilization. Every time the United Nations debates a new resolution, every time rumors surface that Israel or the United States will launch a preemptive strike against Iran, every time Iranian leaders make bellicose speeches, energy markets respond. So far, none of these events have spiraled out of control, but should that happen, the energy world would reel. Once panic sets in, markets can be affected for a very long time. To be sure, there are countervailing forces. Even during the prolonged disruption of supply from Iraq after the U.S.-led coalition invaded in 2003, the Saudis ramped up production in order to offset the loss to the would market. But the Saudis may not have that kind of spare capacity in the future. In my view, we are living on borrowed time.

Beyond this type of geopolitical challenge looms the specter of terror. After 9/11 the media focused primarily on the threats posed by terrorists to civilian and military targets. But another very inviting set of targets are energy assets and infrastructure, both here and abroad. During the Persian Gulf War, Saddam Hussein set fire to Kuwaiti oil fields in a dog-in-the-manger gesture once he realized he couldn't keep them. A decade later, during the worst part of the Iraq War, insurgents put most of the country's pipelines out of commission and production ground to a halt. Over the years there have been reports of attempted terrorist attacks on Saudi facilities by indigenous rebel groups, but to date they have been thwarted.

We have probably not seen the last of these efforts. In fact, I believe the potential will increase in coming years. Energy infrastructure, particularly in the Middle East, makes a very attractive terrorist target. First, refineries and oil fields tend to be in isolated areas. Second, an attack on these facilities serves the dual purpose of destabilizing the local regime and damaging the industrial West as well.

In the wake of 9/11, we quickly recognized just how unprepared we were domestically for such a threat. Shortly after the attack on the World Trade Center, Pennsylvania governor Tom Ridge was named to head a newly created White House Office of Homeland Security. His new team and senior personnel from the Department of Energy began looking at the energy infrastructure in the United States and soon saw the challenges we faced. The most daunting problem was that, except for nuclear power plants, none of our energy facilities came under federal regulatory control. Washington could establish security procedures for nuclear reactors but not for any other source. The security of oil refineries, natural gas power plants, hydroelectric dams, and the electric grid was basically in the hands of their owners.

Over the next months Governor Ridge and I did everything we could to provide information and support to the energy sector. In the process, we learned a lot about the potential of a terrorist attack. What we learned was chilling. In brief, the threat to our energy supplies is not limited to faraway targets.

Of course, the financial markets recognize the risk of terrorist attacks and incorporate this into energy prices. This has been called the "fear factor." After 9/11, as the price of oil and natural gas began to climb, it became obvious that the fear factor was having a big impact on energy prices. It has abated a bit in recent years, but there is no doubt that a successful attack anywhere in the world would quickly cause prices to spike. Unfortunately, the likelihood of an attack remains high and will stay that way. Indeed, as safeguards are implemented to protect population centers and government facilities, energy assets could become even more attractive targets.

Geopolitics also comes into play when consuming nations start entering long-term contracts with producing nations in an attempt to lock up their oil. China has become the major player here. In recent years, China bought much of its oil from Saudi Arabia; in fact, it has become the Saudis' biggest customer. Then in 1997 the Chinese announced a long-term agreement with Saddam Hussein and Iraq. They would provide technical expertise and investment capital in exchange for a guaranteed future oil supply. When the invasion of Iraq threw Iraq's oil supplies into confusion, China turned to Angola, then a relatively small player, and announced an identical long-term agreement in which China would become the African nation's main oil customer. Finally, when oil prices experienced a big run-up in 2008, China renegotiated its deal with Iraq's new government and signed a twenty-two-year agreement for oil at a long-term price of somewhere around $100 a barrel, which seemed low at a time when oil was selling at $150 a barrel, but now appears high.

This approach is relatively atypical in the energy world. In the past, large energy companies in the United States and Europe have sought mineral rights throughout the world for the purpose of selling product worldwide. China, however, is seeking exclusive deals primarily for its own consumption purposes, not resale. Some people argue these deals are irrelevant because oil and natural gas are fungible. If China's buy price turns out to be low, it will sell oil on the international market to make a profit. If it turns out to be high—as the $100 per barrel price looks in 2010—then it will stockpile the oil or try to renege on the deal or end up taking a big loss.

But this calculus could fall apart if China or any other international player should corner a large share of the market in a scarcity situation. Efforts to corner agricultural products and other minerals were common in the early days of American capitalism. They were rarely successful, but when they came close they often set off brief panics that caused considerable disruption in the commodity market.

As ominous as cornering the market on an energy commodity is the control some countries are gaining over other nation's energy access. The prime example here is Russia's control over the pipelines that provide Europe and many former Soviet republics with natural gas. That Russia is willing to take advantage of this situation has become increasingly clear. In March 2005 a dispute broke out between Russia and Ukraine over the price of gas being delivered from Russian fields in Siberia. The argument escalated, and on January 1, 2006, the Russians cut off gas supplies altogether, leaving the Ukrainians freezing in the middle of winter. Tempers calmed and the Russians restored service by January 4, but the Ukrainians really could not afford the newly negotiated price and started piling up debts. In October 2007 the Russians started trying to collect the debts, and by March 2008 the argument erupted again, and Russia once more reduced the flow of gas. By January 2009 the dispute had spilled into Europe, and eighteen countries found themselves short of gas because the Russians would not allow it to flow through Ukraine.

All this can be seen as nothing more than a landlord trying to collect rent from a tenant and having the argument spill out into the street. But the international stakes are very, very high. Obviously, this market leverage can be used to exercise political power as well. When Russia briefly invaded Georgia in August 2008, the muted response from NATO was, in my view, influenced by the possibility that Russia could cut off Europe's gas. Both Georgia and Ukraine have applied to join NATO but have been rejected—even though Georgia has sent two of its best military brigades to serve in Iraq. Hanging over these negotiations is the worrisome consideration that Europe is now almost completely dependent on Russia for a large portion of its energy supplies.

So what does this all portend? It is my belief that in the decade ahead any one of a series of energy-related geopolitical events could undermine not only the energy markets but international security as well. First, it is important to recognize that the world is a very different place from the one that existed during the early days of OPEC. Back then, because there was so much spare production capacity, it took the coordinated efforts of the entire Organization of Arab Oil Exporting Countries (OPEC's eight Middle Eastern members plus Egypt and Syria) to disrupt world supplies. (See Daniel Yergin, *The Prize: The Epic Quest for Oil, Money, and Power.*) Today, though, during periods of peak demand, there is so little spare capacity in the world that a single major producer could have a very disruptive impact if it so chooses.

What does this mean? Well, for starters, a country such as Venezuela or Iran could single-handedly undermine the energy market. Trade works both ways, of course, and these countries are dependent enough on their energy revenues that there is obviously a strong disincentive against such actions. Under the right circumstances, however, it could happen.

This is the challenge the United States and the Free World face in the years ahead. As we try to prevent Iran from developing uranium enrichment capacity and possibly building a nuclear weapon, we have to recognize that Iran now has a powerful oil weapon. If Hugo Chávez decides to escalate his harsh anti-American rhetoric into some specific action, he has the capacity to roil energy markets as well. The possibility that such adversarial countries might act in concert makes the threat to our security even greater. We not only face the frustration of sending billions of dollars a year to potentially hostile countries, we could also find ourselves facing serious economic consequences if a major producer decides to turn off the spigot. As we work our way through the recession of

2009—which many economists argue was kicked off by the oil price run-up of 2008—the last thing we need is another shortage of crude oil.

Of course, America has itself been the target of accusations that is has played politics with energy. Most recently, many people accused the United States of going to war in Iraq solely to enhance our access to energy supplies. "No blood for oil" was probably the most frequent slogan seen on antiwar protest banners. The same charge is made routinely in diplomatic circles.

It will probably never be possible to disprove this assertion. (My experience has been that, when it comes to oil, people will believe almost anything.) But I can say from my vantage point that, both during the time the invasion was being carried out and in the postinvasion effort to rebuild Iraq, oil was not an issue. Other than a small number of technical experts who offered advice in repairing some of Iraq's infrastructure damage, no Department of Energy official—and certainly no high-level officials—played a role in any of the wartime decisions.

To the contrary, it was understood from day one that the people of Iraq would be making decisions regarding the country's energy reserves. And since the new government has been in charge that is precisely what has taken place. Iraq was one of the five founding members of OPEC—indeed, the organizational meeting took place in Baghdad in 1960. Today Iraq remains a charter member of OPEC and sees its oil interests through the lens of a producing country. If we were in Iraq merely to requisition their oil, why is it China was able to sign a deal locking up a significant portion of the country's output right in the middle of the occupation? Lastly, I would note that those who asserted the Iraq War was fought over oil have been noticeably silent on the issue of late.

While the Iraq War was not fought over oil, I definitely would not rule out the possibility that future confrontations may occur over energy supplies. In just the past few years, the United States and Russia have gone nose to nose over the question of whether Russia should provide Iran with nuclear technology. Likewise, as noted, we have watched the Russians punish their neighbors over natural gas bills and, consequently, cutting off nations farther down the pipeline. The margins of error are getting very narrow.

While none of these events has yet led to a direct confrontation, the possibility of such an occurrence taking place in the future is growing. If it is true—and I believe it is—that the era of inexpensive oil is over, it is not at all inconceivable that such confrontations might take place. For these reasons, I believe it is vital that political leaders across the planet begin trying to anticipate these challenges and work toward a consensus on energy issues that go beyond matters such as climate change.

It would be nice if we only had to contend with the frustration of sending hundreds of millions of dollars a day to other nations for our energy supplies, but as we have seen, the threats of geopolitical disruptions are just as great. Terrorist attacks, confrontations over access, and the broad use of energy resources as a political weapon—all are certainly possible. Indeed, I believe it is highly likely that one or more such incidents will occur within the next five to ten years.

For America, this means we must develop more domestic energy security through more production and efficiency, enlarge the scope of our international energy relationships, work to both protect our own energy assets and assist others in protecting theirs, and institute a far greater degree of communication and collaboration on energy issues within the international community. Perhaps such efforts can avert the nightmare scenarios. If so, they will have been well worth it.

CHAPTER 5

Environmental Threats

For more than a decade, and especially since Al Gore made his movie *An Inconvenient Truth* in 2006, attention has been focused on the problem of global warming. Gore's vision of an environmental apocalypse served as a convenient club with which to bash the Bush administration. Now that the Obama administration has taken over, however, it has discovered that broad public fervor for regulating large portions of our economy in order to prepare for a crisis that may not arrive for many years is less than overwhelming.

The result has been a stalemate. The Obama administration has proposed cap-and-trade legislation, a complex system where carbon emitters must buy permits that they can trade among themselves. The idea is that, by sorting out among themselves who will spend for expensive clean-up methods, they will reach the overall cheapest way of reaching the desired reductions. Critics, on the other hand, have called it a straight tax on the economy—"the greatest tax increase in history." Although the bill, which passed the House, was hugely watered down in its final version—to the point where it may not have accomplished much at all—the threat of taking a huge bite out of the economy in the wake of the 2008–09 recession finally proved too awful to contemplate, and so the bill stalled in the Senate. The result of our trying to do too much has been to do almost nothing at all.

We have ended up with the extremes. On one end are the global warming alarmists who swear that the world will end soon in disaster if we don't change our evil ways. (At one point in August 2009, U.N. Secretary-General Ban Ki-moon warned we only had four months to come up with a solution to the problem.) The emergence of serious questions about the accuracy of various climate studies and research in late 2009 and early 2010 has further clouded the picture. On the other end, there are various loud skeptics in Congress, the scientific community, and the business world who call the whole thing "the greatest hoax ever perpetrated on the American people." Neither approach seems very promising.

I don't want to play one of those "triangulating" games that Bill Clinton made so famous, but I think there is a middle ground that leaves much more room for action.

Let me outline my position. First, I believe we should strive to continue reducing pollution. We should also embrace the principles of sustainable development. I also think there is reason to believe that we may be affecting the earth's climate by putting so much carbon dioxide back into the atmosphere.

It is generally believed that the earth's atmosphere was once largely carbon dioxide, just as Venus's atmosphere is today. Photosynthetic plants and algae came along and pulled much of that CO_2 out of the atmosphere, so that it makes up about 387 parts per million of our air today.

The greatest carbon sink on the planet, besides carbon-rich limestone and dolomite rocks and the deep oceans, is the vast deposits of coal that lie beneath the ground all around the globe, laid down hundreds of millions of years ago. In fact, it is now generally believed that coal was created when the planet "developed a case of indigestion." The bacteria and microorganisms that break down dead plants and trees and other organic matter today hadn't evolved at the time of the coal age. As a result, dead organisms *did not* break down but were instead buried in the geological strata. This prevented huge quantities of carbon dioxide from being recycled back into the atmosphere and so cooled the earth in the process.

So it makes sense that if we burn coal for our energy and release large portions of that carbon back into the atmosphere, we can end up re-creating a planet similar to that which existed before these deposits formed. The world is believed to have been much hotter before the Carboniferous period. Therefore it isn't unreasonable to hypothesize that it could be that way again.

So I think it's important to try to do something about carbon emissions. It makes sense to try to reduce them wherever we can. But I don't believe it's worth risking our economy and the world's when we still don't know exactly how urgent the problem is. You can see how enthusiasm for doing something about global warming plummeted when the recession hit in late 2008. Imposing an uncertain, potentially costly carbon regime that would risk damaging the economy became politically untenable. The challenge is to find an approach that does not create such economic disruption that it becomes unsustainable.

Getting there requires some perspective. Perhaps the best approach is to recognize that concerns about coal—which is a key aspect of the climate debate—are not at all new. We have been wrestling with coal and its pollution for the better part of the last century. We were actually on the verge of solving it in the early 1970s—until the Arab oil embargo and exaggerated fears of nuclear power interrupted this effort. Coal has a whole variety of contaminants—sulfur, mercury, particulate matter—that have been considered a health problem since the 1960s. The truth is we haven't been as successful as we would like in cleaning up this kind of pollution, either. The Environmental Protection Administration estimates that 24,000 people still die each year as the result of lung conditions caused by air pollution, with coal being the biggest contributor. Let's look at how these concerns about pollution originally arose and how they have been addressed.

In October 1948 a temperature inversion settled over Donora, Pennsylvania, a coal-mining town twenty miles south of Pittsburgh in the Monongahela Valley, and blanketed the region for a week with warm air. Coal smoke from iron and steel factories in the valley became trapped in the lower atmosphere. In the little town of

15,000 people, 68 died immediately of acute respiratory problems, and hundreds suffered permanent damage to their heart and
lungs. (See John Esposito, project director, The Ralph Nader Study
Group, *Vanishing Air,* also Bjorn Lomborg, *The Skeptical Environmentalist: Measuring the Real State of the World.*)

The Donora disaster set off a national debate over the growing
dangers of coal smoke. The result was the National Air Pollution
Control Act of 1955, which required that the federal government
gather information about the health effects of air pollution. Writing
and enforcing legislation was still left to the states, however, and
nothing much happened. The favorite tactic used to evade the law
at the time was to locate your power plants near the state line so the
smoke and pollution would blow over into other jurisdictions.

Nothing had really improved much when another temperature
inversion settled over New York City in 1966 for the three-day
Thanksgiving holiday. It killed 168 people. Concern about air pollution had been rising, and this event was a cause of alarm. The
result was the Clean Air Act of 1970, which was the first real attempt to deal with air pollution on a national scale. The primary
focus of attention was on coal. The portion of the nation's electricity
generated with coal had been rising steadily since World War II. In
1940, over 33% of our electricity was generated by hydroelectric
dams built by the Army Corps of Engineers after the great conservation era of Theodore Roosevelt. The New Deal had boosted this
effort during the 1930s, establishing the Tennessee Valley Authority
to harness the rivers of the Midsouth and promoting the Bonneville
Power Authority and Hoover Dam in the West.

After World War II, however, suitable dam sites had become
harder and harder to find. In addition, there was growing opposition from nature-loving groups such as the Sierra Club. The group
had split with Roosevelt's conservation movement as early as 1910
in the dispute over whether to dam the Hetch Hetchy Valley in Yosemite National Park in order to provide drinking water and hydroelectricity to San Francisco. The dam was built. When army
engineers proposed damming Glen Canyon on the Colorado River

in the 1950s, the Sierra Club once again objected, and held up the project for several years. The dam was finally completed in 1966, but by then it was obvious that there were few usable dam sites left, and those that existed would raise fierce environmental opposition. Coal was going to be king in terms of future electrical generation.

All this might have raised concerns about energy supplies except a new technology had appeared on the horizon—nuclear power. Since the splitting of the atom, scientists had recognized the nucleus to be the greatest storehouse of energy in the universe. Dropping the atom bomb in 1945 had been a baptism of fire and made people associate the word "nuclear" with weaponry. But scientists knew all along that this same storehouse of energy could be a source of clean power capable of running an industrial society without the vast land requirements of hydro or the air pollution of fossil fuels.

In December 1953, President Dwight D. Eisenhower took the first step in the development of commercial nuclear power with the Atoms for Peace program, which deemphasized the military aspects of nuclear energy and concentrated on its benefits. In a historic speech at the United Nations, the president offered to share American technology with the rest of the world. Earlier, in 1951, Congress had funded development of the nation's first nuclear-powered submarine, *Nautilus*. It was developed under the direction of Admiral Hyman Rickover and launched in 1955. Then President Eisenhower instructed Rickover to build a slightly bigger reactor—60 MW as opposed to 48 MW—and bring it ashore to create the nation's first commercial nuclear plant.

Given the desire to reduce air pollution derived from coal emissions, it was no accident that the first site chosen was Shippingport, Pennsylvania, ninety miles northwest of Donora, on the banks of the Ohio River. Western Pennsylvania had been plagued by coal smoke since the nineteenth century, and the populace enthusiastically welcomed the reactor. The next commercial reactor was commissioned at Indian Point on the Hudson River, twenty-five miles north of New York City. The plant would allow Con Edison to retire some of its oldest coal-fired plants.

In addition to nuclear as a coal substitute came a movement to switch electric boilers from coal to low-sulfur oil. Although domestic supplies were not really sufficient, there were plenty of new low-sulfur oil discoveries around the world in places such as Kuwait and Indonesia. Oil import quotas imposed for national defense purposes by the Eisenhower administration had kept these imports to a minimum. In the late 1960s, however, under pressure from environmental groups, the floodgates were open to foreign low-sulfur oil. From 1968 to 1972, America's coal consumption *declined* for one of the few times in history. The combination of new nuclear construction and foreign low-sulfur oil appeared to be putting our air pollution problems behind us.

Then the Arabs embargoed oil exports to America and the dream of powering the country with cheap, low-sulfur foreign oil quickly vanished. That still left nuclear power. But fears for its safety were beginning to creep in, and opposition to that grew as well. Subsequently, the Carter administration curtailed two major alternatives to coal when it canceled the construction of several western dams and ended nuclear fuel reprocessing, thereby creating the problem of nuclear waste. Instead, it embraced a revival of coal. In his various energy addresses, President Jimmy Carter called America "the Saudi Arabia of Coal" and promised to double our consumption over the next twenty years. That promise was fulfilled. In 1976, when Carter took office, the nation consumed 500 million tons of coal a year. Today it is over 1 billion tons.

Not all nations went in this direction. In the 1980s in Great Britain, Prime Minister Margaret Thatcher promised to break her nation's dependence on coal, both because of its pollution effects and because it had given the coal miners' union a stranglehold on the national economy. Thatcher engineered a transition to North Sea gas, which still stands today—except that those gas supplies are rapidly declining. France renounced coal, oil, and gas—it had very little of these resources anyway—and deliberately embraced nuclear technology. As a result, France now has one of the cheapest electricity rates in Europe and the second-lowest level of carbon emissions as well.

When the Carter administration embraced coal, concerns about global warming and carbon emissions had not emerged. Instead, concern focused on air pollution. The 1970 Clean Air Act had identified five main pollution streams in coal—sulfur dioxides, nitrous oxides, carbon monoxide, coal ash, and particulate matter. The sulfur dioxides come from the traces of sulfur in coal combining with oxygen in the air. Nitrous oxides result when the high temperatures of combustion cause nitrogen and oxygen in the atmosphere to fuse together. Carbon monoxide comes from incomplete combustion and not enough oxygen. (If combustion is complete, it produces carbon dioxide.) Fly ash is the unburned portions of coal that escape up the smokestack. It may contain all kinds of trace elements—chromium, cadmium, mercury, lead, arsenic, and even uranium—which become a concern when they get into soil, air, or water. Finally, the particulate matter is tiny fragments of ash that escape most filters and are very difficult to capture. PM 2.5—particulate matter less than 2.5 microns across, far less than the width of a human hair—is now regarded as the biggest threat because it easily passes into the human lungs, where it can cause a variety of diseases.

Starting in the 1970s, the Clean Air Act tried to deal with these pollutants by what is called "command and control." The EPA would set standards and then figure out how to meet them. This would involve going around to each and every emitter and telling them what they had to do. The possibilities for delay were endless. Individual companies would argue they were being asked to shoulder more than their fair share of the burden. The EPA would constantly have to justify its decisions, even though they were often somewhat arbitrary.

Several questions about how to go about reducing pollution became extremely contentious and awkward. The first big issue pitted older, high-sulfur eastern coal interests against the emerging low-sulfur coal deposits of Wyoming and Montana. The favorite technology for removing sulfur in the 1970s was the newly invented sulfur scrubber. The scrubber removed sulfur traces by combining them with limestone (calcium carbonate) to form gypsum (calcium sulfate), which has a variety of industrial uses. Scrubbers are expensive, however, and eastern coal interests feared that utilities would reduce their sulfur emissions by switching to low-sulfur western coals. So they pressured Congress to rule that utilities would have to install scrubbers whether they used low-sulfur coal or not, thereby erasing western coal's advantage. This led to a lot of unnecessary expenses.

Offsetting this, however, was the decision to grandfather in old coal plants under the regulations. New coal plants could build in sulfur scrubbers without too much unnecessary expense. But retrofitting old plants might become so expensive the plants would have to close down. So Congress ruled in 1970 that any coal plant that had a permit to build by 1973 would be exempt from the regulation. However, if old plants desired to update and make "major repairs," they were to be treated as "new sources," which would require them to install the same types of expensive equipment as new plants. The argument then became what constituted a "major repair." This battle was fought throughout the Clinton and Bush Administrations. In many instances utilities have postponed needed repairs so they would not have to add scrubbers. The end result is that nearly half the coal plants in the country still do no have this 1970s technology.

Another technological breakthrough was pulverization, where coal is ground into very fine particles and then blown into a furnace so that the particles are almost completely combusted. Temperatures inside such boilers are higher than those in a nuclear reactor. This way of burning coal reduces carbon monoxide and fly ash. Getting rid of very small particulate matter that causes most of the health damage has proved far more difficult. Of course, nitrous oxide emissions actually *increase* with the high heat.

In the early years, the EPA chose "ambient standards," meaning measurements in the area right around the plant, to determine who was in violation of pollution rules. "The solution to pollution is dilution" became the byword, so utilities began building huge smokestacks to scatter their effluents to the four winds. By the late 1980s, however, scientists realized that the sulfur emissions were combining with water in the atmosphere and falling back to earth as acid rain. This became the major environmental crisis of the decade and produced demands for even greater reductions in coal exhausts.

When George H. W. Bush was elected president in 1988, he vowed to become the "environmental president." The first issue on his plate was acid rain. Removing sulfur from coal smoke had been a prime goal of environmental legislation for almost twenty years, but it was clear that enforcement efforts hadn't been too successful. Something more was needed. The Democratic Congress, of course, was ready for even more regulation, but President Bush, as a conservative Republican, didn't want another layer of bureaucracy. So Bush proposed something different—market mechanisms, or what eventually became known as "cap and trade."

The idea of cap and trade had first been proposed in the 1960s by a University of Wisconsin graduate student named Thomas Crocker. Crocker was writing a doctoral dissertation on controlling air pollution from Florida fertilizer plants when he came up with the idea of selling "pollution permits" to the plants and then letting them buy and sell among themselves. The "cap" would set the maximum amount of pollution allowed. The decision on how to clean up would be left to the polluters. Those that could clean up more cheaply than others would opt for new technology or some other kind of approach. Those who found it expensive would bid up the price of the permits. The desired level of pollution would be achieved in the cheapest possible way *with no bureaucracy*. Decision making would be left to the polluters and the market.

Crocker presented his idea at a conference in Washington the following year, three years before the passage of the Clean Air Act. Then, in 1968, John Dales, a professor at the University of Toronto, published *Pollution, Property and Prices,* which outlined the marketable rights concept in much greater detail. The book is still considered a classic.

The idea caught on among conservative economists and by the 1980s had been argued in numerous magazine articles and public debates. And so the Bush administration was ready to give it a try. Environmentalists resisted at first. "It legalizes pollution," "It's pay-to-pollute," "The rich will be able to pollute all they want," were the kind of demagogic arguments that obscured the logic of the system. The Bush administration hung tough, however, and in the end, given the choice of cap and trade or a presidential veto, Democrats in Congress decided to go along.

The cap-and-trade program on sulfur emissions is now regarded as perhaps the great triumph of environmental legislation. When the bill was passed in 1990, the EPA was estimating that cutting sulfur emissions in half, to what was considered an acceptable level, would cost between $3 and $20 billion per year and take twenty years to accomplish. In fact, with cap and trade, sulfur emissions were halved in less than ten years at a cost of only $700 million per year. The cleanup even went beyond the stated goal—a benefit that Crocker and Dale had predicted, since the financial incentives to clean up remained as long as the permits had a price. Consequently, environmentalists became the big supporters of cap and trade. This is the reason the Obama administration and congressional Democrats have chosen cap and trade as the instrument for dealing with global warming.

So it might seem that dealing with carbon should be simple: just set a cap on emissions and allow those who put carbon into the atmosphere to trade the permits among themselves. Unfortunately, it isn't that easy.

First of all, carbon dioxide isn't really a pollutant in the traditional sense. Air pollution to this point has been caused by *contaminants* within coal and fossil fuels. Sulfur is the biggest culprit. It contributes nothing to combustion and can be removed without changing the energy output. The same goes for mercury, lead, chromium, uranium, and all the other contaminants of coal. (There is actually more energy potential in the traces of uranium than in the coal itself, and many people have suggested mining coal for the uranium in it instead of burning it.) Carbon dioxide, however, is the *unavoidable by-product* of burning carbon fuels. Carbon is the source of the energy itself. Cutting out carbon means cutting energy output.

It is also worth noting at this point that the Clean Air amendments of 1990 did not really lead to "cleaning up" sulfur emissions from coal. As will be discussed later, almost all the gains were achieved by substituting natural gas for coal. The removal of gas price controls in 1988 marked the point when natural gas suddenly started becoming abundant again. By 1990 environmentalists were becoming enamored of it and they successfully pushed to have the Carter-era ban on burning natural gas for electricity eliminated. We didn't really clean up sulfur after 1990; we substituted a fuel that has no sulfur.

While this doesn't mean a cap and trade system won't work with carbon, it does leave more uncertain the question of how costly such a program would be. The fact that cap and trade proved to be less expensive than anticipated in its application to acid rain, and that attainment goals were achieved sooner than predicted, was principally the result of the reintroduction of natural gas power generation. No one really knows what the cost or duration of the effort would have been if emitters had had to accomplish their mandates exclusively through the development of new technologies and systems capable of reducing sulfur emissions from coal plants. This uncertainty has, in turn, played a major role in the slow pace with which cap and trade has moved through the Senate.

So that's a short history of our federal efforts to address environmental concerns. It is, in my judgment, a history of significant achievement. But there is more history to be written. The linkage between energy production and use and the environment is obvious, and no long-term energy strategy can afford to ignore the environmental implications of energy policy. Thus, in outlining a twenty-first-century energy strategy, we must take into account and address the energy-related environmental threats that confront us, especially those associated with carbon emissions. In my view, there is sufficient risk associated with the current and projected levels of carbon emissions to make their reduction a significant component of our energy strategies for the future. Moreover, reducing carbon emissions can go hand in hand with enhancing our energy security. The question is whether such strategies can be crafted consistent with economic growth and budgetary constraint. As we proceed through the remainder of this book, we will attempt to answer this, and in that context, return to the subject of congressional efforts to reduce carbon emissions.

BOOK 3

Why We Have Failed to Address Our Energy Security Threats

Introduction

We face a wide array of energy threats and challenges as we enter the second decade of the twenty-first century. The worldwide increase in energy demand during periods of economic growth has and will continue to make energy markets extremely tight, because it is so difficult to quickly ramp up energy supply. Moreover, there is a growing concern that we have reached, or nearly reached, peak production of oil and cannot possibly meet projected demand levels in the coming decades.

All of this is made more complicated because of the geopolitical factors that affect the energy world. Whether from internal strife in energy-producing countries, the desire of individual energy producers to utilize their products to gain political leverage, or the potential of terrorist attacks on energy assets, we face many complex problems.

Finally, our efforts to develop a successful energy strategy are further influenced by our desire to minimize the environmental consequences of energy production and use.

These challenges did not simply emerge in the last year or two. American policy makers have been wrestling with them for decades without success. During that time, a number of approaches have been undertaken, yet we still find ourselves facing these threats and challenges today.

So, in addition to gaining a clear understanding of the serious energy and environmental threats we face, we have to have a better understanding of why the policies we have pursued in recent decades have not been successful.

In the following chapters, I will attempt to analyze some of the significant public policy strategies that have been implemented to address America's energy concerns in recent years. In discussing those strategies and policies, I will provide the reader with a better sense of what those policies have attempted to do and how they have fallen short. Only by grasping the reasons why our current policies fall short can we develop more effective approaches in the future. As the reader will see, there is enough blame to go around. From the left and right, from environmentalists and business leaders, from one administration to the next, there have been a lot of mistakes.

The reader will also see that adherence to several of the energy myths discussed in chapter 1 has contributed to our political failure. All too often our political leaders have been willing to accept these myths as reality in order to avoid making the tough decisions required to address the energy challenges of our times.

CHAPTER 6

Mistakes Have Been Made on All Sides

For years our political system has not been up to the task of fully addressing our energy challenges. This failure has been the result of mistakes made on both sides of the aisle, by both the executive and legislative branches and by outside players as well. This chapter outlines just a few examples of the political mistakes that have cost us much time and opportunity.

The Congress

Let me begin with a look at our legislative branch. One thing I discovered in Washington is that it is easy to motivate public officials to solve problems when there's a crisis, but when there's no imminent threat, it's difficult to get them interested. That's why everybody walks around Washington describing their particular hobbyhorse as a "national crisis." One week it's the lack of flu vaccine, the next it's the Y2K crisis, and on it goes. Claiming there's a crisis is the only way to get attention.

Probably the most memorable example during my tenure was the Great Northeast Blackout of 2003. Just before departing on their annual summer recess that year, both the House and Senate had approved comprehensive energy legislation. The bills were somewhat different, and so a House-Senate conference committee was scheduled to reconcile them when the legislators returned in the fall.

Before Labor Day, however, the whole Northeast and parts of Canada were turned upside down by the August 13 blackout. Power was out for at least a day in most cities. Before two hours had passed, nearly every politician in the Northeast was calling the Department of Energy demanding action.

In conjunction with our Canadian counterparts, we immediately went to work trying to restore power. Then we set about trying to figure out what had gone wrong. Not to be outdone, the House of Representatives Committee on Energy and Commerce also swung into action, scheduling a hearing when Congress returned just after Labor Day. I was told to expect a long and difficult interrogation. Notwithstanding my protests that it would take weeks to determine exactly what caused the blackout, the congressional leadership made it very clear I had better be ready with some answers.

On hearing day, I made my way to Capitol Hill with great trepidation. The Energy and Commerce Committee of the House is one of the largest in Congress, with more than fifty members. Republicans were in the majority, but that was small comfort. Despite our efforts to set an agenda, the committee leadership decided that standard hearing rules would apply. This meant every single member of the committee would be entitled to a five-minute opening statement before my testimony began.

Because the blackout was such a hot topic, almost every member of the committee showed up. Eager to get their C-SPAN or evening news coverage for the folks back home, virtually everyone decided to make an opening statement. And so it went, on and on. The opening statements lasted for hours. Under the rules, I was required to sit at the witness table and say nothing until it was over. Predictably, half of the members spent their time claiming their district had been hardest hit and professing to be outraged about the blackout. (As you may have noticed, unlike the rest of the country, where people usually retain some balance in troubled times, people in Washington are always "shocked" when things go wrong. If not shocked they're "appalled," "indignant," "furious," and "frustrated.")

Finally, I was able to speak, by which point, I might add, many of the members had departed. Now I would get to answer members' questions. Unsurprisingly, the most frequently asked question was "What can we do to prevent future blackouts?" Even though we did not yet know precisely the cause of the August outage, I offered a sound general answer. The United States did not have any enforcement powers with regard to running the grid. While we could advise transmission companies on how to operate, we could not punish them for failing to adhere to any specified standard of conduct. As a result, while companies were vulnerable to civil liability actions, they could not even be reprimanded for failing to maintain their own networks. What we needed were enforceable reliability standards to govern the electrical grid.

Happily, language allowing the development of enforceable reliability standards had already been included in both the competing House and Senate energy bills. As the hearing wore on, member after member proudly informed me that Congress had already acted and that it would only be a matter of days before a bill was on the president's desk. As congressmen took their bows, nearly spraining their arms patting themselves on the back, I remember thinking they seemed a bit overconfident. Those of us who follow conference committee deliberations know that a few controversial provisions often stall legislative action and sometimes stop it altogether. And there definitely were some showstopper issues in the two competing bills.

Soon my worst fears were confirmed. Instead of days, it took weeks for a bill to emerge from conference committee. The final version passed by a small majority in the House. Because of Senate cloture rules, however, sixty votes are required for final passage in that chamber. When certain senators started raising objections to other parts of the bill, the whole thing died. So much for swift congressional action to prevent future blackouts.

There is no doubt in my mind that if a vote had been taken within a few days after the blackout, the bill would have sailed through uncontested. Once the crisis had passed, however, momentum died, and things returned to normal. Trivial concerns and special interests took precedence. And so the solution was put off for another day. Almost two more years passed before we finally got Congress to enact an energy bill and adopt an enforceable grid reliability standard.

The Bush Administration

Congress hasn't been the only problem when it comes to energy. We in the Bush administration made our share of mistakes as well.

As I said earlier, the California blackouts were taking place the first day I took office. Rather than run off half-cocked, President George W. Bush did a very intelligent thing. He created the National Energy Policy Development Group to survey the entire situation and devise a comprehensive plan to deal with energy. It was obvious that California had contributed to its troubles by blocking the construction of many new electrical generation plants for two decades. But that was only one aspect. Natural gas prices were soaring. Our oil imports were steadily climbing. Coal was under fire because of concerns about global warming. Nuclear power had been dormant for two decades. What the nation needed was a broad look at our entire energy economy to see what we should do next. Vice President Richard Cheney was named head of the task force. The secretaries of Interior, Agriculture, Transportation, Energy, Treasury, and Commerce along with the heads of the Environmental Protection Agency and the Office of Management and Budget, among others, were assigned to sit in.

Over the course of several months the task force worked on developing a comprehensive strategy, including legislative proposals and actions to be taken by the executive branch. In the end, we came up with a very detailed proposal that included over one hundred recommendations. The report was issued in April 2001. Almost as soon as it was off the presses the study was denounced, even though almost nobody had read it yet.

Environmental groups, Democrats in Congress, and the media immediately attacked. They claimed the problems were being exaggerated and the task force was overreaching. The whole thing was said to be nothing more than a smokescreen to permit drilling for more oil and gas. During the 2008 presidential election, when energy once again became a central topic, I thought back on this whole episode with amusement. By then the critics were alleging that we hadn't gauged the magnitude of our energy problems. But in 2001 it was still possible to argue that the Bush administration was exaggerating the whole issue.

So what went wrong? Although neither President Bush nor Vice President Cheney would have ever been given an easy ride on energy policy, I will be the first to admit that we did make some mistakes. Probably the first was in assigning the chairmanship to the vice president. It's not that he wasn't qualified or that he didn't do an excellent job, but there were reasons why he probably should not have been in charge. First, as the former chief executive of a major energy services business, Halliburton Company, the vice president was susceptible to the accusation that he was not impartial. Of course, anybody capable of overseeing the development of energy policy needs to have some serious experience in the field. But politics is a perception game, and the vice president's background made him vulnerable.

Second, the White House probably made a mistake by making our deliberations secret. At the time it seemed appropriate, since it allowed people to be candid in offering their views. In retrospect, however, this was unnecessary. I attended almost every meeting, and there was nothing said that was unfit for public consumption. Conducting at least some of the sessions in public would have been very beneficial, although I admit I did not foresee this at the time.

Because our deliberations were shrouded in secrecy, critics immediately charged that we had only heard the industry side of things and had not given environmental groups and advocates of alternative energy a fair hearing. This was not true, as even a cursory look at our recommendations would reflect. It was just that we did not make a very convincing case. Vice President Cheney's remark, "Conservation may be a virtue but it is not an energy policy," was a self-inflicted wound. No one was against improving energy efficiency, and most of us were highly in favor of it, but even the top energy experts did not seriously believe that conservation alone was going to solve our energy problems. However, once the perception was formed, our proposals were doomed. I spent the remainder of my tenure as secretary trying to get at least a few of our recommendations through a Republican Congress—without much success.

This image, more appearance than substance, carried over to other energy issues as well. The Bush administration spent much of its time fending off charges that it was not concerned with climate change. In reality, President Bush dramatically expanded the nation's commitment to research and technology in this area, with increased budgets for climate science and clean energy technologies, but no one remembers.

During my first year in office I sat through innumerable discussions about the science of global warming. We heard from experts on all sides as to whether changes in the earth's temperature were actually taking place and the degree to which human activity was responsible. We concluded that some change was indeed taking place, but the amount could not be determined with sufficient precision to warrant drastic actions. Accordingly, we adopted substantial increases in research funding.

What followed was almost comical. Even as we were ramping up our investments in research, the public was being given the impression that the Bush administration was indifferent to the whole subject. So instead of getting credit for our efforts we found ourselves in a defensive posture on all fronts. (It should also be noted that only a few years before, the United States Senate had rejected the Kyoto treaty by a vote of 95–0 even before President Bill Clinton signed it.)

In my opinion all this could have been avoided. As soon as our cabinet working group finished its deliberations, we should have started informing the public of the actions we were taking. Instead, we kept a low profile, creating the impression we were doing little. We should have confronted, head-on, the question of whether

America needed a carbon regulatory system. Instead, we appeared to be disengaged. By the time legislation on climate change began to gain strength in Congress, the public impression was that the administration was lagging far behind.

The Environmental Community

Yes, we in the Bush administration made mistakes that contributed to the failed energy politics of recent years, but it is fair to say that many in the environmental community also contributed to the current impasse. Most notable has been their intransigent opposition to nuclear energy. Because no new nuclear plants have been built in the United States for thirty years, we necessarily burn more coal and natural gas.

The environmental community has also been wrong in its near constant opposition to domestic energy development. Certainly some resource production and facility projects justify resistance, but for too long various environmental groups have worked to stop virtually any new development. I fully recognize the tension that exists between meeting our energy needs on the one hand and protecting the environment on the other, but the simple fact is we must find common ground. That is nearly impossible to do if either side adopts a completely inflexible position. Too often that has been the case with environmental groups on energy production issues, and this stance has, in my opinion, helped lead to the political failures we have endured.

The Media

Not to be overlooked is the media. In chapter 1, we discussed a series of myths about energy that have contributed to the stalemate that has gripped energy policy making. In my view the media has played a central role in keeping some of these and other energy myths alive and has therefore contributed to our current energy impasse.

Also, as with many matters it covers, the media has tended to divide the world of energy into good guys and bad guys. Environmentalists and their organizations have tended to receive good-guy treatment, while energy companies and their executives usually find themselves stereotyped as bad guys. All of this, of course, adds to the tension that characterizes most energy debates. This has, in turn, made it even more difficult for people of diverse opinions to come together and advance a strong energy agenda.

Business

Business has also contributed to the mess. Let's start with Enron. More than anything, the misconduct of that one company reinforced the notion that all energy companies are bad and act to keep the cost of energy artificially high. Enron's actions inflicted severe damage on the entire industry. And Enron was not the only offender. As we discovered during the 2003 blackout, a lot of energy companies cut corners. The failure of one utility to keep the trees trimmed around its transmission lines shut down the entire East Coast.

In addition, many energy companies who have joined the green revolution have stopped making the case for energy production from traditional sources. I applaud companies that invest money in renewable energy and call for sustainable development; I have less praise for those that fail to tell the whole story. The latter have helped perpetuate the impression that we can become both energy independent and environmentally pure by simply building a lot of wind farms. That may help their corporate image, but the lack of balance allows politicians and citizens to believe there are easy solutions to our energy problems.

The Department of Energy

As the reader will recall, my pathway to the job of energy secretary was a somewhat unusual one. In the Senate I had been a cosponsor of legislation that would have abolished the department and assigned its various duties and responsibilities to other agencies. Thus, I carried to the secretary's office a certain amount of skepticism about the effectiveness and capacity of the department I was about to head. The department's employees were, if anything, even more skeptical of their new secretary, who they assumed had little respect for either the department or the people who worked there.

Four years later, I walked out the door a very changed man. While it could be argued that the Department of Energy in some ways contributed to the problems we've encountered in devising energy strategy, I don't really believe it has been a serious part of the problem. To the contrary, I came to deeply respect the men and women who constitute the department's workforce, whose leadership was indispensable to any success I achieved during my tenure.

If anything, the department and its employees were victims of the political process I've alluded to in this chapter. At heart, the department is really a technology and science agency. It runs our national laboratories and oversees countless research programs and grants. As we will later discuss, the meddling of politicians has frequently derailed these science and technology efforts, to the detriment of our nation. Rather than micromanage DOE research and attempt to substitute politically expedient priorities for those based on sound science and good strategy, Congress and the White House need to provide more discretion and flexibility to DOE's experts as they pursue solutions to our various energy challenges.

The nation would also benefit by giving DOE greater investigative authority. During the California blackout the department and I were largely incapable of investigating the true causes of California's energy crisis. This lack of authority undermined us in other situations as well.

Finally, because the Department of Energy resulted from the aggregation of numerous predecessor entities in the late 1970s, it has consistently wrestled with the question of its mission. When the department was created, Congress and the Carter administration cobbled together a wide array of programs, offices, and agencies.

As we have seen with the Department of Homeland Security, it is not easy to assimilate a wide, diverse group of government entities under a new umbrella. At DOE there is still a fair amount of adjustment going on more than thirty years after its inception.

For this reason, it is hard to focus the department on overriding priorities and mission. People whose office was originally responsible for science research feel that they work for the Department of Science. People whose offices oversee the cleanup of nuclear weapons sites feel that they belong to the Department of Cleanup. And so on. During my tenure I attempted to create a sense of an overall mission for DOE. My theory was that the department was first and foremost a national security agency. Whether people were working on nuclear nonproliferation, energy security, scientific advancement, or environmental remediation, they were trying, first and foremost, to make America a safer place.

I believe that is the proper definition of the department's mission and feel that it would make the DOE a more effective institution if we could formulate a strong national consensus that this is, indeed, the department's objective. I am confident such efforts would increase DOE's effectiveness.

Spencer Abraham

Now, let me turn the spotlight on myself, because I, too, made mistakes. As previously noted, I confronted the California energy crisis my first day in office. During the early stages, almost all the evidence we had in Washington indicated California was suffering from rolling blackouts because the state had experienced enormous population and economic growth but had not adequately expanded its power generation or in-state transmission capabilities. We also believed California had exacerbated the situation by poorly handling its electricity deregulation reform efforts—installing a partial deregulatory approach that deregulated wholesale prices but not retail prices.

I remember laying out this argument several times on Capitol

Hill. Congressional representatives from the Golden State, on the other hand, insisted they were victims of evil out-of-state forces. When they did, I would cite various statistics suggesting they were wrong.

Many months later, when the full story came out, it wasn't pretty. Yes, California had not devised the soundest electricity deregulation framework, and yes, they had not adequately invested in power generation to meet their rapid growth. However, as Enron imploded, it became clear that that company and other energy players had engaged in nefarious activities that contributed to California's hardships. My failure to look beyond the data was a mistake. I was new in the job and, because the Department of Energy does not have authority to interrogate individuals or subpoena records, we had not been able to garner all the facts. But I should have seen more. As a result, we might have been able to do more to alleviate the crisis.

Another mistake I made was in not meeting more often with environmental groups. As a senator from Michigan, the auto industry state, I had butted heads with environmental groups throughout my career. These organizations, having worked tirelessly to defeat me in both my Senate races, were not enthusiastic about my becoming energy secretary.

Once I took office, I was largely ignored by these groups, who generally sought audiences in other parts of the administration. In return I tended not to pay enough attention to them. In retrospect, I should have reached out more. Later, I took more initiative, and some returned my overtures. In the end, I forged a good working relationship with a number of organizations, such as the U.S. Green Building Council and the Alliance to Save Energy. But in my early days at the department this wasn't the case.

I also made a mistake in not being more candid with the American people about the basic laws of supply and demand and their impact on energy. I've discussed how the energy secretary is always under fire when gasoline prices go up. At those times, we were under tremendous pressure to appear to be doing something, rather than explaining to people that larger forces were at work.

For example, at one point we created a "price gouger" hotline where people could call and report gas stations they thought were artificially raising prices. In fact, gas stations were just responding to supply and demand like everybody else. Instead of establishing a hotline (which by the way, received only a few calls), we should have given the American people the blunt facts about energy. It might not have been politically popular, but it might have prevented us from kicking the can farther down the road.

The Public

Last but not least, I must point out some mistakes made by the public itself. Knee-jerk opposition to almost every energy project is not healthy. Whether it is power plants, transmission lines, or solar collectors on a neighbor's roof, the instinctive response "Not In My Backyard" runs rampant across our nation. I fully understand that nobody wants some ugly structure anywhere near them. But these facilities have to go somewhere. It's time for the American public to recognize that "Not In My Backyard" behavior is a major reason we face so many energy threats.

If we're ever going to break this impasse, all the players have to give ground. It's time to put away the sharp rhetoric, personal attacks, doctored research, and media mythmaking and work together. Unfortunately, we have instead avoided tough decisions and settled for an array of politically correct solutions that just don't work. In the following chapters, I will outline a few of these failing strategies and show how they have tempted us into avoiding the tough calls. As the reader will recognize, continuing down this road is a prescription for disaster.

CHAPTER 7

The Failure of Politics: You Can't Have It Both Ways

Developing public policy is not simply a function of who has the most experts or better research on their side. It is also very much a function of what real people—the voters—think and believe. And it is in no small measure the case that our energy policy stalemate stems from the fact that, on energy, Americans embrace various opinions that are often inconsistent. Thus, as elected officials strive to maintain their popularity, they frequently pursue policies that are contradictory and thus destined for failure. In this chapter I will step away from policy a bit to examine the political landscape of energy and outline how trying to address the politics of energy has produced a policy train wreck.

When the subject of energy comes up, most people's minds conjure up a vision of drilling rigs and black liquid gushing from the ground. They think of oil and of refineries and of gasoline stations. They also think of billionaire oil sheikhs in the Middle East and of billionaire businessmen in Texas. To most people, energy is all about oil, and the price of oil is what most people think about when the words "energy crisis" appear in headlines or on TV.

Unfortunately, most people are not well informed about the modern world of oil production. For most people, an oil well means one of those tall, black structures seen in movies like *Giant* or *There Shall Be Blood*. They tend to assume that oil wells are drilled indiscriminately in the most sensitive ecological areas of the world, without regard to either the environmental consequences or the cost of a failed project. But even if people believe that the oil production process is insensitive and unpleasant, they generally don't care so long as the end product is cheap.

During the time I served as secretary of energy we faced countless challenges and crises. We had rolling blackouts in California, security breaches at our national weapons laboratories, the Northeast blackout of 2003, and all manner of other serious problems. Yet nothing produced more consternation and concern on Capitol Hill and in the media than high gasoline prices. And, remember, the price of oil stayed under $50 a barrel during my tenure on the job.

I've already chronicled the reaction I received whenever oil prices rose. The response was consistent across the political spectrum. Everybody was angry and wanted something done immediately. Senators who railed about reducing oil imports suddenly wanted us to go beg OPEC for more oil. Congressmen who worried about national security wanted to draw down the Strategic Petroleum Reserve. Put simply, there is an overwhelming national consensus that Americans deserve cheap oil.

Almost as powerful is the consensus for energy independence. Of course, it is never really certain what that means. Does it mean reducing our imports to zero, to less than 50%, or to some happy medium? What is clear is that Americans do not like the idea of being beholden to other nations for our energy supplies.

Complicating objectives one and two is a third point of view shared widely by Americans, which says we need to produce and use energy without harming the environment. These advocates would like to see us expand our mass transit systems, increase the fuel efficiency of motor vehicles, minimize our onshore and offshore energy development, and so on. It is difficult if not impossible to pursue all three of these objectives at once. The tireless efforts of our political leaders to try to pursue these contradictory objectives represent yet another failure of our political process, since it has resulted in our undertaking a set of inconsistent and consequently unsuccessful policies.

For instance, there is no question that the price signal is the most powerful tool available to discourage the use of a commodity. If the price of something goes up people will buy less of it. If it goes down, they will buy more. It's simple economics. With energy, this principle works the same as everywhere else. Despite what anyone says about energy being different or a necessity or a basic right, when the price of gasoline reaches a certain level, people start reducing their demand.

But here's where the inherent contradictions begin. A number of commentators have called for increases in the tax on gasoline in order to discourage consumption. This would reduce our dependence on imports and conserve natural resources. However, an increase in the gas tax means higher gasoline prices. And so, the desire to protect the environment and increase energy independence will inevitably be challenged by the desire to keep gas more affordable. You could call an increase in the gasoline tax an energy-freedom tax, an energy-independence tax, an anti-OPEC tax, or an anti-global-warming tax, but chances are Congress won't be inclined to pass anything if it directly increases the price at the pump.

The Obama administration has found this out in its efforts to regulate carbon. The simplest thing to do would be to place a tax on carbon and let the price of oil and coal and natural gas adjust accordingly, but politicians found this too dangerous: It would be too easy to blame Washington for increases in the price of energy. So it opted instead to try to pass a complex cap-and-trade system that would impose indirect costs on the energy sector that would ultimately fall on the public. Yet even this strategy has bogged down due to the realities of economics and politics.

Another major conflict exists between the desire for energy independence on the one hand and the steadfast opposition of environmentalists to domestic energy production on the other. I used to find it especially frustrating when members of Congress who opposed more domestic energy development would also complain about America's growing foreign dependence. Back in 1995, Congress passed legislation to open up the Arctic National Wildlife Refuge (ANWR) for energy production. President Clinton vetoed it and his veto was sustained. Two of the opposition arguments were that it would take a decade before oil production could begin and that there really wasn't all that much oil up there anyway.

Of course, had the president not vetoed the legislation in 1995, oil would be flowing today. As for the assertion that there isn't much oil in ANWR, no one knows for sure. That's how it is with energy exploration. However, according to U.S. Geological Survey, there could be as much as 16 billion barrels. At peak production, ANWR would then be producing around one million barrels per day. To make this amount seem small, ANWR opponents point out that 16 billion barrels represents only about two years of U.S. oil consumption. Of course, that's not the right way to look at it. Instead, we should recognize that one million barrels of oil per day would reduce America's daily dependence on imported oil by roughly 10%! The bottom line is that it is pretty hard to oppose new domestic development while simultaneously complaining about our dependence on foreign energy sources.

Some have tried to assert that we can be energy independent without more domestic energy development if we dramatically increase conservation in order to reduce our consumption of oil. But, as noted before, getting there isn't very easy. Those who advocate this position usually advocate higher fuel economy standards for motor vehicles, but even the most robust proposals for motor vehicle fuel efficiency standards would not bring us close to the mark. Moreover, as previously discussed, I believe it is somewhat illusory to argue that making cars more fuel-efficient necessarily results in equivalent reductions in gasoline consumption.

In another chapter I will discuss in greater detail the world of energy efficiency, paying particular attention to the work of Mark Mills and Peter Huber in their book, *The Bottomless Well*. Suffice it to say, it is easy to overestimate the energy savings we can get by mandating improved fuel efficiency.

When audiences ask me my opinion of the Corporate Annual Fuel Economy (CAFE) standards, I generally ask for a show of hands to see how many people have an annual mileage plan for their cars. Then I ask how many have an annual dollar budget for their gasoline expenditures. Guess which elicits a raising of hands?

As I've noted elsewhere, not many Americans wake up on January 1 and determine how many miles they will travel in the new year. On the other hand, there are a great many who have a rough budget for how much they want to spend on gasoline per week or per year. If it turns out that their gasoline budget allows them to drive more, chances are they'll use it.

I often ask audiences what would have the greater impact on their fuel consumption, cars that get thirty miles to the gallon or ones that only get five. I'm being facetious, of course, but a case could be made that we would see a lot less fuel consumed if people got only five or ten miles per gallon of gasoline, instead of thirty, because the cost per mile driven would be higher. My real point is this: The notion that we can dramatically reduce our consumption of oil simply by increasing fuel efficiency standards is wrong. A 20% to 30% increase in fleetwide fuel efficiency will have an impact. But the simple fact is that if you make cars more fuel efficient you make them cheaper to drive, and when you make something cheaper you tend to incentivize its use.

Yet another example of how we have been advocating contradictory positions on matters relating to energy policy is seen in our political reaction to high fuel prices. As secretary of energy I was always on the firing line when the price of gasoline spiked. Almost every action recommended in the media and on Capitol Hill during these periods tended to be completely inconsistent with the notion of either reducing our dependence on foreign oil or our consumption in general.

Heading the list of proposals was the perpetual recommendation that we tap our Strategic Petroleum Reserve (SPR) to reduce prices. In other words, we should sacrifice long-term national security for short-term price relief. This, of course, made little sense. The Strategic Reserve is an important backstop against serious dislocations in the world oil market. Depleting this asset is almost impossible to rationalize in an age of terror. Yet, watch what happens the next time high gasoline prices begin to create headlines. The very same people who want us to be energy independent will be campaigning to tap the SPR, placing us even more at the mercy of geopolitical energy factors.

Next comes the predictable demand that we do something about OPEC. Since the 1970s, OPEC has occupied the center stage of the international oil market. Depending on your perspective, OPEC is a force for good or for evil. To its members, OPEC is an effective instrument for bringing stability to world oil markets, a hedge against wild price fluctuations. To the consuming nations, however, OPEC's collaborations are nothing less than an effort to manipulate prices. When those prices seem reasonable, most oil-importing countries pay little attention to OPEC. When prices start to climb, things can get ugly.

As energy secretary, I was regularly interrogated by congressional committees about OPEC. If prices were high, I was asked what we were doing to get OPEC to export more oil. If prices were really high, I was urged to get tough with OPEC and demand that they increase production.

During high price periods Congress has, in recent years, tried to pass a law designed to charge OPEC with violating antitrust laws in the hope of threatening OPEC into producing more oil. This legislation, dubbed "NOPEC," has enjoyed much support on Capitol Hill while raising deep concerns at the State Department and White House because of its broad foreign policy implications. What I find particularly intriguing is that many of the same people who want us to be less dependent on imported energy are also prepared to pass legislation that would, if enacted, almost certainly lead to more foreign dependence.

Failing to pass this legislation, Congress always came back to the same solution. The administration should relieve prices by demanding that OPEC raise its quotas and pump more oil. My response was always the same. Did the members of Congress really want me to go hat in hand to OPEC and beg? When I put it this way, the implications became clear. Begging for or demanding more production would ultimately make us even more beholden to the producer nations.

Some critics never got it, however. They would suggest that the United States start withholding the security support we provide to friendly oil-producing nations around the Persian Gulf. This, of course, would only make things worse. Those nations would then be more vulnerable to internal radical opposition or to regional powers such as Iran, neither of which would be in our interest. Once again, we see our politicians advocating policies that are inherently contradictory and self-defeating.

When it comes to OPEC, all bets are off anyway. During my tenure at Energy, the price of oil was generally in the range of $20 to $30 per barrel. One of our priorities was to hold OPEC to its public commitment to try to maintain prices within a narrow price band of $22 to $28 a barrel. Nearly every time OPEC met in 2003 and 2004, rumors would fly that, due to inflation and fluctuations in the value of the U.S. dollar, OPEC was flirting with the notion of increasing the band to $24 to $30 a barrel. On the eve of each meeting, the United States and other consumer nations would begin informal talks with various OPEC members trying to discourage such actions.

Looking back on those days, I can only smile at our innocence. When oil hit $145 per barrel, I remember thinking how absurd it was that we were once concerned about $30-a-barrel oil. Of course, a lot has changed during the past five years. The market really has grown tighter during peak demand times, virtually wiping out spare capacity. That has left OPEC with less flexibility in holding down prices. Moreover, once it became clear OPEC couldn't maintain a ceiling, speculators concluded the market was headed only one way—upward—and jumped aboard. A lot of people made money on these bets—until the bubble burst.

I also believe OPEC's view of the world has changed in recent years. The rapidly growing demand for oil we saw before the 2008–09 recession nearly has outpaced the producers' ability to expand supply. OPEC no longer has much spare capacity in periods of high demand. Moreover, once the members experienced the benefits of swelling revenues, they quickly got used to it. As both government leaders and their populations adapted their lifestyles to higher levels of revenue, it became difficult to turn back. Now we hear OPEC members talking about reducing their long-term production plans in order to preserve more oil for future generations—a prescription for higher prices.

Moreover, I believe OPEC members have concluded there is not much downside to high prices. During the 2007–08 price run-up, they came to recognize that their greatest fear—the emergence of some alternative fuel or technology to replace oil—was not going to happen. No matter how high the price of oil climbed, serious competition in the form of biofuels, hydrogen-powered vehicles, or oil from nontraditional sources did not occur.

Finally, the emergence of new oil-consuming nations such as China and India has convinced OPEC members they are no longer completely dependent on the United States. Where the United States once stood as the dominant player, there are now a lot of new games in town. This has emboldened the producers. While the United States, with its outstanding technological capabilities and vast resources, might have devised an alternative approach to meet energy demand, the major producers are now confident that they will be able to sell their oil around the world for a long time, no matter what the price.

So what does this mean? It means that our competing political priorities of low energy prices, less dependency, and aversion to domestic energy production are impossible to address simultaneously. Because we want to pursue policy objectives that are inherently contradictory, we haven't made much progress in curbing our oil appetite and enhancing energy security. When we refuse to allow more domestic production, we end up even more dependent on imports. When we take action to reduce prices, we only generate greater consumption. When we push OPEC to produce more energy, we end up more dependent than ever. Either way, we're not making any progress.

Years of debate about energy policy have not really accomplished much. The contradictions outlined here, and similar ones in other energy contexts, always emerge to undermine any momentum we may establish. Just when high prices drive us toward developing domestic resources and pushing for technological change, the price breaks and we go back to our old ways. When prices rise again, our first impulse is to tap the Strategic Petroleum Reserve or ask OPEC for more oil. Like a frog slowly boiling in water, we do not recognize that the long-term trend is not in our favor. What we need are policies that wean us away from dependence and allow us a little room to maneuver in a dangerous world.

CHAPTER 8

"All We Need Is a New Manhattan Project."

"All we need is another Manhattan Project." If I had five dollars for every time I've heard a politician say that with relation to our energy problems, I would be a very rich man.

The original Manhattan Project gave us nuclear energy—at least in the crude form of a powerful bomb. Now all we need to do is follow the same strategy of matching unlimited resources with top intellects, and our problems will be solved. Here's the way author Jeff Wilson puts it in *The Manhattan Project of 2009*:

> When the U.S. committed to producing the atom bomb, the . . .
> government sought out the very brightest minds in the field
> and turned them loose. There were many huge hurdles along
> the way, but in the end they accomplished amazing things in
> just a few short years.

To most listeners, this call invokes memories of President John F. Kennedy's 1961 pledge to send a man to the moon by the end of the decade—a promise that was indeed fulfilled. This excites audiences, appears farsighted, and, most important from the standpoint of a politician, kicks the can a little farther down the road.

This is not reality. The reality is that there are no quick fixes, no silver bullets, no wizards hiding behind the curtain ready to make our energy problems go away. Yet political leaders have long pretended there are shortcuts to the finish line.

One of my most interesting experiences as energy secretary was visiting Los Alamos National Laboratory, the center of our effort to build a nuclear bomb. Altogether, the Manhattan Project consisted of a string of secret government installations with the now-familiar names of Oak Ridge, Hanford, and Savannah River. The heavily secured Blue Room at Los Alamos is where many of the archives are now housed. When I visited, I viewed some of the original handwritten notes of the research scientists who had worked on the project. Although there were some practical adjustments in the theoretical science, most of the basic blueprint for atomic energy had already been devised well before the Manhattan Project was launched.

As I said earlier, there is unfortunately no broad, widely accepted scientific theory about any new form of energy that can serve as a contemporary counterpart. Yes, we can make some progress with respect to new engineering techniques for developing wind and solar energy, but the limitations of these sources are already well established. We may improve energy efficiency, extract more energy from existing sources, and reduce the environmental degradation caused by known technologies, but there is no game-changing source of power waiting around the corner.

Let's look at exactly what happened between the summer of 1939 when Albert Einstein wrote his famous letter to President Franklin D. Roosevelt warning of the possibilities of a nuclear bomb, leading to the initiation of the Manhattan Project, and the moment six years later when Trinity, the first test bomb, was detonated in the New Mexico desert at Alamogordo, 230 miles south of Los Alamos.

The theoretical dawn of nuclear energy occurred in 1905 when Einstein posited $E = mc^2$ as part of his special theory of relativity. Although probably the most famous equation in history, few people even now understand what it actually means.

The equation $E = mc^2$ says matter and energy are interchangeable. Matter can be transformed into energy and energy can be transformed into matter, but the transformation doesn't occur on a one-to-one basis. You have to multiply by that other number— *the speed of light squared*. Think about it. That's a number with fourteen zeroes behind it—something around the order of *ten quadrillion*. It's a number we don't encounter very often in everyday life. What it means is that you don't need much matter to produce an almost unbelievable amount of energy. A set of nuclear fuel assemblies weighing six hundred tons, for example, will sit at the core of a reactor generating 1,000 MW of electricity, enough to power a city the size of San Francisco. When the fuel assemblies are removed after five years, they will weigh about six ounces less than when they went in. The conversion of this six ounces of matter into pure energy is what powers the reactor.

As scientific discovery proceeded in the 1920s, it became clear that, although these transformations back and forth between matter and energy cannot take place in everyday experience, they do take place in what we call the quantum world—the subatomic realm of protons, neutrons, electrons, and dozens of other subatomic particles.

For a long time into the 1930s, some of the world's greatest physicists doubted that large quantities of this atomic energy could be tapped on a controlled basis. Ernest Rutherford, "the Father of the Atom," was violently opposed to the idea, and even Albert Einstein doubted it. But a group of younger scientists pursued the idea anyway and eventually reached success.

In 1931, Leo Szilard, a young Hungarian researcher, recognized that the release of neutrons from one splitting atom could trigger another cleavage, setting off a chain reaction. In 1933, Enrico Fermi discovered he could transform the nucleus of the naturally radioactive uranium atom by bombarding it with neutrons. Fermi assumed he had produced a larger element farther up the atomic scale. But in 1938, Otto Hahn and a younger associate, Fritz Straussman, working in Berlin, reported it was actually barium—an element about half the size of uranium—that was formed in Fermi's experiment. Lise Meitner, Hahn's research partner for twenty-five years who had then fled to Denmark because of her Jewish ancestry, heard the news and ultimately determined what had happened: The uranium had split in half, producing an enormous energy release. "Atomic energy" was possible. (See Richard Rhodes, *The Making of the Atomic Bomb,* also Robert Jungk, *Brighter Than a Thousand Suns.*)

Then Germany invaded Poland and World War II began. Many scientists who had pioneered the effort were Jewish and were driven from Europe. Meanwhile, a few German scientists who were not Jewish sided with the Nazis. Theorists on both sides realized a bomb was possible and soon began racing to beat their counterparts on the other side.

It was under these circumstances that the Manhattan Project was begun. The goal was to build two or three bombs, not change the entire energy structure of a country. The Manhattan Project was an engineering effort, not an attempt to break new ground. Over the course of four years the scientists devised a way to create an instantaneous chain reaction that would produce a huge release of energy. But the source of that energy was already known.

So the question is "Are there any new energy sources waiting to be developed in the same way?" The answer is no. No scientific theory suggests any great undiscovered sources of energy anywhere in the world. At the Department of Energy billions of dollars are spent annually researching energy theories. Countless expert panels help shape the scope and direction of such research, and no one alleges that we are on the brink of a breakthrough on the order of nuclear power. Increasing the department's research and science investments makes a lot of sense, but not because we are on the cusp of a game-changing energy source. Believe me, this is no more a function of failing to tap the brightest minds than it is a function of inadequate resources. For years now the top scientists and laboratories have been working on these issues. They are having a very positive impact, but no one has suggested we are on the verge of a new Manhattan Project achievement—or even close.

This assessment doesn't mean we aren't making headway in our effort to realize the potential of other energy alternatives. We know that solar energy is a huge resource but very dilute. We know that wind energy is even more dilute and requires even greater amounts of space to gather it. We know that photosynthesis is less efficient in turning sunlight into energy than solar collectors, so that growing biofuels will require even more land. Scientists are studying these challenges and trying to address them. But the magnitude of these impediments is substantial, perhaps impossible to overcome. No one expects major breakthroughs anytime soon, no matter how much we spend.

Let's look at just one area—burning organic material. People have been burning firewood for centuries. Then the Industrial Revolution began a switch to coal and other fossil fuels. In both instances, we are tapping solar energy stored by plant photosynthesis.

As problems with fossil fuels have arisen, the possibility has been raised that we should return to burning wood and other plant material, this time under the name of "biofuels." Supposedly this approach will be more "sustainable." But it is not as simple as it seems. Photosynthesis is only 1% efficient in turning the sun's energy into stored chemical energy—far below the efficiency of solar and photovoltaic collectors. The amount of solar energy that a plant can store over a year is not that great. As a result, it would take hundreds and thousands of square miles of biofuel plantations to provide even a fraction of our energy needs. We would have to cultivate all the agricultural land in the United States to replace half the gasoline we put in our cars. Scientists are looking for ways to use materials other than food crops for biofuels, but no one has any theory for addressing the issue of how much land is needed for major biofuel production.

Consider a gallon of gasoline. The octane molecule in gasoline is the most compact form of solar energy ever discovered. It's no wonder we use it in our cars. A full tank of gasoline, fifteen to twenty gallons, will propel your car for about four hundred miles—if it meets CAFE standards. That's a tremendous amount of energy to be stored in a container that can be tucked into your car in a place where you don't even see it. Think of how much "horse power" it would take to pull your car that same distance with real horses! What physicists discovered over the course of the twentieth century is that this energy, too, comes from transformations on the order of Einstein's $E = mc^2$. When you burn a gallon of gasoline, less than *one-billionth* of the mass of the electrons is *completely* transformed into energy. The amount is so small—about the weight of a single proton—that nobody has ever been able to measure it. But when you multiply it by the c-squared coefficient—the speed of light squared—it turns out to be a large amount of energy. That's not going to be easily replicated, nor is there any Manhattan Project on the brink of providing a cheap or simple alternative to gasoline for these reasons.

Altogether, we can expect slow, steady improvements from conservation efforts and "alternate energy," but don't expect any miracles. It doesn't make sense to wait for a Manhattan Project or to think we can conjure one up simply by throwing money at promising technologies. To a large extent, we're going to have to work with what we've got. That means oil, coal, gas, solar, wind, biofuels, conservation, and nuclear. Unfortunately, in the political arena it is often preferable to avoid tough calls, and one way to postpone them is to create the impression that enough money and experts will combine to eliminate them. Creating this fiction is yet another example of the failure of the political process to meet our energy and environmental threats head on.

CHAPTER 9

Relying on One or Two Superfuels Will Not Be Enough

To many politicians and policy gurus natural gas is the dream fuel. It is clean and easy to burn. It has no sulfur or mercury contamination and only about half the carbon emissions of coal. Back in the 1990s it became the fuel of choice until domestic demand began to outpace supply and prices rose. Now we again appear to be blessed with growing supplies. Although gas ran short and prices soared from 2000 to 2006, recent breakthroughs in drilling have made it possible to tap the huge reservoirs of gas trapped in shale deposits. Almost overnight, this technology has increased our potential. T. Boone Pickens wants to substitute gas for oil in our cars and trucks. (T. Boone Pickens, with whom I have had a business association, outlines his theories at www.pickensplan.com.) Meanwhile, environmentalists such as Robert F. Kennedy Jr. are talking about using gas in combination with wind and solar to produce all our electricity.

But there are caveats. Although gas can be employed in transport and electricity, it has much better uses. It is the ideal fuel for home cooking and heating. Gas combusts so cleanly that you can burn it on your kitchen stove without causing dangerous fumes or air pollution. In the basement heating boiler, it converts almost 90% of its energy to home heat. It also plays a crucial role in the chemical industry, serving as a basis for products as widely varying as rubber tires, plastic water bottles, prescription drugs, and farm fertilizer. Indeed, many of these industries moved manufacturing plants out of the United States when gas prices soared after 2000.

For these reasons, it makes sense to take a balanced view of the use of natural gas in generating electricity. Yet this is not what we are doing. More than 90% of the power plants built since 1990 have burned natural gas. This is because nuclear has been in limbo and because coal plants have met increasing opposition. With the unlocking of new shale gas resources the temptation may be to build more gas plants and forget about everything else. One potentially wasteful strategy would be to employ expensive gas turbines as a complement to wind and solar installations, using the turbines' quick starting abilities to match the unpredictability of these renewable resources. That would be a very expensive way of achieving baseload electricity. Some are already touting gas as a "bridge fuel" to a solar-and-wind future but, as occurred with coal in the 1970s and 1980s, that could be a miscalculation.

We need to step back and take a deep breath. A few experts in the gas industry are warning that the new shale wells may play out much sooner than traditional sandstone wells, because the nature of the rock may make it difficult to get out the last remains. In addition, shale gas is expensive and will require high prices to make it economical. If we deploy this gas exclusively on electricity, we could find ourselves facing another supply collapse or price run-up as we did in the past decade. Although natural gas now appears to be a most promising resource, we have to view it in the context of an overall national energy program.

Natural gas—at least the kind we usually discover—is methane, the simplest of all hydrocarbons. It contains one carbon atom and four hydrogen. It is the fundamental building block of all the combustible hydrocarbon forms of "natural gas"—pentane, propane, butane—plus the organic compounds that are the chemical architecture of all living things. Propane is often manufactured from methane, although it is sometimes found in small quantities in natural gas reservoirs. Octane, kerosene, benzene, and all the other carbon fuels are derived from coal and oil. Most methane is believed to be a fossil fuel—although free methane does occur in outer space and may exist in pockets of the earth as well.

In early oil drilling, gas was considered a nuisance, and wells that produced only gas were considered dry holes. A story from the early days in Texas says that if a geologist hit gas three times in a row he was fired. Because it could not be shipped or stored in barrels, gas was flared off at the wellhead. The practice continues today in many parts of the world. We have probably flared off almost as much gas as we have used over the course of history.

Gas did get a start illuminating streets and homes during the fondly remembered Gaslight Era of the nineteenth century, but this was "town gas" produced from coal. The gas works were a common institution in towns across America back then, as was the gashouse gang, a hard-bitten crew that handled the dirty and dangerous job of breathing coal dust all day while turning it into methane.

All this changed around 1900 after improvements in welding made it possible to build leakproof pipelines that could transport gas across the country. Soon gas that would have been flared in Texas was being piped to cities as far away as Chicago and Philadelphia, and town gas was supplanted by natural gas. The oil and gas industry undertook a vast advertising campaign to tout the advantages of this cleaner fuel and persuade Americans to start "cooking with gas."

Such transitions never happen smoothly, however, and natural gas soon became entangled in a regulatory web that would inhibit its development for more than a half century. Because town gas had been regarded as a municipal utility, it had fallen under Progressive Era regulation, which saw basic services such as water, streetcars, telephones, and electricity as "natural monopolies." The theory said that such basic services were best delivered by a single provider who was regulated by the government. We have since discovered that telephone service, electric utilities, and urban transportation can all thrive under vigorous competition. At the time, however, natural monopoly doctrine held sway, and town gas companies were generally awarded municipal franchises.

When the new gas pipelines arrived, they not only had to contend with these monopolies but also with the coal providers. Working with the regulators—as threatened competitors often do—the coal companies were able to persuade municipal officials that pipelines should also be classified as natural monopolies and that only one gas franchise should be awarded per city. Town gas companies would then contest these franchises, arguing that a city was already well served by existing facilities. By the 1920s, northern states had become a crosshatch of regulated gas utilities, with municipal and state officials empowered to set their prices. Since pipelines reached across state lines, however, this state authority was limited. Then came the New Deal. In its first phase, the National Industrial Recovery Act of 1933, many industries were organized into government-run cartels that were allowed to fix prices and limit production. Natural gas was not included. But northern consumer states began arguing that, although production was concentrated in a few states of the Southwest, it should be covered since gas was sold nationwide.

In 1936 the Roosevelt administration finally responded to this pressure by creating the Federal Power Commission and authorizing it to regulate interstate pipelines. Following natural monopoly theory, the FPC immediately began *limiting* pipeline construction on the premise that too much competition was wasteful. Bowing to political pressure from northern states, the FPC also kept gas prices low. The result was that northern states were able to exploit the producing states—mostly in the Southwest—for their resources.

Still, the FPC only had control over gas once it was *in* the pipeline. Wellhead prices remained unregulated. Soon the consuming states were working on that as well. Northern attorneys general brought a series of lawsuits arguing that the FPC should have authority over wellhead prices. Finally in *Phillips Petroleum Co. v. Wisconsin* (1954), the U.S. Supreme Court ruled that *any* gas put into interstate commerce should be regulated by the FPC *at the wellhead*. Northern consumer states, which had the most political muscle, would now be able to dictate a favorable price that the producers, who were mostly in Texas and Louisiana, would be forced to accept. The entire national gas industry, consisting of thousands and thousands of small wildcatters and independent drillers, had now been declared one vast "natural monopoly."

It was an awkward and explosive situation that was bound to come to an end at some point. Although the Sunbelt had not yet emerged as a political force, Texas and Louisiana had congressional representatives in powerful committee chairmanships. Even without help from Congress, the producing states still had one simple solution. *They could refuse to sell their gas out of state.* Federal price regulations did not apply if the gas never entered an interstate pipeline. So, by the early 1970s, Texas and Louisiana were keeping large portions of their output in state. Meanwhile, in parts of the industrial belt, consumers were waiting six months to get a hookup from the gas company.

All this came to a head during the brutal winter of 1977, three years after the Arab oil boycott. With homeowners and businesses trying to switch from oil to gas to avoid high prices, supplies suddenly collapsed. As *Time* reported in a cover story:

> *A genuine crisis [has] developed in the natural-gas industry. Suppliers put into effect emergency plans, cutting all deliveries to thousands of industrial users. Company officials pleaded for school closings, shortened business hours, and thermostats to be turned down to teeth-chattering levels in private homes. . . . The Labor Department estimated that some 500,000 workers had been laid off in plants shut down by fuel shortages. . . .*
>
> *Thousands of schools in at least a dozen states, including virtually all those in Georgia, were closed for varying lengths of time. The longest period was in Dayton, which planned a month-long shutdown. Energy emergencies were declared in Minnesota, New York, Pennsylvania, Ohio, and the city of Milwaukee. . . .*

The natural-gas shortage was called "a nightmare" by Joseph Solters, the Federal Power Commission's gas expert.

In office only a week, President Jimmy Carter struggled to get control of the situation. He was soon horrified to learn that while homeowners in Pennsylvania and Ohio were literally freezing to death from lack of natural gas, Texas and Louisiana were awash in it, and burning it to produce half their electricity.

Instead of deregulating this vast, atomized industry, however, the Carter administration decided to extend federal regulation into Texas and Louisiana as well. What followed was a bitter intersectional conflict. In places like Texas and Louisiana the attitude became one of indifference to the plight of their northern neighbors with slogans like "Let the Yankees freeze in the dark," emerging from the feud. Southern congressmen, largely aligned with the Democratic Party, stonewalled legislation for more than a year. Finally, in the Natural Gas Policy Act of 1978, Congress reached a compromise. Natural gas prices would be deregulated, but not until 1988, ten years down the road. Meanwhile, the sale of natural gas in producing states would be brought under federal regulation. At the same time, burning natural gas to produce electricity would be *illegal*.

The 1978 act might not have changed pricing practices much, except the FPC—now the Federal Energy Regulatory Commission (FERC)—was soon stocked with Reagan administration appointees who began deregulating prices. Spurred by the prospect of a free market, wildcatters began exploring new areas of the country. They soon hit finds in the overthrust belt of the Rockies and other western areas where exploration had never taken place. Gas prices fell during the entire decade of the 1980s, and by 1990 the nation was experiencing something it had never encountered—a surplus of natural gas.

It was at this point that some politicians and environmentalists began thinking natural gas might be the answer to all our energy problems. As I said before, sulfur emissions from Midwestern coal plants were suspected of causing acid rain, which was damaging forests in New York and New England. President George H. W. Bush, asked Congress to act. The administration proposed "cap and trade," which was wildly successful. As also noted before, though, cap and trade didn't primarily bring about these results by triggering a technology revolution. Instead, natural gas simply replaced coal because it was once again permissible to burn gas for power generation. It was a solution that would eventually pose problems when domestic output hit a peak in 2000.

One thing spurring the boom in natural gas was the invention of combined-cycle generators. Conventional power plants boil water and then use the steam to drive a turbine. The efficiency of conversion of fuel into electricity is only about 30%. With combined-cycle gas boilers, however, the exhaust from the gas turbine drives another turbine—something that can't be done with coal, oil, or nuclear energy. This achieves upward of 60% energy conversion.

The most common use of natural gas, however, is in what are called "gas turbines." These are essentially jet engines bolted to the ground. They do not boil water. Instead, the exhaust gases drive the turbine, just as in a jet airplane. The great advantage of gas turbines is that they can be started and stopped in a few moments, which makes them invaluable for dealing with surges in peak demand. They are also relatively cheap to build and can be thrown up in a short amount of time. In New York and California gas turbines have been mounted on barges and docked in industrial areas, since they make a great deal of noise. Because the highest peak demands may only occur on a few hot days of the year, they sit idle most of the time, but they have become the essential tool in matching supply to demand.

This dream that we might be able to run huge portions of the electrical grid on clean natural gas came to an end in 2000 when supplies suddenly ran short and prices rose from $2 per thousand cubic feet (mcf) to $11 per mcf—a run-up greater than the oil price increase during the Arab oil boycott. Soaring natural gas prices helped exacerbate the great California electrical crisis of 2000–2001. They also mothballed a lot of new electrical generating stations. Today, though natural gas makes up 39% of our generating capacity, it produces only about 20% of our electricity. This is because it is used so much for peak power and because gas plants have become expensive to run. Ninety percent of the cost of gas plants is in the fuel, so even when gas prices are low, gas-powered electricity tends to be high-priced. When gas prices peak, it's the most expensive form of generation we have. Therefore it is not likely to become the superfuel that can single-handedly solve our energy problems.

Why did natural gas supplies suddenly fall? The foremost reason was the drying up of conventional supplies. Most gas is found in conjunction with oil, and America's oil production has declined steadily since 1970. Once the distortions caused by price controls were flushed out of the energy system, natural gas surged, but eventually hit a peak as well. Then, too, there is the issue of whether we should drill offshore, in sections of the overthrust belt, or in the Arctic National Wildlife Reserve, most of which drilling has been banned by Congress. Although environmental groups like the idea of burning natural gas, they do not always like drilling for it. For these reasons, supply was unable to keep up with demand.

The effect on gas-dependent industries was devastating. From 2000 to 2007, according to the American Chemistry Council, the plastics industries lost 120,000 jobs. Dow Chemical closed twenty-three plants and Goodyear cut U.S. tire production by 30%. By 2003 the heads of large U.S. chemical companies began announcing that they were moving major operations abroad to countries in Europe and the Middle East in order to be closer to cheap and reliable gas supplies. Half the fertilizer industry decamped for Mexico and the Persian Gulf to locate next to gas wells.

From 2000 through 2006 natural gas production in the Lower 48 remained perfectly flat, while demand rose steadily upward. To deal with this imbalance we imported more gas, following the same pattern that occurred after oil production peaked in 1970. This time Canada and Mexico were our main suppliers, and by

2007 North American imports had grown to 15%. Tapping overseas suppliers, however, has proved much more difficult. Pipelines
cannot be extended across the ocean (although Europe has already
built several pipelines beneath the Mediterranean Sea to import
gas from North Africa). Bringing gas to America from places like
Qatar would require a more complicated approach: the use of liquefied natural gas.

Liquefying natural gas means freezing methane to a temperature
of –259°F, which, as you can imagine, takes an enormous amount of
energy. The liquid is then pumped into a tanker at extremely high
pressure for its ocean voyage. At the other end a regasification terminal is also required. LNG facilities are extraordinarily expensive
and carry a whiff of danger, since the gas will escape into the atmosphere if there is a leak. We built six LNG terminals around the
country in the 1990s, but two have since closed. Outside Texas and
Louisiana, the energy workhorses of the nation, opposition has
crystallized against building any more terminals, especially where
they are most needed: on the East and West Coasts.

There is one other problem with imported gas—competition
from other countries. When it comes to a world market, Europe
and China will have much easier access to supplies in Asia and the
Middle East, because they can rely on pipelines, which are a cheaper
means of transport than LNG tankers, and the gas need not be
liquefied. Thus by the middle of the decade, the four LNG terminals in the United States were operating at only half their capacity
because we could not afford to pay international prices.

A second major issue arises from the problematic nature of
some of the sources of the world's largest gas reserves. Most of the
world's natural gas deposits are believed to be in the eastern hemi-
sphere, particularly Qatar, Russia, and Iran. Dealing with these
countries can be full of surprises, both good and bad.

I will never forget my first encounter with a fellow energy minister my counterpart from Qatar. Shortly after I took office, he asked
for a meeting with me while he was visiting Washington. A few
weeks later, Abdullah Al Attiyeh arrived at the Energy Department.

He was accompanied by several aides, all of whom, like him, were dressed in the traditional ceremonial attire worn by Middle Eastern diplomats.

They appeared to be as disconnected from the United States as possible, and I worried that I might not be able to develop a rapport with them. They seemed equally concerned. We exchanged pleasantries, however, and began inquiring about each other's backgrounds. When I mentioned my home was in Michigan, my counterpart's expression changed dramatically. He informed me that he had gone to school there. We were even more astonished to discover we had both attended Michigan State University. It even turned out we were contemporaries, although in a student body of forty thousand we had never encountered each other. I jokingly promised that if he would keep OPEC production levels at a high rate, I would not let our MSU alumni fund-raisers know that he was now minister of energy of one of the world's richest countries. We became close friends and worked together on a number of important issues in the years thereafter. I consider him one of the outstanding energy leaders on the international scene.

Our relations with these natural gas exporting countries cannot always depend on such coincidences, though. Dealing with Russia and Iran will be much more difficult. The Russians have already shown their willingness to play politics by holding up natural gas supplies in the middle of winter. Iran could pose an even greater threat. Even the Canadians are not necessarily happy with having America as its sole customer, especially when politicians start making campaign noises about "renegotiating NAFTA." The Canadians are now building a pipeline to the Pacific Coast so they can export some of their gas to Japan and China. Mexico, despite its considerable supplies, is a net importer of gas, and its domestic demand is rising, so we cannot depend on them, either.

Fortunately, our natural gas prospects have improved immensely since new technology has allowed us to extract supplies from shale. For decades oil and gas explorers have known there were huge reserves in these "tight" formations but found them impossible to access. Shale is hard and impermeable rock, as opposed to the sieve-like sandstone from which gas is usually extracted. We have huge shale gas reserves all over the country, from Texas to upstate New York, yet no one had ever figured out how to develop them.

In the last decade, however, innovative companies began cracking the shale by injecting water and then using new horizontal drilling techniques to release large quantities of the gas. This new technology was first tried in the Barnett Shale of the Fort Worth Basin and has since migrated to other parts of the country. As a result, natural gas production has increased by 10% per year since 2006, a climb that has not been witnessed since the 1980s. The potential is enormous. There are reserves of shale gas in Texas, Alabama, Arkansas, Oklahoma, Colorado, and the entire Appalachian Basin extending from Kentucky to Upper New York State.

Yet once again there are caveats. While shale gas may forestall the need to import from outside North America, it will not change our fundamentals. We cannot simply rely on natural gas to solve all our energy and environmental problems. Shale is not economical at the low end of the price window and in some areas, such as upstate New York, environmental opposition may prevent its development. And don't forget, natural gas is still a fossil fuel. It emits carbon, if only half as much as coal. If a true cap-and-trade regime or carbon tax ever makes it through Congress, the price of natural-gas electricity will rise.

In addition, there are already a few dissenting voices claiming that the bonanza will not be as great as anticipated. Art Berman, an independent Texas oil consultant, has raised hackles by arguing that the evidence suggests that shale wells may play out after fifteen years, far short of the sixty-five-year lifespan forecast by the industry. Critics respond that if the companies keep "fracking" the rock, production can be maintained, but Berman points out that continuous fracking is an expensive proposition. It's probably too early to tell who is right, but the important point is that the future of this new gas is by no means fully predictable.

Moreover, there is the strong likelihood that shale development, because of the dislocating activities involved, will be met with a growing level of environmental opposition. There are already concerns that fracking may contaminate groundwater, and legislation allowing the EPA to regulate in this area is gaining support. This could delay or even stop projects going forward, which will have an impact on future shale production levels.

Natural gas is an extremely valuable resource and we are lucky to find it in so many places within our borders. But the notion of natural gas as a superfuel able to solve America's or the world's energy concerns is not a workable energy strategy. The relocation of gas-dependent industries to the producing countries and the likelihood that growing worldwide demand will force prices upward are all reasons that require a broader energy approach.

In recent years, a second fuel began to emerge as a potential silver-bullet solution to our energy challenges: ethanol. As will be discussed later at length, for all its promise, ethanol has not proven itself to be terribly effective as either a substitute for oil or a means of reducing carbon emissions. Nevertheless, ethanol has enjoyed exalted status in Washington. Favorable tax treatment and, more recently, renewable fuel mandates, have been provided to support the industry. Many people suggest that this infatuation stems from the prime role that Iowa enjoys in the selection of presidents. That may be one factor, but it is also the case that many states have large agricultural sectors and a great many rural voters. These voters are very effective in lobbying their congressmen and senators to keep the ethanol program strong.

As a result, as with natural gas, a false impression has been created suggesting that ethanol can revolutionize our energy market. That is simply not the case. Notwithstanding the merits of offsetting some of our oil consumption with ethanol, it is hard to conclude that, on balance, its benefits outweigh the costs. Unfortunately, by putting as much emphasis on ethanol as we did on natural gas in the 1990s, we have failed to place appropriate focus on other solutions to our energy challenges or make the tough decisions needed for the future.

BOOK 4   **The Road Ahead**

Introduction

Thus far we have outlined the major threats facing America's and the world's energy marketplace and examined in some detail the failure of the political process to effectively address these threats. The rest of this book is focused on the strategies and tough policy choices that must be adopted if we are going to surmount the challenges we face.

I believe the starting point in all of this is to devise a realistic strategy for addressing our energy and related environmental challenges. The past decade's efforts have been marked by political impasse or seen us attempting politically expedient short-term energy fixes—like tapping our Strategic Petroleum Reserve to lower oil and gasoline prices. Neither approach will get us get very far in addressing our real problems.

The election of Barack Obama combined with overwhelming Democratic majorities in the House and Senate seemed to signal that decisive action would take place in Washington. Most assumed that the deadlock between various energy strategies would be resolved. However, to the surprise of many, political reality once again intruded. Quick action on climate change was thwarted by the harsh reality of the potential economic consequences stemming from a carbon regulatory framework. Having had a close call with depression in 2009 few congressmen and senators were ready to risk the possibility of a legislatively created one. Suddenly,

Rust Belt Democrats began to sound like Sun Belt Republicans when discussing the implications on the economy of America's adoption of a cap-and-trade carbon system—especially if countries like China would not do the same.

Another factor was the problems Europe ran into when it tried to apply cap and trade to enforce the Kyoto Protocol. The Europeans put a huge imaginary "bubble" over the continent and then issued permits to meet Kyoto standards. But the biggest emitters claimed they could not shoulder the cost of the permits. Large numbers were given away at the outset. That favored some, and left those who had to buy their permits at a huge disadvantage. Then large numbers of permits were given to Eastern Europe just at the point when the economies of the former Soviet satellites were collapsing. So Eastern European businesses did not use their permits; they sold them cheap to Western European businesses.

Then there was the concern with "offsets," a practice that has crept into all cap-and-trade programs. If you can't clean up your own emissions, perhaps you can clean up those of somebody else and get "credits" that will reduce your own obligations. But the nature of these offsets soon became highly contentious. Does planting trees in Africa really offset burning coal in Central Europe? Such a program has also been subject to scams. In recent years there have been charges that Chinese entrepreneurs were building dirty factories just so they could be torn down again to sell the "credits" to European polluters.

All these problems were already on the record when Congress and the Obama administration began its push to adopt cap and trade in 2009. It wasn't long before the problems surfaced then as well. Once again, major coal-burning industries pleaded they could not clean up fast enough or afford the permits, so in the House of Representatives they were awarded permits for free. By the time the giveaway was over, 75% of the permits had been awarded gratis. This was only six months after President Obama was talking about reducing the federal deficit with the revenues from cap and trade. Then particular sectors of the economy started complaining that they were victims of discrimination. While coal utilities in the Midwest were given permits, for example, oil refineries were completely excluded. This discrimination threatened to close down some of the remaining refinery capacity in this country.

The problem of offsets also set off alarms. What practices will be allowed and how will they be calculated? The spectacle of movie stars buying offsets, like papal indulgences, to atone for their private jet flights to global warming conventions has raised public doubts. Even environmentalists are concerned that in all the paper shuffling nothing much will be accomplished.

Finally, the so-called Climategate affair that emerged in late 2009 further roiled the waters. The concern that some of the climate research has been tainted only added to the skepticism and discouraged passage of a controversial bill. So while House passage was secured, the Senate held back.

In light of this background, most experts now believe congressional passage of a comprehensive carbon program, such as a cap-and-trade bill, is unlikely until at least 2011. And if the 2010 elections return a smaller Democratic majority in the House or the Senate or a new Republican majority in either chamber, prospects for a carbon bill will likely decline even further.

Congress now finds itself in roughly the situation that has existed for more than ten years: running in place. Despite the projected growth in energy demand and the looming environmental and geopolitical threats, we are not making the tough decisions required to move us ahead. Unfortunately, we are rapidly running out of time.

The inability of Congress to act has also brought EPA into the picture. In December 2009, on the eve of the United Nations meeting to address climate change in Copenhagen, the agency ruled that carbon dioxide constitutes a hazard to health and, based on that ruling, embarked on an effort to regulate it. This approach had been anticipated for some time as a strategy by which Congress would be pressured into finally acting on carbon. Commentators have speculated that when business and industry contemplate the ramifications of EPA imposing a "command and control" carbon regulatory framework on them they will embrace a cap-and-trade program, or some other congressionally devised approach that would likely be more predictable and less expensive (not to mention more easily manipulated via lobbying).

It remains to be seen how this will ultimately play out. Any EPA-imposed framework will be met with countless lawsuits that will drag out the process for years. In the meantime, if Congress does not act (and many suspect that Congress will be more than happy to have this contentious issue taken off their plate), the Obama administration will be held accountable for EPA's proposed actions and face accusations that they have unilaterally attempted to impose a gigantic energy tax on the nation. With the 2012 elections not that far away, this may not be a politically viable position—especially given the nation's economic and fiscal problems of recent years.

I believe there is a better path. I believe that we can take actions that improve our energy security, strengthen the energy marketplace, and reduce associated greenhouse gas emissions in a way that is acceptable to most Americans and makes economic sense. What follows is a brief outline of how I believe we should proceed.

Let's start with the environment and, in particular, with carbon emissions. While there might not be a clear consensus on climate change, I believe that a substantial majority feels that it would be preferable to reduce our emissions of greenhouse gases, if that can be done consistent with a strong economy and without dramatically increasing federal spending. With these objectives in mind, we can begin, logically, with power generation. If we are going to reduce carbon, we will need to reduce the demand for electricity and find ways of supplying it that release less carbon.

In the past when we have attempted to reduce emissions, we have, as previously discussed, either empowered EPA to impose a "command and control" regulatory process that requires polluters to reduce their harmful emissions or legislated cap and trade.

Given the inability of Congress to enact cap and trade and rather than waiting for the EPA to try to address these issues via a protracted, heavily litigated, and politically unpopular regulatory effort, I believe we should take a much more practical approach.

The place to begin is with a broad, long-term vision for the electrical marketplace. I would propose that we establish a blueprint for the composition of our power generation sector and then take actions to achieve it. Already many policy makers have concluded that it makes sense to set a renewable energy mandate. If that's true, why does it not make sense to create a mandatory minimum amount of power generation from other sources as well?

I say it does. And I think that it will be far easier and cheaper to reach power production goals aimed at increasing energy security and reducing emissions than to try to legislate and then implement a highly complicated and potentially uncertain regulatory system for carbon reduction.

Let's try to lay out such a power generation strategy, in terms of the next twenty years. I have designated my approach the 30–30–30 by 2030 plan. As the table on page 125 indicates, it is my view that we should strive to establish a power generation mix of 30% nuclear, 30% renewable sources (including hydro) plus energy efficiency gains, and 30% natural gas plus coal gasification (with full carbon capture) by the year 2030. As we will see, these are attainable goals consistent with a growing economy and budgetary sanity. Furthermore, the strategy I suggest will not be subject to the uncertainties of a cap-and-trade regime or the potentially onerous burdens of a command-and-control EPA enforcement process. Instead, utilities and clean energy producers will receive an incentive-laden set of options designed to help us reach our goals. It won't be free, but I believe the costs of such an approach should not be prohibitive, since a good deal of the capital will come from private investment.

I am going to be a little unorthodox and suggest that the government bear roughly half the construction costs of the more politically risky and innovative power plants, especially new nuclear

builds. This could run the costs to the government into the neighborhood of $150–$250 billion over twenty years. (Such numbers
don't sound as bad as they used to, do they?) But as will be discussed later, the government would have an ownership interest in
those plants where it provides capital, and it could sell its interest
once they are up and running in order to recoup its investment.
Altogether, the costs are not out of line with what we have done in
previous decades building our infrastructure, and certainly less
costly than the expense associated with implementing a cap-and-
trade or an EPA command-and-control approach. Here is a brief
outline of what I am proposing:

A. Nuclear Power: 30%

The first leg of this effort requires a substantial increase in nuclear
energy. Today nuclear reactors provide 21% of our electricity. I
believe we should strive to increase this percentage to 30% by the
year 2030. That would mean building about fifty new reactors over
the next twenty years. That won't be easy, but if it is established as
a national priority and government agencies at all levels work together, it can be done.

B. Renewable Sources Plus Energy Efficiency: 30%

1. Hydropower: 5%
Here we begin with the fact that hydro already produces 6% of our
electricity. That number is likely to go down as the pie increases
but the number of dams does not.

2. Other Renewable Sources: 15%
Under the renewable power generation mandate that Congress has
attempted to set, renewable energy must make up roughly 12% to
15% of our power production by 2020. In my judgment that will be
difficult to attain, but can almost certainly be reached by 2030 if
we provide the right incentives.

3. Energy Efficiency: 10%

In addition to ramping up our use of renewable sources, our blueprint for the power sector must also include significant gains in energy efficiency. I have little doubt that over the next twenty years we can substantially reduce the projected growth in power demand through the deployment of a variety of existing and soon-to-be devised energy efficiency technologies and the development of an energy-saving smart grid infrastructure. I believe it is realistic to garner as much as a 10% improvement in efficiency between now and 2030. In fact, achieving a 10% or greater improvement should be viewed as only a first step in terms of addressing our broad energy challenges. As will be seen later when we discuss efficiency in more detail, there are potentially huge improvements in energy savings possible throughout our society.

Our goal must be not only to employ smart or intelligent grid technologies and products like energy-efficient lightbulbs, but also to bring about the adoption of energy consumption monitoring—and incentive-based reductions in energy use—by as broad a group of businesses and individuals as possible. By marrying twenty-first-century information technology that can provide energy users with real-time information about their energy consumption and carbon footprint, with incentives to reduce consumption and carbon emissions, the goal of reducing projected growth in energy demand by at least 10% can be achieved and even exceeded in coming decades. This must be our mission.

C. Natural Gas Plus Clean Coal Gasification With Carbon Capture: 30%

1. Natural Gas: 25%

Today natural gas provides nearly 20% of our base load electricity—the generation that must be kept running without interruption, night and day, in order to maintain voltage balances on the grid. As noted earlier, though, we have sufficient power plants that operate on natural gas to dramatically increase this number. A key factor in increasing the natural gas share of our power mix is the price of gas itself. Fortunately, the emergence of many new gas supplies in the United States in recent years suggests that it will be possible for us to utilize more of our gas generating capacity. Because natural gas–fired plants emit fewer greenhouse gases than coal-fired plants, this increase is significant.

2. Clean Coal: 5%

America has significant reserves of coal, and they will be used. The opportunities to burn coal in a cleaner fashion are growing. We are now at a point where these technologies can be deployed to substantially decrease the emissions from coal-fired energy generation. I believe we need a comprehensive national strategy designed to launch a fleet of clean coal-gasification plants that capture high percentages of carbon emissions and effectively dispose of them. In my view, by the year 2030, it will be feasible to generate at least 5% of our power from this type of clean coal facility. To do so we would need to build approximately twenty-five of those units in the next twenty years. I believe that can be done as well.

The Result

If we were to accomplish all these objectives by 2030, then we would bring about a very substantial change in America's carbon emissions. I would estimate a reduction of more than 10% in the power-generating sector alone. More important, I feel that the formula outlined here is not only feasible but can be attained without undermining the economy or excessively burdening the U.S. Treasury.

Rather than continuing the failed approach we have been taking, we need a new direction that has a greater chance of being enacted. In my view, we can address our energy security threats and have a very significant impact on our environmental chal-

Power Generation Sources Today and in 2030, in Percent

	2009	2030
Natural Gas	19	25
Coal Gasification	0	5
Total Natural Gas and Coal Gasification	19	30
Nuclear	21	30
Hydro	6	5
Other Renewable Sources: Wind, Solar, Tidal, Biomass, Geothermal	3	15
Total Hydro & Renewables	9	20
Total Natural Gas, Coal Gasification, Nuclear, Renewables	49	80
Conventional Coal	50	19
Others:	1	1
Additional Energy Efficiency Savings	0	10

lenges with a straightforward program of building an effective mix of new facilities to meet the challenge. We already know that our utility companies will be building many new power plants over the next fifteen to twenty years. To me it makes sense to sculpt the composition of those new plants along the lines outlined above, thereby achieving the objectives of our environmentalists, businesses and industries, and the American people.

What this plan will do, as the chart above indicates, is reduce the role of conventional coal in our power sector from providing about 50% of our electricity in 2010 to under 20% by 2030. This is a significant reduction and will translate into an enormous reduction in emissions associated with power generation. Also, by launching a clean coal gasification industry, we will be laying the groundwork for the ultimate replacement of aging coal plants with clean coal facilities on a widespread level. This is the case because with the development of each new clean coal gasification plant, the utility industry will increase its knowledge about and comfort with these projects. Undoubtedly construction costs will come down as developers become more accustomed to building these plants and the construction process (siting, permitting, etc.) will likely become less cumbersome and slow. That will, in turn, increase the confidence level of the industry and translate into more plants in the future. While we may not see the elimination of all conventional coal plants, I believe their number will continue to decline once coal gasification emerges as an alternative.

What this plan will not do is address the carbon issues related to emissions from nonpower generation sources. In later chapters, however, I will address other strategies I believe we should pursue that will, in part, speak to carbon emissions from other sources. In particular, I believe a strong emphasis on carbon sequestration research is called for in the hope that we can dispose of some of the carbon associated with smokestack industries. I also feel that by ramping up advanced automotive propulsion and fueling research—including hydrogen—along with battery-technology R&D, we will likewise lay the groundwork for reducing carbon emissions. While it may not be the case that these reductions will match those contemplated in cap-and-trade legislation, we must not forget that such legislation has not passed and might never become law. My bottom line is simply this: Rather than losing more time while waiting for passage of an elusive carbon bill, let's adopt a strategy that addresses many of our objectives and minimizes the fiscal and economic dislocations that have deeply concerned so many policy makers.

In the following chapters I will discuss in more detail each of the key elements of this strategy. In doing so I will attempt to outline the specific actions needed to bring about the goals I have described.

Now let's consider a strategy for addressing the energy security and geopolitical threats we also confront.

As we think strategically about security in terms of both market threats and geopolitical challenges, an interesting conclusion emerges: Many of the strategies that address our environmental concerns also help us accomplish our security goals.

For example, every improvement we make in energy efficiency reduces our demand for energy and thus our dependence on imported energy. That, in turn, reduces the extent to which we are vulnerable to geopolitical threats in the energy marketplace.

Increasing the share of our power production derived from nuclear power and renewable sources also reduces the extent to which we must rely on energy imports. It also ensures that we will be able to use our coal reserves for an even longer period of time. Finally, by facilitating the development of clean coal power, we can lay the groundwork for the long-term use of our vast coal reserves, and that will help keep energy prices affordable while decreasing the emissions from future coal plants.

But we must do more. Let's face it, our greatest concerns regarding energy security relate to the amounts of oil we import. Since we do not use very much oil for power production, increasing our use of nuclear power and renewable sources will not significantly affect America's reliance on oil. One option of course is to impose some form of tax on oil in order to curb demand. However, such a tax would most likely fall on those least able to pay, and while there might be ways to refund some of these dollars for equity reasons, chances are it would not be easy to devise a truly workable approach. Moreover, the first time oil prices rise significantly, such a tax will likely be abandoned. Sooner rather than later we would be back to square one.

So what do we do? First, it's time for us to take a more realistic view of domestic energy production. While there is no evidence that America could eliminate its dependence on imported oil by drilling in every location that is currently prohibited, it is also unmistakably the case that if we maintain an exploration and development moratorium on an ever larger amount of promising geography, we will only increase our dependence on foreign energy no matter how many "cash for clunker" programs we devise, or how effectively auto manufacturers increase fuel efficiency.

In short, we need to make some hard decisions about domestic oil production. This simply cannot be left to the normal political process. In my opinion what is needed is an unelected high-level panel, like the Base Realignment and Closure Commission that decides the fate of military installations. Such a commission could make decisions regarding both offshore energy development and production on federal lands. Only by removing these critical matters from special-interest leverage can we ever hope to meet our energy needs.

There's more. As has been discussed in earlier parts of this book, there is no general agreement on whether or not we've reached the level of peak oil production on a worldwide basis. But one thing on which most experts agree is that there will certainly be a day when our global oil reserves begin to diminish. So we must be prepared. This means ramping up our investments in energy research, especially for advanced fuel systems technology and battery technology.

Finally, it is important that we recognize the extent to which energy security challenges are not America's alone. When it comes to the physical security of energy assets we must work in closer collaboration with other producers and consumers to avert disaster. We must also play a more active role in fostering the development of energy in places like West Africa, the Caspian region, and other emerging energy areas. Not only will these new energy producers require capital to be successful, they will need our technological help and the political support of the United States and other large consuming countries as they build up their industries.

As this overview indicates, dealing with the threats that confront us in the energy marketplace will not be easy. There are no simple strategies or silver bullets at our disposal. As the following chapters indicate, the steps we must take to implement the strategy I have outlined here are complicated and require fortitude on the part of public officials. For too long we've seen our political process fail to make the tough decisions required to achieve our energy objectives. Unfortunately, we no longer can wait.

CHAPTER 10

Nuclear Power

If we are really going to control carbon emissions and provide ourselves with enough energy, there is really one overriding critical choice. We have to take another long look at nuclear power.

While I was secretary of energy we did our best to get started. We reactivated federal and joint international nuclear research efforts. We attempted to step up the licensing process at the Nuclear Regulatory Commission and cleared the way to store spent fuel rods at Yucca Mountain. These efforts were successful enough that people began talking about a "nuclear revival."

But we still have a long way to go. As noted, our goal should be to build at least fifty reactors over the next two decades. That would allow us to expand the portion of nuclear electricity from 20% to 30% of our total generation. The main impact would be to replace aging, polluting coal plants with clean new nuclear reactors. Meanwhile, we should set reasonable goals for other technologies—30% renewable sources plus efficiency, 30% natural gas plus coal gasification. If this could be accomplished, then we would have an energy economy that achieved significant emissions improvements, while ensuring an affordable and sufficient supply of electric power to spur economic growth.

But nuclear is the lynchpin. We can't expand the other technologies without stretching resources, gobbling up vast amounts of land, and generally causing environmental disruptions.

Expanding nuclear, however, will mean abandoning some of the irrational fears that have held us back so far. But the rewards will be great. Look at what has happened in France. The French now get 80% of their electricity from nuclear power and have inexpensive electricity and low carbon emissions. They store all their unusable spent fuel—the so-called nuclear waste—beneath the floor of one room in their facility at La Hague. What more could we want? It's time to take a long second look at nuclear power.

Because irrational fears play such a big part in discussing nuclear, I will spend the first part of this chapter dealing with issues that prey on people's minds: (1) reactor safety, (2) terrorist attacks, (3) the proliferation of nuclear weapons, and (4) the problem of "nuclear waste." (I put that in quotation marks here because in a very real sense there is no such thing as nuclear waste.) Then I will outline the steps I think we have to take to get started again on nuclear construction.

The thing to keep in mind throughout this discussion is the tremendous *energy density* of nuclear power. The energy releases from the nucleus of the atom are *2 million times* greater than the energy releases we get from the same weight and volume of fossil fuels. Furthermore, fossil fuels themselves are ten to fifty times more powerful than the kinetic energy we derive from wind and hydro or the diluted radiative energy of solar power. With that kind of energy density, nuclear power can't help but have a much smaller impact on the environment.

REACTOR SAFETY. Perhaps the biggest obstacle facing nuclear is that people tend to conflate it with a nuclear bomb. They are two very different technologies. The fissionable uranium isotope, U-235, is the source of energy in both a power reactor and a nuclear bomb. U-235 makes up only 0.7% of the natural ore. At that level it is not concentrated enough to release energy for either bombs or power plants. In order to produce the self-sustaining chain reaction that occurs inside a power plant, the U-235 isotope must be "enriched" to 3% to be usable as what is called "reactor grade." This is a very tedious process. The United States has long operated a huge enrichment plant (not privatized) in Paducah, Kentucky, that burns almost 1,000 megawatts of electricity night and day to produce approximately 50% of the reactor fuel we get from our own domestic enrichment efforts.

In order to build a nuclear bomb, on the other hand, natural uranium must be enriched to 90% U-235. During the Manhattan Project, producing enough bomb-grade material for a single weapon took three years. Because the uranium enrichment process is so tedious, almost all the nuclear weapons built since then have used plutonium. The Iranians have been at work at it for years. Even when you have bomb-grade material, you have to design a device that can bring two halves of a critical mass together with the speed of a bullet in order to make them explode. Enriching uranium and turning it into a weapon is not something a group of terrorists can do in a garage. It takes a state enterprise.

It is because reactor-grade material and bomb-grade material are two entirely different substances that *a nuclear power plant cannot blow up.* A reactor is not a bomb waiting to go off. Worrying that a reactor will explode is like worrying that a jar of Vaseline in your medicine cabinet is going to blow up and set your house on fire. Vaseline is, after all, "petroleum jelly." Napalm is jellied gasoline. But of course there is a vast difference. The volatile fractions in Vaseline are nowhere near the same amounts as in napalm. Similarly, the fissionable U-235 isotope is not anywhere near as concentrated in reactor fuel as it is in an atomic bomb. A reactor cannot blow up in a nuclear explosion as so many antinuclear advocates suggest. All it can do is the slow, controlled "burn" that produces enough heat to generate electricity.

A nuclear reactor can, however, "melt down," which is what happened at Three Mile Island. The reactor lost its cooling water and overheated, melting the fuel rods. But the consequences turned out to be much less catastrophic than expected. Imaginative scientists had envisioned a "China Syndrome" in which the fuel element would continue to melt right through the steel reactor vessel and the concrete containment structure and then right through the earth until it hit groundwater and caused an explosion that would "make an area the size of Pennsylvania uninhabitable" (as the movie *The China Syndrome* put it).

All this was *disproved* by Three Mile Island. The overheated fuel didn't go anywhere. It simply dripped down to the bottom of the reactor vessel, where it remained. The heat wasn't even enough to melt through the chromium alloy at the bottom of the vessel head. Three Mile Island was a serious industrial accident, but it was exceptional in that no one got hurt.

The important thing to remember about all American reactors is that they have a built-in fail-safe mechanism that keeps them from getting out of control. The water circulating throughout the core serves three purposes. First, it cools the fuel rods and keeps them from overheating. Second, it carries heat away from the core (this heat is what creates the steam to drive the turbines). Third, *it makes the chain reaction occur.* When neutrons escape from a splitting uranium atom they have to be absorbed by other nuclei to keep the chain reaction going. However, they are generally moving too fast to be captured. What is needed is a "moderator." This is a small atom with which the neutron can collide without being absorbed. The hydrogen atom in water fulfills this role. What this means is *the water is necessary to keep the reaction going.* You can't have a "runaway reactor." If the coolant is lost, the reactor automatically shuts down. The only heat left in the core is "decay heat" from the previous reactions. That is why the China Syndrome can't happen.

Chernobyl was a different story. Here we have to thank Soviet science—or should I say arrogance. The Russians were so confident of their abilities that *they didn't even bother to build a containment structure around the reactor.* No American reactor has ever been built without a containment structure. In addition, the Soviets had designed the reactor to produce plutonium for bomb material as well. This is a different technology. Instead of using water for a moderator—the fail-safe technology—they used graphite, which has what is called a "positive void coefficient." In simple language, this means that *if you lose the coolant, the reaction speeds up*. Unlike American technology, you can have a "runaway reactor." Finally, and perhaps most important, once you have a runaway reactor and temperatures are soaring to dangerous levels, *the graphite can catch fire*. Graphite, after all, is compressed carbon.

That's what happened at Chernobyl. The runaway reactor caused a steam explosion, blowing the lid off the reactor. Then the graphite caught fire and burned for four days. The effect was a chimney, sending radioactive smoke and debris high into the atmosphere, where it eventually scattered all over the world. More radioactive elements fell on the area around Three Mile Island from Chernobyl than from the Three Mile Island incident itself. You could hardly engineer a worse scenario if you tried. But a Chernobyl accident could never happen again. Even the Russians have now put containment structures around all their reactors.

In short, there are obvious dangers associated with nuclear technology, and accidents can happen, but the stakes with a nuclear accident are not as high as popularly supposed. In 2006, the United Nations World Health Organization issued a twenty-year evaluation of Chernobyl, easily the worst nuclear accident in history and probably the worst imaginable. According to the report, sixty people died, most of them soldiers who were rushed to the scene as emergency rescue workers. Some of them were sent to a rooftop to throw off radioactive debris with their bare hands. They died in large numbers. There were also five thousand cases of thyroid cancer in the surrounding population, most of them children, who are more susceptible. Fortunately, thyroid cancer is treatable and only two of these youngsters died. Within days of the accident some 135,000 people were evacuated from neighboring Pripyat. A seventeen-square-mile exclusionary zone has now been set up around the site, but about ten thousand people, most of them elderly, have returned to the area because they want to be at home. No adverse health effects have been reported among them. A U.N. report issued on the twentieth anniversary in 2006 said that the main effect on surrounding populations had been mental depression resulting from dislocation and the misapprehension that something terrible had happened to their health. In the absence of human civilization, wildlife has thrived in the exclusion zone. Rare and endangered species have returned to the area, which is now regarded as one of Europe's biggest wildlife sanctuaries.

Other industrial technologies pose much greater risks. The chemical explosion at Bhopal killed 4,000 people. There are about ninety natural gas explosions each year in the United States and fifteen people die annually. The toll from lung diseases caused by coal, of course, is far higher—24,000 a year, according to the EPA. At the same time, federal data show that working in the nuclear industry is one of the safest occupations in the country—safer than the FIRE (finance, insurance, and real estate) industry. As Patrick Moore, the cofounder of Greenpeace who has become a convert to nuclear power, puts it, "I'd be happy to live *inside* a nuclear reactor. It's one of the safest places you can be."

The important thing to remember is that *a reactor cannot blow up*. Once you get over the idea that a nuclear power plant is a "silent bomb" waiting to explode, you can begin to see that the dangers of nuclear power are not terribly different from other industrial operations.

Another thing to remember is that the newest reactor designs are even safer than those that presently constitute the U.S. reactor fleet. It always amazes me when I hear that nuclear activists are opposing the construction of new plants in the name of safety. It seems a bit inconsistent to contend that we shouldn't build new and "safer" reactors while we continue to allow nuclear plants built in the Three Mile Island–era to operate. In a similar vein it doesn't make sense not to build new safer reactors because thirty years ago Three Mile Island took place. Failing to acknowledge, let alone take into account, safety improvements in the nuclear industry has largely undermined efforts to launch new builds. It is indefensible. It is like refusing heart bypass surgery in 2010 because back in the 1970s open-heart surgery wasn't as safe as it is today.

TERRORIST ATTACKS. The nightmare continually conjured up by opponents of nuclear power is that terrorists will hijack an airplane and steer it into a reactor, breaching the containment structure, setting off some kind of explosion, and producing a volcano of radioactive debris that would poison the landscape for miles around. Antinuclear activists have even speculated that had one of the hijacked airplanes on September 11, 2001, been steered into the Indian Point Nuclear Reactor in Upper Westchester County, far more people would have been killed than at the World Trade Center.

In fact, had the hijackers tried to attack Indian Point instead of the World Trade Center, it would have been a blessing. Three thousand lives would have been saved. All that would have happened is a spectacular plane crash. To see exactly what would have happened, go to YouTube and search "Plane crashing into wall." In the 1990s, the Department of Energy mounted an F-4 Phantom jet on a railroad track and crashed it into a four-foot-thick concrete wall at 500 miles per hour. The jet simply vanishes, vaporized by the impact. The wall barely budges. As Manhattan Project nuclear scientist Ted Rockwell says, "If you wanted to penetrate a concrete wall, the last thing you'd use is a hollow metal tube."

Critics argue that a jumbo jet, which weighs five times as much as an F-4, would have a greater impact, but this isn't necessarily true. The impact depends on the mass and the velocity of the moving object, with the velocity playing a more important role. (Remember, energy equals mass times the velocity *squared*.) A jumbo jet flying at 300 mph—a speed at which it could be controlled—would have only slightly more impact than the F-4 at 500 mph. It is also possible that the larger plane would spread out the impact. The explosion of jet fuel would not make much difference, either, since it would not last long enough to create enough heat to melt the concrete. The World Trade Center was vulnerable because it was made of glass and steel. Had it been built like a nuclear containment structure, the planes would have vaporized there as well. Nuclear reactors are built to withstand such terrorist attacks.

Another scenario has the jet striking the pool where spent fuel rods are stored. Now it is indeed a tragedy that so much spent fuel is still being kept on-site at nuclear reactors. This is because we have abandoned reprocessing and have been unable to develop a storage repository to handle it. Notwithstanding where we are, the on-site storage pools still do not make a very plausible terrorist target. Many storage facilities are within the containment structure or in well-constructed buildings nearby. Crashing a commercial airliner into a storage pool would be like trying to land a plane in someone's backyard swimming pool. The most experienced pilots—let alone an amateur hijacker—would find it very difficult.

Even if the plane scored a direct hit, the radioactive debris would not scatter more than a few hundred yards. The scenario imagined by antinuclear activists is that the storage pool will drain and the fuel rods will melt down and cause some kind of Chernobyl-like catastrophe. But remember, it was the graphite moderator that caught fire at Chernobyl. There is no graphite in American reactors or in storage pools. Once the fuel rods have been in storage for a few years they are not hot enough to melt anyway. The water only serves to shield their radioactivity. A plane crashing into a storage pool would be an on-site disaster, and workers would have to be shielded while cleaning up the site. But it would not be an area-wide catastrophe.

One final scenario has terrorist commando units storming a nuclear plant and taking control of it, either to blow it up or melt it down or initiate some other disaster. Now we get into the realm of sheer action-movie fantasy. Reactors are well guarded by security forces with live ammunition that take target practice regularly. Reactors are now designed with so many backup safety systems that the operators themselves probably couldn't melt it down even if they tried. At one reactor I visited, the control room had a steel barricade so the operators could bar the door against attackers. It would be much more practical to steal a nuclear bomb from the military and explode it somewhere than to try to fashion a nuclear reactor into some kind of catastrophe.

Finally, let's not lose sight of a very basic point: There are already 104 operating nuclear reactors in the United States. If terrorists want to attack a nuclear facility they could do it tomorrow. Building new nuclear reactors won't create any larger risk of a terrorist assault than currently exists. It simply doesn't make sense to judge a technology by the number of fantasies people can make up about it.

NUCLEAR PROLIFERATION. Somewhere back in the administration of President Jimmy Carter, the idea took hold that we were going to be able to stop the proliferation of nuclear weapons around the world if America gave up nuclear reprocessing in this country. This thinking is what has created the problem of so-called nuclear waste.

The argument didn't make a whole lot of sense in 1976 and makes even less sense today. Somehow we had the idea that nuclear technology was a big secret and we could keep it from the rest of the world. With fifty plus reactors under construction in thirteen countries around the world, and none in the United States, it is getting harder and harder to maintain that illusion. All we have done is handicap ourselves by abandoning reprocessing technology while others pushed ahead with it. As I already mentioned, France now stores all its nuclear waste beneath the floor of one room at their reprocessing center.

Yet even today the Department of Energy is holding up reprocessing by saying France's system isn't good enough. We must develop some new reprocessing system so that—you guessed it—we can prevent the proliferation of nuclear weapons. The truth is what we do with our own spent fuel in this country will have no impact on whether other countries develop their own nuclear programs or utilize reprocessing to deal with their nuclear waste. It is time we wake up and realize what is going on in the world.

The issue of proliferation centers on plutonium, the only other element besides uranium that can serve as bomb material. Plutonium is a man-made element created when U-239, the nonfissionable uranium isotope, absorbs a neutron and moves up two notches on the atomic scale. Only a short time after the discovery of uranium fission, the plutonium isotope Pu-239 was also found to be fissionable. ("Fissionable" means the atom will split nearly in two, whereas "radioactive" means that only small bits such as protons or electrons are emitted.) The first test bomb at Alamogordo was made from plutonium. The Hiroshima bomb was made from enriched uranium, and the Nagasaki bomb was again plutonium. Most subsequent nuclear weapons have been made using plutonium.

By the time the fuel rod is spent, it is 1% plutonium. While Pu-239 is the first isotope formed from U-238, if the plutonium stays in the reactor long enough it absorbs more neutrons and turns into other plutonium isotopes that "poison" the material for bomb use. One isotope, Pu-241, fissions too quickly, while Pu-240 and Pu-242 do not fission quickly enough.

In the 1970s the U.S. Army conducted a series of tests in which they found that reactor plutonium could be exploded—although the yield is much smaller and there is a chance the bomb won't go off at all. If you want bomb-grade material, the best strategy is to run the reactor very fast for about five months and then take out the plutonium before other isotopes begin to form. This is what the Soviets were doing at Chernobyl. It is also what North Korea did with its reactor (built from a British model published in 1956 as part of the Atoms for Peace program). When the Koreans closed down the reactor after only a few months and extracted the fuel rods, we knew they intended to make a bomb.

In 1975 there was some reason to think we might be able to stop proliferation by hoarding this technology. India had just extracted plutonium from a research reactor given to them by the Canadians and used it to make a weapon tested in 1973. The fear was that this would be duplicated around the world. As President Gerald Ford prepared to run for reelection in 1976, the call to ban reprocessing became so strong that he temporarily suspended it. Then when Jimmy Carter came to office, he permanently shut down the Clinch River Breeder Reactor, which was to burn reprocessed fuel. That ended America's reprocessing effort. Meanwhile, France, Canada, Britain, Russia, and Japan all went on with reprocessing.

While it made sense to exercise caution in giving the technology to other nations, the idea that ending reprocessing in this country would keep other countries from developing nuclear weapons was foolish. The premise was that if we isolated plutonium somewhere in America, someone would steal it and give it to terrorists or foreign nationals. (The alternative theory was that if the United States used reprocessing, other less sophisticated nations would follow America's example and they would be unable to protect their isolated plutonium.) This was a bit like worrying that someone might steal some of the gold from Fort Knox. Instead of stealing our bomb material, other countries just went ahead and made their own. South Africa developed a bomb, Israel developed a bomb, Pakistan conducted a test in 1998, and North Korea followed in 2006. Iran is still working on it. Meanwhile, countries like France and Japan use reprocessing, and no one has stolen their plutonium.

Instead, by sacrificing our technological lead, we have left it open to other countries to proliferate their own nuclear technology. France, Russia, Canada, and Japan are all selling their technology around the world. China will soon be doing the same thing. Some of this will go to countries that we don't regard as particularly friendly. Russia is now building a reactor for Venezuela's Hugo Chávez. Could one of these exporters look the other way or simply fail to be sufficiently vigilant, while their clients stole a little plutonium to make their own bomb? Who knows?

The Obama administration's continuing belief that we are somehow making the world safer by piling up plutonium in spent fuel rods, instead of extracting it and putting it to use in nuclear reactors, is just another example of how far out of touch we have gotten with the rest of the world when it comes to nuclear technology. The cat is already out of the bag. It's time we took the lead again before we lose our technological edge altogether.

NUCLEAR WASTE. When Congress addressed the issue of nuclear waste back in the 1970s and early 1980s, it decided the best course was to build a permanent underground repository in which to store it. Because, as noted in the previous section, reprocessing had been deemed a proliferation risk, the only real alternative was to store the material in a central repository.

After the threshold decision to store waste underground occurred, the federal government expended huge sums of money to determine where the repository would be located. Ultimately, based on a variety of factors, such as seismic volatility, volcanic and other destabilizing activity, isolation and other factors, Congress voted that the repository would be located under a place called Yucca Mountain, about seventy miles outside the city of Las Vegas, Nevada. It was probably inevitable that the nuclear waste repository siting decision would ignite a firestorm of protest. Thus, it probably should come as no surprise that the people of Nevada launched what has now been a multidecade effort to prevent the site from ever opening.

The Nuclear Waste Policy Act, under which Yucca Mountain was created, set forth an extremely expensive and elaborate method of determining whether the site could be made safe for nuclear storage, and called upon the EPA to set safety requirements. It likewise set a target date of 1998 for the secretary of energy to make a recommendation on the site's feasibility to the president of the United States. Finally, the legislation provided the state of Nevada with the right to veto such a presidential determination, but also permitted the Congress to override that veto by a simple majority.

By the time I became energy secretary in 2001, we were three years late in formulating a recommendation. Because of the importance of having a pathway for nuclear waste, I decided it was a priority for me to make a go/no-go decision with respect to the project. Because the law specifically empowers the energy secretary to render a recommendation, I decided to study all of the available material on Yucca Mountain. Hence, over the course of several months, I studied thousands of pages of documents, countless research projects, and all other available literature.

Also in accordance with the law, we conducted public hearings all over the state of Nevada where citizens could comment. Various senior department officials attended the hearings, and I chose to attend one of the largest, which took place in Las Vegas. Not surprisingly, most of the attendees were local residents who opposed the repository. Let me give you a feel for the meetings. At the Las Vegas hearing, a man wearing a Santa Claus outfit and claiming his name was Chris Kringle informed me that he would be watching me closely to see whether or not I would be naughty or nice. He made it clear that if I recommended going forward with the repository I would be naughty.

My conclusion was that the repository should be built. The federal government had spent billions of dollars to research every possible argument against the repository, no matter how far-fetched. We have studied whether seismic disruptions might expose nuclear waste. We researched whether volcanic activity could undermine the repository. We even investigated whether a new ice age might envelop the western states and later thaw in such fashion as to cause massive drainage into the underground repository, sufficient to release radiation. (All this was back at the turn of the twenty-first century before we began really focusing on global warming.) In each and every case, our experts concluded that the heavily sealed casks, buried more than a thousand feet underground in a special secure chamber, would be safe. And not just kind of safe. In fact, the standard we had to meet required these containers to be so safe that in ten thousand years they would not give off enough radiation to cause a person living near Yucca Mountain to be exposed to a level of radiation roughly equivalent to what an individual gets making two transcontinental airline flights. In my opinion the repository could be built to meet this standard.

If you ever visit Yucca Mountain you'll be struck by the extent of its isolation. It is above an aquifer it shares with Death Valley. There are no humans in the immediate neighborhood either, except for a group of people who work in businesses that are located at a highway crossroads several miles away. In formulating my opinion, I boarded a helicopter on top of the mountain and toured the entire area covered by the EPA's safety standards. The only thing I saw was the aforementioned crossroads, which had a couple of convenience store–gas station structures and a one-story building nearby. I asked my tour guides on the helicopter what the building housed. They informed me that it was a place called the Cherry Patch, one of Nevada's notorious legalized brothels. That's it. No one else is anywhere near the place. Nor is anyone likely to move there once we start sending nuclear waste to the area.

(By the way, I asked my tour guides what the disposition of the employees of the Cherry Patch was toward Yucca Mountain. I was informed that they were overwhelmingly in favor of it because during the construction period it would mean a lot of new clientele in the neighborhood. I didn't ask how my guides had ascertained this.)

Once I made my recommendation, the process moved forward in a highly predictable way. The president affirmed my recommendation, Nevada vetoed it, and Congress began considering whether to override Nevada's veto. This produced a variety of meetings and hearings in which I traveled to Capitol Hill to make the case for building the project. Because of the quality of the research we had amassed about the safety of the site, nuclear opponents decided to build their case around the notion that transporting nuclear waste to Yucca Mountain would be dangerous. This, despite the fact that since we began producing nuclear waste in this world, *more* than the amount that will be sent to Yucca Mountain has already been transported without one single injurious emission. Nevertheless, environmental groups and key legislators tried to stop the project. The most heated exchanges took place in the House Energy and Commerce Committee. There Congressman Edward Markey of Massachusetts, a well-known opponent of nuclear energy, claimed that moving the waste would set up the possibility of terrorist strikes or worse. Calling the program a "mobile Chernobyl," Markey insisted that the risk of transporting waste to Yucca was too great for it to be built.

In my response, I asked Congress a simple question: If terrorists really wanted to attack nuclear waste, why would they wait the ten or more years it would take to build the Yucca project, and then still be required to identify which among all the moving trucks and railroad cars in the country contained nuclear waste *and then* take on what would be heavily protected convoys, when they could go online, learn the current locations of any of our nuclear power plants and, in some cases, their spent waste pools and attack them tomorrow? No one provided a coherent response.

Ultimately, Congress voted overwhelmingly to override Nevada's veto and let us move forward with the project. Unfortunately, opponents went to court and ultimately secured a decision that argued that the standard of safety, which had been set by the Environmental Protection Agency, was insufficient and needed to be adjusted. I was astonished at this outcome. As I previously mentioned, the standard we were asked to meet was one that would require the area be safe from any significant radiation leakage for ten thousand years. The courts, though, seized on the fact that a National Academy of Sciences study indicated that radiation from nuclear waste might have a lifespan of more than a million years to argue that we needed an even longer-term safety standard. Obviously, it never occurred to the appellate court that we might go forward with the EPA standard and develop a post–12,000 A.D. standard sometime in the next ten millennia.

As a result, Yucca Mountain is still unfinished and unlicensed, and nuclear waste is still piling up outside of reactors all over America. President Barack Obama waited less than six months before attempting to drive a stake through the heart of the project by having his secretary of energy, Steven Chu, announce that virtually all funding would be suspended and the project placed in limbo. Instead, Secretary Chu declared his intentions to form a blue-ribbon committee to study the whole problem again from scratch. Although the Commission is made up of a number of very able individuals, Washington's "Blue Ribbon Commissions" tend to be synonymous with putting off tough decisions to someone else's watch.

So what should we do with our nuclear waste? Basically the question is a bit misleading. There is very little in a spent fuel rod that can really be called "waste." Thinking of the by-products of nuclear energy as waste is actually a leftover from the era of fossil fuels. Coal, oil, and gas do indeed produce waste.

The by-products of nuclear power production are entirely different. First, they are amazingly small. This is because the energy releases from the nucleus are 2 million times greater than the releases from carbon chemistry. One-third of the fuel rods are replaced in a reactor every eighteen to twenty-two months, so a fuel rod lasts almost five years. When it comes out of the reactor it looks exactly the same way it did when it went in except that it is now highly radioactive. Make no mistake, this is dangerous stuff. If a spent fuel rod suddenly became uncovered, it would kill everyone within about a hundred yards. But it can be handled remotely by machinery and robots. That is why all the nuclear waste that has ever been produced in this country can be stored in large "swimming pools" at each reactor site.

Even then, the highly radioactive portion of a spent fuel rod is very small. Recall that a fuel rod is only 3% U-235, the isotope that can split in two, releasing large amounts of energy. The rest is U-238, which gives off only low levels of alpha radiation. After the fuel rod is spent, *95% of it* remains the relatively harmless U-238. This is just natural uranium, the same stuff that comes out of the ground. The U-235, however, has morphed into several highly dangerous isotopes.

One percent of this is plutonium. This is very poor bomb material, but it can be mixed with the spent U-235 to form a mixed oxide fuel (MOX) that can be burned in special reactors. Another 1% is the unburned U-235, which can also be extracted and used for more fuel. Two percent is the "fission products"—highly radioactive isotopes of barium, cesium, strontium, and zirconium. The remaining 1% is actinides, man-made elements that are higher than uranium on the periodic table. (Plutonium is one of them.) These are also highly radioactive, but many have industrial and medical uses.

Some fission products are used as medical tracers. Technetium-99, a purely reactor-made product, is now the most common medical isotope in the world, used forty-thousand times a day. Glenn Seaborg, the former chairman of the Atomic Energy Commission from my native Michigan, won the Nobel Prize for his discovery of plutonium. But he always said he was much prouder of his discovery of technetium-99 because of its prominent role in nuclear medicine. Yet we now import virtually all our technetium and our other medical and industrial isotopes from Canada, because all our isotopes are trapped in the nuclear waste debate.

We are never going to be able to deal with global warming or energy dependence without reviving nuclear power. We simply have to overcome the myths and vanquish the fear about nuclear energy. We also have to revive our own technological base. The vast majority of nuclear engineers in this country are over age fifty-five and about to retire. We probably don't have enough specialty welders to build reactors right now. And there is the ever-present problem of finding investment money for projects that will cost billions. Much of the early expertise and investment may come from other countries. The nuclear industry estimates that as much as 70% of the parts in our first new reactors will probably be machined abroad. That is how far behind we have already fallen. But it can only get worse. The time to start reviving nuclear power in this country is now.

As stated earlier, both our energy security and environmental objectives can be enhanced if we were to substantially increase the percentage of our power supply derived from nuclear energy. In the introduction to this section of the book, I outlined a potential formula for how we might shape our future power generation, suggesting that by 2030 we should strive to add at least fifty new nuclear power plants to our current 104.

Given the costs of construction of nuclear plants and the ongoing political opposition to any form of nuclear energy, this will not be an easy undertaking. But it can be done. Our first step in the process must be to set a clear goal.

Once we have a national commitment to expand our nuclear fleet by fifty plants, we must put our money where our mouth is. A new plant is likely to cost, on average, $6–$10 billion. That means the full program will cost $300–$500 billion over the next twenty years. Undoubtedly, the utility industry will be building far more than fifty new power generation plants over the course of the next two decades. The question is what it will take to incentivize the industry to make sure that fifty of them are nuclear?

To try to prompt new nuclear construction, the 2005 Energy Bill included provisions that would provide federal loan guarantees to support the construction of new nuclear plants in America. Unfortunately, not one guarantee was issued during the final three years of the Bush administration, or until the second year of the Obama presidency. In 2009 Republican senator Robert Bennett proposed adding $50 billion to this $18 billion program as part of the economic stimulus bill Congress was devising, but, while it made it through the Senate, the provision was ultimately dropped from the final bill due to the apparent opposition of both the House and the Obama administration. Then, in a surprising turnabout, in his 2010 State of the Union address, President Obama called for a $36 billion increase in the program (to $54 billion) as part of his 2011 budget.

While there is no question that loan guarantees are better than not providing any federal support for new nuclear plants, I am not confident that the loan guarantee program will be sufficient to trigger the construction of the fifty new nuclear plants we need by 2030, whether the funding is at $18 billion, $54 billion, or $68 billion. In my view a better way to insure the construction of a fifty plus fleet of new nuclear plants, and truly usher in a nuclear renaissance in America, is through direct government co-investment in new plants.

I would propose that the federal government contribute up to

50% of the cost of these new facilities in exchange for up to 50% of the ownership. This kind of financial partnership will not only encourage the construction of nuclear facilities, but also put the government in the position of providing what will be, in essence, political risk insurance to help ensure these facilities will actually be built. In the alternative, the federal government would commit to directly finance all cost overruns above the projected plant cost, in exchange for a proportionate ownership share, thereby providing investors with certainty as to their potential exposure. Under my proposal, utilities and rival states would vie for the projects through a competitive process.

Over the years I have had numerous debates with advocates from both the right and left on the subject of providing government support to facilitate nuclear builds. Conservative advocates of small government recoil at the prospect of spending federal money to support what they view as essentially private sector initiatives. The usual argument is that if building nuclear reactors made sense to the market, sufficient capital would be invested to build plants. On the left, liberal critics (many of whom oppose nuclear energy on principle) argue that utility companies and nuclear technology firms are profitable enterprises that don't deserve government handouts.

Here is a response to such contentions. To conservatives I would argue that building nuclear reactors is an indispensable component of achieving energy and, ultimately, national security in the twenty-first century. I would further point out that due to the political uncertainties that surround nuclear power, it is almost impossible to finance nuclear construction. In a perfect world the market *would* capitalize new nuclear power plants, but it is unwilling to do so because of fear that political resistance could cause such delays that the building costs would prove to be unacceptably high, as we have seen in projects such as the Shoreham reactor on Long Island. There a $6 billion fully built nuclear plant was never opened due to strong opposition from environmental groups and New York governor Mario Cuomo. Eventually, the costs were passed on to Long Island ratepayers, but we should assume that in the future such risks will be borne by shareholders and investors. Only by offering a high degree of government support are we likely to provide investors with sufficient confidence in the ultimate success of projects to bring about capitalization. In short, the issue really isn't whether the market would support nuclear, rather the issue is that market signals have been distorted by political factors that are preventing the market from acting rationally. Government support of new nuclear builds is the only way to transcend this distortion and is worth providing because of the overriding national security interests associated with building new nuclear facilities.

To liberals I would argue that first and foremost, it is impossible to fight global warming and oppose nuclear energy at the same time. More nuclear plants are an indispensable component of any program to reduce carbon emissions. If we allow nuclear to wither away, it will be nearly impossible for us to address carbon issues.

If we can ever get past the long-standing knee-jerk opposition to nuclear that has been so pervasive on the left, I would argue that there is little difference between providing incentives to utilities and nuclear industry firms and giving subsidies to those who provide renewable sources. The truth is that they are often the same companies. When we provide production tax credits for renewable energy, the ultimate beneficiaries are investors, utilities, and firms who provide components for renewable facilities. It might somehow feel better to subsidize a wind farm than a nuclear plant, but there is scant difference in terms of who receives benefits. Moreover, in each case we are facilitating the construction of a non-emitting source of power production.

I recognize that some may question whether the approach I have laid out here would result in the construction of fifty new nuclear facilities over twenty years. I am confident it would. I believe communities, the states, and the power generation industry would be lined up to partner with Washington in building these plants. If sufficient funds are provided to make sure the licensing process is carried out in a timely fashion, I have no doubt the goal set forth here can be achieved.

Once plants are up and operating, they are certain to be profitable as well as valuable. I have confidence that the government will be able to sell its shares in these new facilities, at a profit, to private-sector investors once they are constructed. In the meantime, the government will be investing approximately $7.5–$12.5 billion a year in exchange for a dramatic increase in energy independence and a dramatic decrease in carbon emissions, as these new nuclear facilities replace aging and obsolete coal-fired power plants. Thus, by the early 2030s, the federal government will be turning a profit on their investment in these facilities and the American people will be reaping the benefits of a nuclear renaissance.

In addition to helping provide political protection and upfront capital for a new nuclear fleet, the federal government must also seriously address the issue of how we deal with nuclear waste. It is remotely possible that the Obama administration's blue ribbon commission could produce a new and more popular set of solutions to the waste issue, but scientists worldwide have been working on this challenge for a long time without devising any new ideas. At the end of the day, it still comes down to either storing the waste somewhere or, as is the case in so much of the world, reprocessing it for reuse.

Having invested so much time in studying the viability of Yucca Mountain as a storage site for nuclear waste, I remain comfortable with that path. In the alternative, should it be decided that Yucca Mountain is not a politically feasible option, we could, of course, leave the nuclear waste outside of the existing nuclear facilities (where it currently reposes) and return the money sent by ratepayers for the disposition of the waste back to the utilities so they can spend it to better protect and store the waste on site. But in my view that is both a less safe and less prudent course.

A better alternative is reprocessing. Maintaining a reprocessing system in the United States will not pose a proliferation risk any greater than that presented by similar systems in France and Japan.

We have passed the point where we can say that because the United States does not reprocess its nuclear waste, other nations won't. The rest of the world has ignored America's approach on this issue, to our detriment. The notion that America's example will dictate the course for other countries is simply not valid in this context, and we should put an end to this myth. Instead, we should allow private companies to vie for the opportunity to build reprocessing facilities as the soundest way to dispose of our nuclear waste.

Finally, for a large number of new nuclear plants to be built we must have a streamlined and efficient process for their licensing and regulatory approval. Remember, the Nuclear Regulatory Commission has not had much recent experience in the licensing of new nuclear facilities. For it to work efficiently, safely, and expeditiously (and these are not mutually exclusive capabilities), the NRC will need the staff and resources to get these licensing programs on a fast track. Thus, it will be essential that NRC budgets be adequate for this challenge.

Building a new generation of nuclear plants can help us deal with many of our energy security issues and reduce our carbon emissions. It is an essential ingredient in any twenty-first-century energy strategy and should be initiated with no further delay.

CHAPTER 11

Renewable Energy

There is no more shining vision in the energy debate than a world run on "clean, renewable energy." It seems to be the answer to all our problems, providing us with all the energy we need, with no ugly pollution and a minimal environmental impact.

I am a strong advocate of renewable and clean energy and feel it must be a big part of our energy solution. Some environmental activists might find that statement surprising given the relationship between the environmental community and the Bush administration over the years, not to mention my frequent debates with environmentalists over U.S. auto industry issues during my service as a senator from Michigan.

But by my calculus, ramping up our deployment of renewable energy is just as important as ramping up our use of nuclear power. We simply cannot pursue the goal of enhancing our energy security or reducing our emissions without both of these components. Over the years, I have grown increasingly frustrated when I hear nuclear power enthusiasts dismiss the arguments of advocates of renewable sources and vice versa. It is impossible to strengthen America's energy security position without more renewable sources *and* nuclear power. Likewise, it is impossible to address climate change without more renewable sources *and* nuclear. In my opinion, much of the recent stalemate in Washington on energy policy stems from the unwillingness of either nuclear power proponents or renewable proponents to embrace the other side. We are simply not going to be able to address our energy challenges by building only nuclear plants. Nor are we going to be able to address those challenges by building only renewable energy sources.

Fortunately, some individuals on both sides have begun to exhibit the leadership required to bring about progress. For instance, Patrick Moore, one of the founders of Greenpeace, is now a strong backer of nuclear energy. Similarly, a number of large utilities and companies that have specialized in nuclear energy have embarked upon major renewable energy development efforts. I am hopeful that others on both sides will follow suit and help break the impasse that has contributed to our current energy difficulties. To me, the sensible approach is to embrace both these power sources and work hard to advance them in the coming twenty years.

That said, we must understand that renewable sources, like natural gas in the last decade, cannot do the job alone. Thus, in addition to understanding its benefits, we must also recognize the limits of renewable energy as well.

To begin, we might ask what exactly we mean by "clean and renewable energy." These things can sound good on paper or as an abstract alternative to the "dirty" and "nonrenewable" resources of fossil fuels. But the reality often turns out to be much different. When we envision windmill farms, are we really prepared for thousand-square-mile installations of sixty-story structures covering mountaintops and midwestern farmland? When we talk of solar collectors, are we really ready to sacrifice hundreds of square miles of desert? When we promote biofuels, are we aware that we may be taking food out of the mouths of people in tropical countries?

When we say "clean" we usually mean free of the by-products of fossil fuels—both the contaminating pollutants, like sulfur and mercury, and the inevitable by-product of carbon combustion, carbon dioxide, which is not a pollutant. Wind and solar power are free of pollutants and carbon dioxide, but then so are the uranium and thorium that are the source of nuclear energy.

"Renewable" is a trickier concept. No energy is really "renewable." The second law of thermodynamics says, in effect, that energy cannot be recycled. Every energy transformation produces a quantity of low-grade "exhaust" that is of no use. Reassembling it to make it useful would cost more energy than could be recaptured. This is why a perpetual motion machine is impossible.

When we say sunshine and wind are "renewable," what we really mean is they are recurring and appear to be inexhaustible. The sun will keep shining and the wind will keep blowing no matter what use we make of them. But this does not mean that solar and wind energy is available in *unlimited* quantities or that they will be there whenever we want them. Both have physical limitations as to their quantity and availability. It is best we be aware of these before we establish our strategy.

So, for example, it is a grave mistake to call biofuels "clean and renewable" and think of them as inexhaustible or even "sustainable." Biofuels have great limitations in that they require prodigious amounts of land to produce them. If biofuels were truly inexhaustible, humanity would never have had any problem finding enough to eat.

Finally, it is often argued that wind and solar energy are "free" and therefore we would be foolish to turn them down since they are a gift from nature. But this is a bit of a wordplay. Oil, gas, coal, and uranium are also "free" in that they are lying in the ground waiting to be taken. But that doesn't mean they are costless. The cost considerations are (*a*) it takes effort to extract and deliver them, and (*b*) someone usually owns the land by which we gain access to them. The same factors limit all forms of renewable energy. They may be free for the taking, but gathering them and turning them into some useful form has costs, whether it is land access, infrastructure costs, or transmission expenses.

Most forms of alternative and renewable energy have promise if we satisfy ourselves that they have strengths and limitations. Solar energy will work well to meet peak electrical demand. Wind can provide the reserve that utilities are required to carry for emergencies. Biofuels may cut a little bit into our oil imports, although even that isn't entirely certain. But none of these will ever be able to fully provide our base load energy needs. Each has a key role to play, and if we pursue them wisely we can reach the goal we set forth earlier for 2030.

Let's look at the main forms of "renewable" energy—solar, wind, hydro, geothermal, biomass, ethanol, and other gasoline substitutes, and see what we can expect from each.

SOLAR ENERGY. The amount of solar energy that reaches the earth every day is enough to power America's energy needs for one-and-a-half years. Al Gore's Repower America claims that we could power the entire country with solar collectors covering Metropolitan Atlanta. (Although he doesn't mention it, Metropolitan Atlanta covers 8,300 square miles.) But before we start covering Fulton and Gwinnett counties with photovoltaic cells or high-gloss mirrors, we should take a look at exactly how such a system would work.

Solar energy reaches the earth's atmosphere at an intensity of 1,000 watts per square meter. That means it would power ten 100-watt lightbulbs sitting on the average card table. But much of that energy is lost as sunlight penetrates the atmosphere. By the time sunlight reaches the ground, it averages about 400 watts per square meter—enough to light four 100-watt bulbs. However, the best technologies are able convert only about one-quarter of this energy to electricity. Photovoltaics have a theoretical maximum of 25% conversion to electricity. Using mirrors to focus sunlight to boil steam does slightly better at 30%. Such thermal electricity has to be transported, however, so it is safe to say that, at best, solar energy can provide us with enough power for about one 100-watt light bulb per square meter of rooftop. (Fortunately a lot of research is currently focused on improving these yields with the hope of enhancing them by 2030.)

What this suggests is that there's enough rooftop space in the country to provide us with a lot of electricity—maybe enough to provide lighting, refrigeration, electric clocks, a few kitchen gadgets, and perhaps run our television sets, at least during the daytime. This constitutes about 15% of our electrical consumption. Going beyond that to power an industrial society, however, would require gargantuan amounts of land. In January 2008, three leading solar scientists, Ken Zweibel, James Mason, and Vasilis Fthenakis, proposed a "Solar Grand Plan" for America on the cover of *Scientific American.* They proposed we could provide all our electrical needs by 2050 by putting solar collectors—both thermal and photovoltaic—on 46,000 miles of Southwestern desert. That's about one-third the size of New Mexico, the nation's fifth largest state.

That's only the beginning. Such solar collectors would only produce electricity when the sun is shining. There would be no output at night, when lighting needs are the greatest. If New Mexico suffered a cloudy day, the whole country could shut down. This means such a solar driven system would require backup or electrical storage or both.

The writers of the *Scientific American* article suggest we put our solar collectors in the desert because there is rarely a cloudy afternoon. But remotely locating a solar farm of this magnitude would require upgrading the entire national electrical grid in order to deliver power across the country. Most transmission lines now carry 345 kilovolts (kV), which lose 10% of their power every three hundred miles. New 745 kV lines would reduce these losses nearly to zero, but reaching this capacity would involve rewiring the entire grid. This would be about the equivalent of rebuilding the Interstate Highway System.

I don't think I encountered any issue more difficult as secretary of energy than siting long-distance transmission lines. It seems like anywhere you place them it's alleged they run right past a church or a school or a park or some sacrosanct site. Moreover, as we discussed in chapter 1, there are the persistent rumors that transmission lines cause cancer. Electrical engineers now talk about America having a "third world grid" in part because it is so difficult to get people to accept high-tension wires in their neighborhoods. Now some supporters of renewable energy are talking about *rewiring the whole country* in order to ship electricity from remote areas to urban centers. Such an undertaking will not be cheap or easy, and it risks creating a new hazard. Building a new grid will likely divert attention from our efforts to expand renewable production. Planners already face strong resistance to siting renewable projects; adding the challenge of siting an entire new grid is most likely to produce opposition to both the new grid and the projects the new grid is designed to support.

In addition, there is the issue of storing surplus electricity produced during peak daytime hours. Electrical storage is a very difficult proposition, and probably more expensive than generating the electricity. That is why the proposal to power America with thousands of miles of solar collectors does not really scratch the surface of the requirements. The solar collectors would only produce sufficient electricity at maximum output. The need for nighttime electricity would mean devoting tens of thousands of square miles for this additional storage capacity.

The authors of the *Scientific American* article suggest a national network of caverns storing compressed air. This would be used to fire natural gas boilers so they would burn at a higher rate and thereby recover some of the stored power. They estimate the scale to be the same size as all facilities in the country now used to store oil and gas. That's a lot of storage space. Some developers are also working on thermal storage systems where the fluids heated by the sun's rays retain their heat for six or seven hours and so keep generating after the sun goes down. Once again, though, this means producing extra electricity—and therefore taking up even more space—in order to do this double duty.

Another rarely mentioned challenge with remotely located solar is the need to clean the mirrors or photovoltaic panels. Any sand or dirt that begins to accumulate on these ultrasensitive surfaces diminishes their output. Most solar panels must be cleaned about once a month—with water. Where in the middle of the desert are we going to find enough water to clean 35,000 square miles of solar panels?

Where solar may work best is on rooftops and in urban areas providing peak power that does not have to be transported over long distances. Such a system would be able to replace gas turbines for peaking needs.

In short, solar can be a key part of our energy mix, but it has its limits. Solar cannot provide us with base load electricity. It cannot provide nighttime electricity. It cannot provide anything on cloudy days. It is not as strong in northern parts of the country. It is only one piece of the puzzle. However, if we accept these limitations, solar energy can play an important part in our energy future.

WIND. Probably no form of renewable energy has caught the public fancy more than wind power. Windmill companies put out 9,922 MW in 2009, the equivalent of six plus 1,500 MW coal or nuclear plants. Installed capacity now stands at 35,500 MW in thirty-five states, and the American Wind Energy Association says another 10,000MW is to be added in 2010. "In 2008 we passed Germany as the largest source of wind power in the world," says Randall Swisher, executive director of the association. "We're well on our way to contributing 20% of the nation's electricity by 2030." A 2008 U.S. Department of Energy study, *20% by 2030,* claimed it could be done.

So is wind going to solve our energy problems? Once again, it is not as easy as it looks.

It is very unlikely that wind will ever be able to provide us with base load electricity due to the fact that it is intermittent in nature. At best it can serve as a supplementary source of power that will give coal plants a rest. Or it may replace some natural gas, since gas is the most expensive electricity and likely to be withdrawn first. But those plants will not be shut down; they must be available for lulls in the wind.

There is also the challenge of project financing. A 1.5 megawatt windmill costs well over $1 million, which puts building a 1,000 MW windmill farm into the $1 billion range, even without considering the 30% capacity factor. A 1,000 MW reactor now costs $6.1 billion but offers a 90% capacity factor. Importantly, windmills are being built with the benefit of generous tax credits, and half the states have passed laws mandating renewable energy. Every time the federal production tax credit has been removed, windmill construction has collapsed. Europe has had the same experience. There may never have been a windmill built anywhere in the world without a government subsidy in recent times.

Denmark has pioneered wind power. A tiny country of 5.4 million inhabitants, smaller than New York City, Denmark has no oil, no coal, and no mountains for hydroelectricity, as neighboring Scandinavia has, and so it has embraced wind as the solution to its energy problems. These days it's hard to travel anywhere in the Danish countryside without seeing a windmill. The country claims to get 24% of its installed electrical capacity from wind and is now aggressively marketing its technology to the rest of the world.

Still, there are cracks in this picture. First and perhaps most important, there is a huge difference between *installed capacity* and *generated electricity*. All electrical plants have a "nameplate" capacity, indicating their maximum output when they are running at full speed. But electrical plants do not run at full capacity all the time. Nuclear reactors do this best because they have been designed to such high standards and because the fuel elements only have to be changed once every eighteen months. America's entire nuclear fleet is now running at a remarkable 90% of capacity— meaning reactors are up and running 90% of the time.

Coal plants operate at about 60% of capacity. They close down every two weeks or so to "give the boiler a rest." They also need constant cleaning and maintenance. Natural gas runs at only about 40%, mainly because gas is relatively expensive and makes up 95% of the operating costs. The gas is generally turned off at every opportunity. Hydroelectric dams run at only 25% of capacity because rainfall varies with the season. They must maintain reservoir capacity and release water in a way that does not endanger fish life. Fossil fuels, nuclear, and hydro are regarded as "dispatchable" because they can be summoned at any time.

Wind is an entirely different animal. It is not dispatchable. Its output depends on whether the wind is blowing. Unlike solar, its periods of peak output do not measure up as well with periods of peak demand. In fact there is no real pattern except that the wind tends to blow stronger at night and during the fall and spring—all periods of *low* demand. As a result, although wind makes up 24% of Denmark's generating capacity, it provides less than 18% of the country's electricity. Despite all its windmill construction, Denmark has not been able to close a single fossil fuel plant.

Power from a windmill can vary minute to minute. The wind is constantly shifting, and output varies with the cube of wind speed. These kinds of fluctuations can potentially cause havoc on an electrical grid. All this can be masked as long as wind remains only a small portion of generation, but once wind gets above 20%, the fluctuations can no longer be disguised. Without extensive backup or some system of electrical storage, it will be impossible to power more than 20% of a grid with windmills. Thus, the popularly stated goal of "20% wind by 2030" is not just an optimistic figure; it may also be a *maximum*.

One solution to the variability problem is to put windmills offshore. The flat ocean surface means the wind blows at a steadier rate and the problem of disrupting landscapes can be minimized. Much of Europe's new wind capacity is being built offshore. Transmission costs, however, mean that offshore wind must also be built near population centers. This is not a problem in Europe, where population density is greater and much of it is located near the coast. Denmark, with its long and densely populated coastline, is an ideal place for offshore wind, and it is no surprise that the Danes are leaders in wind generation.

In the United States there are also highly populated coastal areas that are attractive for offshore wind. The New Jersey coast, Long Island Sound, and the Massachusetts shoreline provide ideal conditions. Of course, many of these areas are also vacation spots, and people living along the coast do not want their view "spoiled"—as Massachusetts has discovered in trying to build windmills within sight of Nantucket Island. The answer may be to move these windmills out to deep water where they are not in sight of land. Already, several projects are in the development stage. I am very bullish on offshore wind as a key energy resource, but there are some hurdles to surmount. Only in 2009 was it determined that the Minerals Management Service of the Interior Department would have jurisdiction over offshore wind. Consequently, the rules of the road are new and will take time to be clarified. If the MMS has sufficient resources, it should be possible for offshore wind operations to make significant progress if there is a commitment to devise a safe but expeditious regulatory approach.

HYDROELECTRICITY. Hydroelectricity provides 6% of our electricity today, but the figure is not likely to grow. In 1940 we got over 33% of our electricity from hydroelectric dams, and west of the Mississippi it was close to 70%. This is because of the remarkable federal efforts in dam construction during the early part of the twentieth century.

Theodore Roosevelt and Gifford Pinchot, early leaders of the conservation movement, saw dam construction as a "wise use" of natural resources. Dams controlled rivers that had created catastrophic flooding, such as the Mississippi River flood of 1927, which wiped out vast areas. They also offered recreation and scenery. Often water was redirected for agricultural use. Ultimately, dam spillways could be harnessed for the generation of hydroelectricity. It was a perfect combination of natural enhancement and productive use.

Beginning with the damming of Hetch Hetchy Valley in Yosemite National Park in 1920, the Army Corps of Engineers began damming rivers all over the West. Hoover Dam, begun in 1931, harnessed the Colorado River, bringing significant amounts of electricity to Los Angeles and Southern California. With the arrival of the New Deal, the Bonneville Power Authority was funded to start building dams along the Columbia River. After World War II the aluminum industry moved into the region to take advantage of the cheap electricity.

When the army engineers renewed construction in the 1950s, however, it began to run into opposition from the Sierra Club, which had been founded by John Muir in 1892 for the formation of national parks. The Sierra Club had actually opposed the proposal to dam the Hetch Hetchy Valley in 1910, causing a split between Roosevelt and Muir. Now the "preservationists" began finding more legal tools at hand and gathering more public support.

The Sierra Club opposed the Glen Canyon Dam, just north of Grand Canyon. In its stead the club proposed a nuclear plant, since nuclear did not require drowning whole valleys and did not create air pollution. When the army engineers gave up plans to build the Echo Park Dam, which would have flooded Dinosaur National Monument, the club relented and withdrew its opposition to Glen Canyon. Sierra Club president David Brower later regretted the decision, however, calling it one of the biggest mistakes of his career. (See David Ross Brower, *For Earth's Sake: The Life and Times of David Brower*, also John McPhee, *Encounters with the Archdruid*.) Four years after Glen Canyon was completed, the National Environmental Protection Act of 1969 instituted environmental impact statements for every federal project. No major dams have been built since.

Dams do not last forever. Poorly built structures have been known to fail in other countries and in the United States. Dams have collapsed in Italy and India. A highly underreported failure in 2009 at Russia's biggest dam in the Republic of Khakassia killed seventy-six people—more than died at Chernobyl. In 1976 the Teton Dam in Idaho failed, killing eleven people and causing $400 million in property damage.

The longer-range problem with dams is silting. Both Hoover Dam and Glen Canyon now produce only 80% of their original capacity because of silting. Dams also block fish migrations. The dams on the Columbia River have been held responsible for declines in Pacific salmon populations. Environmental groups are now campaigning to tear down dams, and about thirty are being removed each year.

One constant issue I faced as secretary of energy was "fish mitigation payments." Hydroelectric dams, particularly in the Northwest, have regularly blocked the salmon from making it upstream to their spawning grounds. As a result, fish populations decline. We constructed fish ladders to help them get past dams, but they are never really enough. So every year the Department of Energy allocates compensation to ocean fishermen for their declining catch. The payments formed a considerable part of our annual budget and took up quite a bit of time to allocate. Altogether, the payments constituted another cost of hydropower that is not usually counted on the balance sheets.

Environmental groups now oppose dams to the extent that they resist having them classified as "renewable energy" in portfolio mandates. (Older hydroelectric dams are usually excluded from the equation as well.) Instead, they favor "low-head hydro," small dams that generate no more than thirty megawatts. There are hundreds of older dams around the country that were built for factories or reservoirs but never fitted with turbines. Some of these are being retrofitted for electricity. But the more common pattern is for older dams to be torn down to restore natural flows.

Another suggestion has been "run-of-the-river" power, where turbines are placed on the bottom of a river instead of building a dam. There have been estimates that placing turbines in large rivers like the Mississippi could generate thousands of megawatts. This is another one of these ideas that may sound good until we try it. How will they affect fish populations? I wouldn't want to write the environmental impact statement for that one. Also run-of-the-river turbines cannot be controlled like hydroelectric dams and, as always, will be subject to rainfall and seasonal variations.

Hydroelectricity has played a central role in the electrification of America. But its growth years have waned, and it will play an ever-declining role in the future. We can't count on any expansion of hydropower to solve our energy problems.

GEOTHERMAL. Geothermal energy is really nuclear energy taken out of the ground. The center of the earth is heated to 7,000°F by the breakdown of uranium and thorium in its crust. That's hotter than the surface of the sun. This molten rock occasionally reaches the surface through volcanoes, but it also comes in contact with groundwater, producing geothermal vents. Sometimes the steam rushes to the surface at regular intervals, like Old Faithful. But in most areas there is just a slow release of steam, called a fumarole, which can be harnessed to an electric turbine.

Geothermal resources differ widely around the world. They are most common on volcanic islands or near geological faults where continental plates rub together and earthquakes are common. Hawaii, New Zealand, and Iceland all have abundant geothermal resources. Iceland has proposed powering its entire economy with geothermal energy, siphoning off electricity for a fleet of hybrid vehicles as well. California also has extensive sites because of the San Andreas Fault and gets nearly 5% of its electricity from geothermal power.

As with hydroelectricity, however, geothermal resources are limited by the earth's geology. There are only so many places where molten rock approaches the earth's surface. One way to expand geothermal would be to drill down through the earth's crust into the liquid magma that underlies the continental plates everywhere. This would mean going down perhaps ten miles, twice as deep as the deepest oil wells. Bringing the steam all the way to the surface would be difficult because of heat losses. But locating the turbines ten miles deep seems equally unlikely. How would they be maintained? In 2010 a long-standing effort to drill for geothermal energy near Basil, Switzerland, was called off because it was causing earthquakes. Thus while geothermal may be a regional solution to some of our energy challenges, it cannot be expected to deal with more extensive needs.

BIOMASS ELECTRICAL PRODUCTION. Another area of potential growth within the renewable world is biomass—the burning of various materials for electricity production. Although only a tiny source of power production today, biomass has the potential to make an important contribution to the growth of renewable sources. I especially foresee potential for the deployment of small (50 MW) biomass plants in the coming two decades. For the most part biomass facilities utilize wood and other vegetation as a feedstock. Of course, this could potentially undermine the goal of achieving a significant reduction in carbon to the extent we are engaging in deforestation efforts to collect fuel. However, biomass operators are in many cases seeking to minimize this possibility by planting fast-growing trees to compensate for those removed for biomass production.

This is one area in which innovation is having a growing impact. Researchers are discovering that a variety of seemingly valueless materials including garbage, waste products, and even kitchen grease can be feedstock for energy production. To the extent further breakthroughs occur along these lines, the potential for biomass expansion will be significant.

ETHANOL AND OTHER GASOLINE SUBSTITUTES. Biofuels are generally regarded as one of the most successful efforts in promoting clean energy through government intervention. The effort dates to the Energy Bill of 1978, which offered a forty-cents-per-gallon exemption from federal gas taxes for any fuel that included a 10% mix of crop-based alcohol. Archer Daniels Midland took the ball and ran, building processing plants all over the Midwest and buying up large portions of the corn crop.

But the biofuels effort was not well thought out. The original idea was that we could replace foreign oil by growing our own fuel. As energy guru Amory Lovins put it, "Would you rather be dependent on the Middle East or the Midwest?" But no one ever bothered to calculate whether there was any real energy gain or how much land we would need to make a dent in our oil consumption. Today almost one-third of the American corn crop is going into our gas tanks, and still replaces only 3% of our oil. Obviously, biofuel isn't going to take us very far.

No one has ever even decided whether there is any energy gain from turning corn into ethanol. It takes a lot of energy to grow those crops. Fertilizers, pesticides, and irrigation all consume energy. Then there's the tractors plowing the fields and hauling the crops to market. Distilling corn into alcohol is also energy intensive. Ordinarily the price mechanism would tell us if it was worth the effort, but this is drowned out by the federal subsidy. Extracting ethanol from corn is not very efficient, since only the sugars in the seed can be used. Sugarcane produces eight times as much energy per acre. That's why Brazil's ethanol effort is thriving. But we have a steep tariff on imported sugar to protect our domestic growers. Many advocates of ethanol argue that we should lift these tariffs in order to import more sugar for our gas tanks.

There is a problem here as well. Countries in South America are cutting down tropical forests and turning them into sugar plantations. The same practice is occurring in Southeast Asia, where forests are being cleared to grow palm oil for European biodiesel. The last habitat of the orangutan is being threatened by the process. Many environmental groups have switched gears and are now campaigning against tropical biofuels. They recently persuaded the European Union to limit biodiesel imports from Southeast Asia. Do we want to go through the same experience with South America?

The problem of biofuels competing with food production is so obvious that it is amazing no one ever thought of it early on. By 2005, grain prices soared across the world and, as noted earlier, food riots took place in Mexico, Indonesia, India, and several other countries. In 2008, the government of Haiti fell over the issue. Officials at the U.N. Food and Agriculture Organization directly blamed biofuels, calling them "a crime against humanity."

Biofuels enthusiasts claim the problem can be solved with "cellulose ethanol," derived from the starches that make up the bulk of plant material. Cellulose is a more complicated molecule and does not ferment easily. It must first be broken apart by bacteria. Various researchers have accomplished this in the laboratory, but no one has ever been able to do it on an industrial scale.

It's not an easy task. The bacteria must be cultivated properly and other bacteria are always trying to compete. If the technology is ever mastered, it will be a big improvement in creating biofuels. We will be able to use all kinds of agricultural and forest wastes. Even then, the total land requirements will not be much smaller.

Finally, we have to ask, "What are biofuels supposed to accomplish?" Even with cellulose ethanol, we would have to set aside significant portions of our agricultural land to grow them. The best estimates are that we could replace perhaps 25% of our oil consumption by devoting 100 million acres of farmland to cellulose crops, 30% more than we use to grow corn today. If we encouraged tropical countries to do the same thing, we could be doing greater damage to the environment and, as we will soon see, taking a big step backward on carbon.

Once it became clear that biofuels offered no easy solution to our oil consumption, people began arguing that it was somehow going to help with global warming. The argument is that biofuels are "carbon neutral." By burning them, we are only putting carbon back into the atmosphere that was taken out last year, as opposed to hundreds of millions of years ago with the fossil fuels. Enthusiasts argue that biofuels are "young carbon" while coal, oil, and gas are "old carbon." It's hard to see how this makes any difference. Carbon dioxide is carbon dioxide, no matter where it comes from. If we are trying to reduce carbon emissions into the atmosphere, it hardly helps to be incinerating millions of acres of crops when there are other energy sources available.

The carbon-neutral hypothesis finally blew up in 2008 when *Science* magazine published two articles showing that burning biofuels is hardly different from setting a forest afire. In "Land Clearing and Biofuel Carbon Debt," J. Fargione and his coauthors showed that whenever land is utilized for biofuels, cropland somewhere else is put into cultivation, usually by clearing forests. In "Use of U.S. Croplands for Biofuels Increases Greenhouse Gases Through Emissions From Land Use Change," T. Searchinger and coauthors showed that when a forest is cleared for biofuels, it takes *ninety years* before the carbon debt is repaid.

Altogether, it is hard to make a strong case for biofuels. They are carbon-based and can hardly be expected to help much in fending off global warming. They are a poor substitute for gasoline and may not be producing any net energy at all. Yet they are now firmly imbedded in the network of agricultural subsidies and will be very difficult to revoke. Every presidential primary season now begins with the candidates making a pilgrimage to Iowa to testify to how much they adore corn ethanol.

Renewable energy has an important part to play in our energy strategy. Solar collectors can play an enormous role in meeting the demands for peak electricity. Windmills could one day provide double-digit percentages of power. Hydroelectric dams provide 6% of our electricity although this figure will not grow. Geothermal is contributing almost 5% of California's electricity but it is not available everywhere. In short, although they all have promise, they also have their limits.

In order to speed the development of renewable sources, about half the states have decided to forge ahead with "renewable energy portfolios" or "mandates." In these instances the legislature decides that utilities will have to get a certain percentage of their electricity from renewable sources by some future date. Twenty-seven states have now adopted such mandates, and more are likely to follow.

My proposal to set a national goal of 20% for renewable sources, including hydro, by the year 2030, while tough to reach, is a worthy target. The key is to understand that to meet it we must maintain strong federal support and concentrate on the promising areas of offshore wind, onshore wind, and solar. Similarly, we need to appreciate the potential consequences of subsidizing ethanol.

Washington and various states have already done a lot to help facilitate renewable deployment, but more help is needed. First, we need to extend the production tax credits for wind, solar, and other renewable electricity production for a long enough period—a minimum of ten years—to allow these industries to truly mature and develop. Extending these benefits for short periods and letting them lapse periodically is a poor approach.

Second, we should help pay for these incentives by scaling back the subsidies for biofuels. Until technological breakthroughs dramatically improve the energy production and emission calculus for biofuels, it does not make sense to underwrite this energy source as we have.

Third, we need to sufficiently fund and staff the Mineral Management Service of the Interior Department to allow it to quickly and comprehensively start up an offshore wind industry. Allowing bureaucratic inertia to derail or suppress the development of offshore wind would be a tragedy. At the same time the MMS must set reasonable timetables for the siting, licensing, and approval process of these facilities so that they can be brought online in the near to mid term.

Finally, I believe it is possible, perhaps even likely, that Congress will adopt a federal renewable energy mandate in the near future (at the time this book went to press such a proposal was under serious consideration). Already the House has passed a renewable energy mandate as part of its larger Energy/Climate package. Although that bill is stalled in the Senate, in 2009 the Senate Committee on Energy and Natural Resources approved a narrower energy bill on a bipartisan basis, which included a federal renewable electricity standard but no cap and trade carbon provisions. It would therefore seem that a renewable mandate has a chance to make it through both chambers, which would enhance the possibility of reaching the target I have proposed of 20% by 2030.

Coal—Time to Start Making It Clean

In the early twentieth century, my grandfather came to the United States from Lebanon and found a job in the coal mines of Pennsylvania. While still a very young man he suffered a serious injury and was forced to move to Michigan and live with relatives. That's the reason Michigan is my home state.

My grandfather's experience was not unusual. Over the course of the twentieth century, a hundred thousand Americans died in coal-mining accidents, and many more were injured. Explosions and tunnel collapses that killed dozens of miners at a time were common right through the 1960s, and they occur even today. Other disabilities were ignored. When Black Lung Disease was finally diagnosed in the midtwentieth century, it had already affected hundreds of thousands of miners and caused tens of thousands of deaths. Yet, it still was not acknowledged as a work-related condition by Worker's Compensation laws for years. Only when the Federal Coal Mine Health and Safety Act was adopted in 1969 did compensation for such injuries begin to be offered. Improvements to safety have since lowered the incidence of the disease by about 90%, yet even today about a thousand former miners die each year from the condition.

When it comes to the environmental impact of the Industrial Revolution, coal has also probably been the most controversial product. Coal smoke choked European and American cities from the sixteenth century on, killing thousands by ravaging their lungs—just as it does in China today. The London fog, which characterized that city for centuries, turned out to be coal smoke instead of a meteorological condition. When Britain switched to natural gas in the 1970s and 1980s, the famous fog disappeared. Finally, we have to worry that carbon dioxide exhausts from burning coal and other fossil fuels may be threatening the earth's climate.

Even with all these negative effects, however, we still find coal hard to give up because so much of our industrial society depends on it. Without coal the Industrial Revolution probably never would have occurred. Until the end of the nineteenth century almost every industrial facility in the world ran on coal, unless it ran on wood. Only when electricity was introduced did hydropower begin to assume some of the burden. Yet as dam sites have dwindled, the trend over the last thirty years has been a return to coal.

From 1968 to 1972, as we became aware of the hazards, we actually reduced our coal consumption. Then came the Arab oil embargo. That ended the attempt to replace coal with low-sulfur oil. In 1976 we burned about a half billion tons of coal to produce our industrial power, mainly by generating electricity. Today we burn more than a billion tons. And that's the way it's likely to be with us for many, many years to come if we don't start diversifying our energy mix.

Replacing coal with renewable sources, nuclear power, or natural gas is one solution. Each has its place and must be developed. But we still have vast coal resources—anywhere from one hundred twenty-five to four hundred years' worth of supply by most estimates. And so the question remains, Is there any way that we can keep burning coal in a way that is less harmful to the environment? Is there any way we can continue to burn coal and still reduce carbon emissions? I believe there is.

The technology that offers the most promise right now is called integrated gasification combined cycle (IGCC). Coal is very dense in carbon and short on hydrogen. Many of the molecules are benzene rings and the "aromatic" compounds in which carbon molecules are double- and triple-bonded to each other. In methane, on the other hand, each carbon atom is surrounded by four hydrogen atoms. That is why coal, when it is burned, generally produces twice as much carbon dioxide as natural gas.

The way to deal with this is to break up the carbon bonds with heat while adding hydrogen in the process. The result is a "gasification" of the coal; it turns into methane—in effect, a synthetic natural gas. Most of the soot and ash in coal is unburned carbon. If all this carbon is attached to hydrogen, however, it will burn cleanly and leave almost no residue. Sulfur, mercury, and other contaminants can be precipitated out in the process as well. The result is a very clean product in which the only things that escape into the atmosphere are water vapor and carbon dioxide—although a lot less per kilowatt than if we burned the same amount of coal in the traditional way.

Now let's see what happens if we run this gasified coal through a combined cycle generator. With combined cycle, you recall, the exhaust vapors power one turbine while their heat boils water to power another. You can't do this with conventional coal, oil, or nuclear, only with natural gas. The result is electricity produced with a very high-energy conversion, around 60% as opposed to 30%–35% in ordinary steam boilers. This means you need less fuel to produce the same amount of electricity. When you gasify coal, you get the same result. This makes IGCC a very efficient way of utilizing our coal resources.

But we've still got the carbon dioxide. What can we do with that? How can we "sequester" this carbon so it doesn't pose a threat to anyone? There are a great many potential sinks for carbon dioxide in nature and a whole lot of suggestions on how to utilize them to keep carbon dioxide out of the atmosphere.

There are about 1,000,000 gigatons of carbon in and around the earth, but almost all of it is more or less permanently bound up in carbonate rocks such as limestone and dolomite. It never circulates. Only about 45,000 gigatons are part of what we call the carbon cycle. The biggest repository is the oceans, which hold 38,000.

The atmosphere holds 750, the biosphere 600, and the earth's soils a remarkable 1,500. The biggest carbon sinks outside the oceans are the world's fossil fuels, with coal holding 3,000 and oil and gas only about 300.

What these figures illustrate is the large role that the laying down of coal deposits played in removing carbon dioxide from the earth's atmosphere. Scientists believe that before vegetation invaded the world, CO_2 was a much larger part of the atmosphere—perhaps as much as 40%–50%—and the globe was a much hotter place. Then plants spread across the land and started removing carbon through photosynthesis. But the bacteria and other soil organisms that break down plant material hadn't evolved yet. As a result, the earth "developed a case of indigestion" and huge amounts of plant material—probably in swamps and shallow seas—gradually sank into the earth, to remain there as coal. That is why it is so significant that we are digging up a fair percentage of this coal and putting it back in the atmosphere.

One idea now being widely pursued, of course, is the planting of more trees. This makes sense in areas where trees have been stripped from the land to make way for development. An approach that is being tried in Europe is to cut down trees and bury them underground and so keep them away from the atmosphere in a way that imitates the process that creates fossil fuels.

Another suggestion has been to fertilize the ocean to encourage the growth of photosynthetic algae, which also take carbon out of the atmosphere. Studies have found that lack of iron is the limiting factor that prevents the growth of more algae. Since the 1990s, a dozen international research teams have conducted ocean trials demonstrating that iron can stimulate phytoplankton blooms. The latest, in 2009, involved a 500-square-mile patch of ocean in the South Atlantic. The experiments have only been moderately successful, however, and concern remains that such efforts could upset marine ecosystems.

A modern version of an old practice has also attracted attention. From ancient times wood has been burnt without much oxygen to create charcoal. The resulting fuel is less smoky and has a 50 percent reduction in weight, both of them offering considerable advantages. The method was simple. Large piles of wood were covered with earth or clay and set on fire or they were burned in special kilns. On the early American frontier settlers simply buried the logs and burned them underground. In the 1990s, British environmental scientist James Lovelock, originator of the Gaia hypothesis, proposed that charcoal production be revived, using coal, with the coal left underground to sequester the carbon. His was basically a variation on burying trees to burn them. The drawback? Lovelock's proposal would have to be done on a huge scale to make any difference in global warming.

The most promising technique for carbon sequestration is to pump the gas into underground repositories in geological formations. This is already being done to enhance oil recovery in various oil fields, but the hope is to inject carbon wherever underground geological conditions would allow. In 2008, a twenty-megawatt generator in Spremberg, Germany, became the first commercial coal plant in the world to sequester its carbon emissions. The process is not easy. First the nitrogen—which constitutes 70% of atmospheric air—must be separated out so only pure oxygen is used for combustion. Then the exhausts are run back through the plant for several cycles until they become 98% carbon dioxide. At that point the CO_2 is cooled to $-57°C$ until it is liquefied. At Spremberg, the liquid CO_2 is then trucked to a depleted natural gas field 150 miles away.

As noted above, oil and gas companies have actually employed carbon capture for their own purposes—pumping carbon dioxide back into oil wells to enhance oil recovery. Norway originated its Sleipner Project in the 1990s, which stores a million tons of CO_2 annually under the North Sea. In 2001, eight oil firms, including Chevron and BP, started the CO_2 Capture Project, which has been investigating various cutting-edge technologies both for extracting carbon from fossil fuels and finding a safe place for it. The consortium is now beginning to employ some of them on a pilot basis.

Occidental Petroleum (a firm with which I have a role) has developed this approach in a very extensive way and became a leader in the use of CO_2 for enhanced oil recovery.

Older oil and natural gas fields make excellent sites for carbon sequestration. The problem is that oil fields are often far from the place where the coal is being burned. If carbon sequestration for enhanced oil recovery is to be expanded, it will be necessary to build pipelines to transport captured carbon dioxide from power plants to appropriate geological sites.

During my tenure as secretary of energy, we launched Future-Gen, a demonstration coal plant designed to employ all the technologies mentioned so far. FutureGen was to implement IGCC, gasifying coal and then capturing its exhausts for carbon storage. In the process the plant would produce both electricity and hydrogen. The latter was to be part of the Hydrogen Fuel Initiative, which was seeking to replace gasoline in our cars.

The plant was originally projected to cost the Department of Energy $1 billion. The DOE chose Mattoon, Illinois, as the Future-Gen site in December 2007, after I had left office. Shortly thereafter, the projected construction costs had increased to an estimated $1.8 billion. At that point the DOE withdrew support and decided to focus on carbon sequestration alone.

A greater focus on sequestration makes sense, but stopping FutureGen was a mistake. First of all, the run-up in construction costs occurred at the end of the speculative bubble that eventually led to the economic meltdown of 2008. The price of everything was going through the roof. Given the adjustments that have occurred during the recession—as well as the importance of clean coal—the Obama administration and Congress acted quickly to restart FutureGen. I applaud that decision.

Clean coal funding has always been an area of federal budgetary debate. One incident stands out in my memory. On Capitol Hill, coal's greatest advocate has always been Senator Robert Byrd, of the coal-rich state of West Virginia. Indeed, Senator Byrd had been responsible for most of the appropriations for clean coal technology over the years. When President George W. Bush took office, the Department of Energy and the Office of Management and Budget shifted some of its priorities and diverted some of the Byrd-related coal funds into a new set of clean coal and other programs. Senator Byrd was not very happy with this.

When the Democrats took control of the Senate in 2001 following the party switch of Senator Jim Jeffords of Vermont, Senator Byrd regained the chairmanship of the Appropriations Subcommittee on Interior, which controlled our budget. Around that time, after rigorous debate within the administration, OMB downsized and reconfigured a number of fossil fuel research programs. Everyone knew that Senator Byrd was unhappy, and officials in the DOE's Fossil Energy Division warned me that my testimony in defense of the budget before Senator Byrd's subcommittee would be unpleasant.

As I prepared for my appearance, there was great anxiety at DOE. I was told career officials were taking bets on the likelihood of my survival. When the morning finally arrived, I showed up early and went right up to the dais to say hello to Senator Byrd and Senator Conrad Burns of Montana, the ranking Republican member. As we engaged in pleasantries, I mentioned to Senator Byrd that one of my fondest memories from my Senate term took place September 5, 1996, when my youngest child, a son, was born. Learning of the news that day, Senator Byrd had taken to the Senate floor and offered an extremely touching tribute. To my delight, the senator remembered the event. I then asked if he would be willing to autograph a copy of those remarks from the *Congressional Record*. He readily agreed.

I returned to the witness table and prepared for the worst. Once proceedings began, however, Senator Byrd indicated that he wished to ask me a personal question prior to the official start of the hearing. He then asked me to confirm that I had a son who had been born while I was a member of the Senate. "How old is that boy today?" he asked. I said he was six years old. Byrd smiled and asked what his name was. I responded that his first name was Spencer, like mine, but I wanted the senator to know that his middle name was Robert. At this, Senator Byrd flashed a magnificent smile and indicated that we would only have a short hearing. He and his staff would submit most of their questions to me in writing rather than in a public setting. After some brief statements, and a few sharp criticisms of the budget, the hearing ended, and I escaped intact. I will always be grateful to Senator Byrd for his consideration that day.

Clean coal does have its opponents. Lately, environmental groups have taken out TV ads mocking the idea. In one a clean coal salesman leads the audience through an office door to view "the latest developments" and the building turns out to be a prop with nothing but desert behind it. In another, a family sprays a "clean coal" product around its house and it turns out to be choking coal dust.

It's easy to make fun, but this kind of attitude isn't going to get us anywhere. In fact, the effort to improve clean coal technology is gaining traction. Tenaska, Inc., an Omaha merchant energy company, has announced the start of a $3.5 billion, 500 MW clean coal plant in Taylorville, Illinois. The project was spurred by a new Illinois state law requiring that utilities buy at least 5% of their electricity from companies generating with clean coal. In nearby Cash Creek, Kentucky, a similar project is moving ahead (this is a project with which I have a business relationship). Meanwhile Mississippi Power, another innovative company, is planning a complete 580 MW IGCC plant in Gulfport that will include carbon sequestration. In New Haven, West Virginia, the Mountaineer power plant, built in 1980, is undergoing a series of major changes that will convert it into one of the country's most ambitious clean coal projects. The project team is drilling several deep underground wells that will capture and store up to 300,000 tons of CO_2 annually.

Developing clean coal technology is going to be a big job, but we really don't have any choice. If there's a way to utilize coal for energy without putting as much carbon and other emissions into the atmosphere, we have to find it. This will involve pursuing experiments like FutureGen. It will mean building a network of pipelines to carry CO_2 from power plants to geological repositories. Above all, it will mean taking actions that can jump-start the clean coal industry and, as noted earlier, help it expand to provide 5% or so of our electricity supply. To do that we need to take several decisive steps. First, we need to set the target of building twenty-five clean coal plants by 2030. Then we need to help get them built.

Although building a clean coal plant is likely to face less resistance than trying to construct a nuclear power plant, there is still a probability that construction efforts might be slowed, delayed, or thwarted because of the strong anticoal sentiments in America today. Even if a proposed coal gasification facility is expected to have a very small carbon footprint, and even if efforts are undertaken to make sure that carbon is captured and properly disposed of, there is still the potential for opposition based simply on the fact that the plant uses coal. For these reasons, securing permits and financing for a fleet of clean coal gasification plants will not be easy.

To surmount these problems, I believe that we should provide sufficient federal support to serve as political risk insurance in order to bring about the construction of these important facilities. Here, I do not believe it is necessary to provide half the financing from Washington, as I proposed for nuclear, but I would suggest either a 10% to 30% federal share (in exchange for a commensurate ownership interest), or robust loan guarantees to support up to twenty-five projects. Already Washington has begun to assist a few projects with loan guarantees and I believe that strong federal support is an essential ingredient in bringing about the development of a fleet of coal gasification power plants that can lay the groundwork for the long-term use of our coal resources in an environmentally desirable fashion.

Finally, to fully launch a clean coal industry means making carbon sequestration a research and development priority. That, in turn, means insisting that using CO_2 for enhanced oil recovery is deemed an acceptable means of sequestration in the event we ever adopt a carbon regulatory system. It also means investing in research at the levels needed to bring about the emergence of sequestration capabilities adequate to support a fleet of clean coal plants and, hopefully, other carbon-producing sources. This will mean a major effort on the frontiers of technology, but we've got to do it. Our coal resources are too vast and critical to our energy security.

Energy Efficiency, Part One: General Strategy

As outlined at the beginning of book 4, my plan for energy security calls for an improvement in energy efficiency of 10% between 2010 and 2030 in the power sector. To get there requires both efficiency gains in the way we use energy in our daily lives and significant efficiency gains in the way we transmit electricity from power generation sources to end users. The next two chapters will focus on these two areas. We will look at energy conservation strategies in chapter 13 and electricity transmission and the smart grid in chapter 14.

As I have already detailed, one of the most noted comments about energy in recent years was Vice President Dick Cheney's famous remark, "Conservation may be a sign of personal virtue, but it is not a sufficient basis all by itself for a sound, comprehensive energy policy."

As I said earlier, it's that "all by itself" that is usually left out of the historical accounts. The vice president made the comment because there were people telling us at the time—and are still out there telling us—that all we have to do is conserve energy and we won't have to worry about building power plants. California followed this advice in the 1990s and ended up with a power deficit that contributed to the California electrical shortage of 2000.

Nevertheless, I don't want to knock conservation, because we must reduce future demand growth if we are going to enhance our energy security. We just have to be realistic about what we can achieve.

Nothing in Washington is more fashionable than to claim you're in favor of energy conservation. Whenever a debate about the environment takes place on Capitol Hill, everyone claims to be a conservationist. Republicans take credit for Theodore Roosevelt's efforts to create national parks and conserve natural resources, while Democrats talk of their leadership in setting aside major national wildlife refuges and promoting energy-saving technologies.

I believe most Americans also think of themselves as supporters of conservation and efficiency. Indeed, many families practice what they preach. They recycle their bottles, cans, magazines, and such items. Even those who are less diligent probably engage in some form of conservation in their business or community.

Unfortunately, paying lip service and taking a few modest steps will not be enough to meet the energy challenges of the years ahead. In earlier chapters I described the dramatic increases in energy consumption being forecast for the United States and the rest of the world. The numbers, as you will recall, are daunting. In my view, it may be nearly impossible for our planet to keep up with this dramatic demand. It will be even more so if we continue to play "Not in My Backyard."

So where does that leave us? It leaves us facing not only the challenge of increasing energy supplies in an environmentally acceptable fashion, but also of reducing our demand for energy in a way consistent with a strong economy.

To achieve a 10% improvement in efficiency in the power sector by 2030 will not be easy. Economic growth is inexorably linked to energy. As we have learned in the last decade, even the rise of the information technology age (as opposed to the industrial age) has brought a significant increase in demand for electricity. Enormous amounts of power are needed to run the data centers and other key components of our cyber world. The same is true for plasma televisions, advanced video games, home computers, and all the other fruits of our happy and successful lifestyles. We are even finding that manufacturing solar panels to convert sunshine into useful power requires enormous blocks of electricity.

And we aren't just talking about the United States. I remember traveling to some of the most impoverished regions of the world during my tenure at the Department of Energy. I visited cities where the poor lived in conditions I've never encountered in America. I recall seeing countless buildings in which large extended families resided in one-room apartments. Yet, even then, as we drove by these tenements, you always saw two things: hundreds of satellite disks on the roofs and countless computer terminals through the windows. My point is not to suggest people living in these circumstances shouldn't have these appliances, but rather to underscore that even in the most poverty-stricken places, people are using a lot of energy. They are not going to give up these benefits in the name of energy conservation.

Nor is it always clear that improvements in energy efficiency translate into an equivalent reduction of energy consumption. I have previously mentioned an extremely interesting book, *The Bottomless Well*, by Mark Mills and Peter Huber. The authors demonstrate compellingly that increases in energy efficiency are just as likely to be followed by increases in energy demand as by reductions. This is called the Jevons paradox, a principle first put forth in the nineteenth century by Stanley Jevons, who studied Britain's consumption of coal. He found that with every efficiency improvement to the steam engine, *more* coal was consumed. As steam engines became capable of performing more and better work, people used them for more tasks. Mills and Huber show that the same thing is true for almost all technologies. Even as motor vehicles or computers become more efficient, people begin to do more with them and thus consume more energy.

So as we embark upon this effort we must remember that improvements in efficiency and conservation do not always lead to equivalent reductions in demand. Sometimes it works the opposite way. We can't assume that improved efficiency will mean people do the same amount of work with less energy. They may choose to do *more* work with the *same* amount of energy. They may even choose to do *much more* work with more energy because of the improved technology. This increases overall demand. Our goal must be to accomplish efficiency gains in such a way that enhanced usage does not wipe out the gain in efficiency.

My experience over the years confirms that it will be enormously difficult to reduce the demand side of the equation. We learned this by trial and error at the Department of Energy. For example, over the years, we started several public relations campaigns aimed at persuading people to use energy more efficiently. Probably the best thought out was a program called "Energy Hog."

In 2004, the department's Energy Efficiency and Renewable Energy Division, working with the Ad Council, devised a program aimed at educating young people on how much energy is wasted in America every day. The premise was that children and young adults are far more likely to be receptive to energy conservation ideas than their elders. Energy Hog would utilize a variety of media to inform young people on how to avoid wasting energy. Not only would we train a generation of young Americans to conserve more, they might even pass the lessons on to their parents and grandparents as well.

The program featured an animated hog intent on wasting energy. The cartoon would appear in TV public service announcements and on a Web site with interactive elements to attract young people. Everybody at the department loved the concept. In conjunction with the Ad Council, we proudly announced our program to the media at a major press conference in hopes of jump-starting a high-profile rollout. Except the media didn't show up.

We had expected great press coverage because, on the whole, the press had been strongly supportive of energy conservation—not to say constantly critical of the Bush administration for supposedly *not* pursuing conservation strategies. We were wrong. There's nothing more frustrating for a politician than playing to an empty house. Believe me, I'm an expert. It is often said in politics that being ignored is worse than being condemned or criticized. Yet here we were, along with the leaders of the Ad Council, sitting in a large auditorium at the Department of Energy before a national media contingent of two.

And so Energy Hog got off to a less than rousing start. Unfortunately, our target audience, young people, had only slightly more enthusiasm than the media. Kids did see our ads and log onto our Web site, but they didn't seem to find the topic very interesting, either. We didn't make much headway. And that was the case with most of our efforts to promote energy austerity. It's a pretty hard sell.

Another energy efficiency project that has had more success is Energy Star. A combined effort of DOE and the Environmental Protection Agency, Energy Star is designed to provide consumers with accurate information on the efficiency of household appliances. If a product has an Energy Star label, buyers may pay more for its purchase, but they know they will save energy costs in the long run. I was and remain a big fan of Energy Star. A lot of consumers depend on it, and I believe we should continue to expand the program of Energy Star certifications. Still, I'm not convinced we will ever significantly expand the number of Americans who rely on the Energy Star endorsement.

Trying to explain the program better, the department went on the offensive with a promotional campaign. Among other things, I was dispatched to a recording studio to tape a short video explaining why people should look for the Energy Star label. I was told that major retailers like Sears and Best Buy would be playing the video on monitors in their appliance sections.

Of course, anyone who's ever run for public office salivates at the prospect of having this kind of exposure. Shortly after the taping I was informed that hundreds of copies were being distributed across America and would soon be airing in stores from coast to coast. Since that time I have probably been in several hundred stores that sell Energy Star products. I have never once seen myself on a monitor. My point here is not to criticize the retailers, but only to reiterate that energy efficiency is a very hard sell.

One thing that works—but is very likely to generate all kinds of political conflict—is conservation mandates from the government. In addition to Energy Star, the DOE has also been responsible for developing enforceable efficiency standards for equipment and appliances. This requires the department to engage in lengthy rule making. During this procedure, manufacturers, consumer groups, and other interested parties—all of which have a big stake in the outcome—get the opportunity to comment. At the end, the department establishes a standard that is binding on manufacturers.

But the process gets complicated and political because any such process involves picking winners and losers in the marketplace. As a result, interested parties spend substantial sums to lobby the decision to their advantage. Then congressmen start to get involved, intervening on behalf of favored corporate constituents, and the whole process becomes immensely partisan.

For example, the Clinton administration in its closing days finalized a rule setting the standard for residential air conditioners. Every air conditioner sold in the United States after 2006 would have to have a 13 Seasonal Energy Efficiency Ratio (SEER), a measure of the unit's cooling efficiency. A 13 SEER is very powerful. It also adds to the cost of the unit. In parts of the country such as New England, where the need for air-conditioning is not as great, people would be spending extra money they would probably never recover through reduced electrical bills. As a result, advocates from these regions argued that a 12 SEER standard was sufficient. They were joined by conservatives who opposed the idea of federal air conditioner regulations altogether.

The new Bush administration stepped into this thicket on January 20, 2001. As a general matter, we decided to review each new rule passed in the final hours of the Clinton administration, including this one, an approach that most new administrations undertake. Ultimately, it was decided a 12 Seer standard would do. Then things really erupted.

Remember now, we're talking about the difference between a mandated 20% versus 30% increase in the efficiency for residential air conditioners. No one was arguing against conservation. Yet the Bush administration was attacked for being oblivious to the needs of the planet. It responded by arguing that Democrats were trying to foist expensive and unnecessary standards on the American people. Lost in the cross fire was that under either approach we were still improving energy efficiency. My conclusion from all this is that establishing mandatory standards for products can save energy, but our present system has become so politicized that it needs significant reform.

Even more effective than efficiency standards is the price signal. For almost any form of energy consumption, there is a price point at which people will modify their behavior because the cost is too great. During the dramatic run-up in gasoline prices in 2008, for instance, we saw Americans reach the breaking point. Consumption began to level off when prices reached four dollars per gallon. There was a decline in gas-guzzlers and a big increase in sales of fuel-efficient cars. Of course, behavior modification works in the other direction as well. When gas prices fell dramatically in the fall and winter of 2008–09, Americans began to resume their old buying habits.

The price incentive is not confined to gasoline. The same holds for home heating fuel, utility bills, and pretty much everything where ratepayers feel the pain of high prices or the lack of pain in lower ones. In short, all the public-service commercials and government mandates in the world will never have the impact of a sharp price change.

As we previously discussed, however, it's one thing for prices to fluctuate because of tight markets and another for the cost of energy to be elevated artificially. Voters may be frustrated with their public officials because they have failed to deal effectively with OPEC, but they probably won't vote them out of office. Their attitude will be far different if public officials try to raise the price of energy by imposing energy taxes.

As secretary of energy, and in my subsequent private-sector career, I have delivered many speeches around the country. I don't think I've ever made an appearance where a member of the audience hasn't suggested raising energy taxes to reduce demand. Not only is the question always asked, but it's almost always the same individual who asks it. He is inevitably a well-dressed, middle-aged man in a business suit (even when the rest of the audience is casually dressed) who considers himself well read and intellectually superior to the rest of the crowd—and presumably to me as well. Rather than just asking in direct terms, "Does it make sense for us to raise energy taxes?" he always poses the question in a condescending manner. "Haven't you people ever thought of raising taxes on energy in order to reduce demand?" He then turns to the audience with a smug look on his face, as if to say, "How is he going to talk his way out of that!" This guy always thinks he's the first person on the planet who ever thought of the idea.

I eventually discovered the most effective way to deal with this question was to point out how frequently I encounter it. Sometimes I even exaggerate the numbers in order to burst the ego of the questioner. "That must be the five hundredth time this year I've been asked that question," I will say. I relish watching the interrogator's reaction.

Theatrics aside, the men who ask this question do have a point. Higher prices, whether from taxes or market run-ups, definitely encourage conservation. But, as I noted in chapter 3, raising taxes on anything is not an easy process. People do not look favorably on politicians who want to raise their energy bills. President Obama's effort to cap carbon emissions had a fair amount of support until it suddenly became clear that what it amounted to was an indirect nationwide energy tax.

Bottom line: In the absence of a war or other major crisis, a majority of Congress is not likely to vote for an energy tax in order to reduce consumption. Instead, they are much more likely to perpetuate the myth that low energy prices are some kind of constitutional right.

So here we are. We know there will be dramatic increases in energy consumption in the decades ahead. We also know it will be hard to meet that demand while protecting our geopolitical interests and preserving the environment. Therefore we need to address the demand side of the equation. What follows are several recommendations on how we should proceed.

To begin, we should recognize that price signals can be used in a variety of innovative ways. As secretary I met with officials of the Puget Sound Energy Company of Washington State fairly early in my term. Puget Sound, like most utility companies, faces a challenge in meeting peak demand for electricity. People don't use much electricity after midnight, but they use a lot during the day, particularly on hot summer afternoons. The cost of meeting this demand—either by running gas turbines or buying on the spot market—is very high. To reduce peak demand, Puget Sound decided to provide its customers with information about their energy consumption and the cost of using electricity during various hours of the day. They also provided suggestions on how to move consumption from peak times to periods of slower demand. Finally, they offered customers benefits if they were able to reduce their energy consumption by a certain percentage. According to company officials, the approach has been very successful. Other utilities have adopted similar programs since then. The conclusion is that positive price signals can help significantly to save energy. Our goal should be to persuade every utility to adopt this type of energy savings initiative.

A second strategy to improve energy efficiency involves the building sector. A huge percentage of our energy is consumed by residential and commercial real estate. Given the rising costs associated with building operations and residential utility rates, there is no question that owners of property would respond well to cost savings related to their real estate energy expenditures. The question is how to make it happen.

First we should note that numerous strategies and technologies to reduce energy consumption in buildings already exist. For many years the U.S. Green Building Council has provided a blueprint for more efficient buildings. Their grading system, called LEED (Leadership in Energy and Environmental Design), awards structures silver, gold, and platinum honors based on how well they conserve energy. The challenge is to persuade as many homeowners and business operators as possible to make their houses and offices LEED-certified structures.

Right now, less than 5% of existing commercial buildings meet LEED standards. The opportunities for savings are therefore enormous. It is clear to me that whether or not we adopt a carbon regulatory framework in the United States, a high percentage of businesses are already focused on their contributions to carbon emissions and are trying to do something about it. For many companies, monitoring their carbon emissions has become an important part of their corporate culture. In addition, of course, these businesses are also trying to save money.

Commercial property owners already have at their disposal lots of tools to conserve energy. First, they have the opportunity to retrofit their properties to make them green buildings, utilizing such technologies as advanced lighting systems, energy-efficient heating, ventilating, and air-conditioning (HVAC) equipment, and a variety of other off-the-shelf products. In addition, they can do such things as paint the roofs of their structures white or cover their roofs with grass, or other vegetation, in order to reduce heating and cooling requirements or reduce atmospheric carbon. They also have the option to install on-site renewable sources such as solar panels and small wind turbines. Providing incentives for businesses to deploy these types of improvements will help take us toward meeting our 2030 goal.

Residential properties can also benefit from conservation efforts. What we need is to better educate the public about the potential savings from retrofitting their homes and thereby hopefully encourage them to do it. Even though the benefits to homeowners are substantial, it will not be an easy sell. Therefore, it will also be important to make the whole process as uncomplicated and workable as possible.

One idea is to encourage utilities to play the role of general contractor and, perhaps, banker in the process. Because existing state and proposed federal renewable mandates are requiring utilities to build a lot of green power or improve conservation, they already have a strong motivation to conserve energy. And, since a lot of energy can be saved if people retrofit their homes with new HVAC equipment, insulation, windows, lights, and so on, it makes sense for utilities to facilitate as many retrofits as possible.

One role they can play is to identify capable firms to handle this work and make sure their residential customers know which home improvement companies to hire to ensure quality performance. Utilities might even be able to help reduce costs for customers by aggregating interested homeowners into groups and negotiating with providers and vendors on their behalf.

I also believe it makes sense for utilities to help finance energy-saving home improvements for regular and dependable customers. The biggest impediment to retrofitting a home is the up-front capital investment. Why wouldn't it make sense for utilities to offer creditworthy customers home improvement financing for retrofits that save an agreed-upon amount of energy and then recoup their investments from the homeowners in their monthly utility bill? Paying back the utility company lender out of the monthly savings that the residential customer earns will leave the homeowner whole (and with new equipment) and help the utility meet its efficiency target.

For these reasons I favor providing very favorable tax treatment for energy-saving conversions, both in commercial and residential buildings. We already provide a variety of tax write-offs for building-related energy savings investments, and I propose we double them in order to bring about widespread investment in this area.

The best way to reduce energy consumption is with the price signal. But raising energy taxes to dampen demand is a political nonstarter. Instead, what we need is to utilize incentives to bring about the adoption of practices that reduce the use of energy. A well-crafted program combined with the active leadership of our utilities can have a significant impact on energy efficiency and bring our 2030 goal within reach.

Perhaps the biggest long-range potential for improving the way we use energy lies in the possibility of computerizing the distribution of electricity to tailor it more precisely to the demands of consumers. There are many other advantages as well in what we call the smart grid, which is what we will turn to next.

CHAPTER 14

Energy Efficiency, Part Two: Electrical Grids, Smart and Otherwise

The need to improve energy efficiency and incorporate more renewable sources has suddenly made us realize that a lot depends on making vast improvements to our national electrical grid.

The grid, as Phillip F. Schewe of the National Institute of Physics has written, is "the largest, most complex industrial machine ever invented." Coast to coast, it is composed of 200,000 miles of high-tension wires and 5.5 million miles of smaller distribution lines, largely forming one big, interconnected electrical circuit. "Everything is connected to everything" is an adage environmentalists used to recite, and in this case it is literally true. If a sagging high-tension wire brushes against a tree branch on a hot summer afternoon in Ohio, people all up and down the East Coast may find themselves without electricity, which is exactly what happened during the Great Northeast Blackout of 2003.

Because the electric grid *is* essentially one big electrical circuit, supply and demand must be balanced constantly. Most of our electrical equipment is designed to operate at a potential of 120 volts. This voltage must be constantly maintained. If demand exceeds supply, brownouts and blackouts will result. If supply exceeds demand, there will be power surges that damage electrical equipment. Electronics such as computers are particularly susceptible. That is why you have a surge protector between your wall outlet and your computer.

In today's grid, voltage balances can only be adjusted at a central headquarters by the systems operator. These are the people who are constantly making decisions to take a coal plant offline because demand has sagged or to rev up a few gas turbines because consumption is about to climb toward its peak. It is systems operators who have the job of incorporating windmills and other intermittent sources and trying to smooth out their supply curves so they correspond with demand.

The idea behind a smart grid is to computerize this entire system so that decision points are distributed all across the network. In a smart grid, monitors would be constantly reading voltage levels at various points and making adjustments. Small transformers could be cut in and out of the system to adjust voltage at the local level. If power suddenly surged, it could be isolated instead of cascading through the system—the pattern that causes widespread blackouts. The overall result would be to flush waste from the system and make the whole grid operate more efficiently.

Ideally, the distribution of decision making on the smart grid would extend right down to individual smart meters in every home. Homeowners would receive real-time pricing that would allow them to adjust their consumption to available supplies. This would help alleviate the problems encountered during peak-demand periods, which generally occur in the late afternoon, particularly on hot days when everyone turns on the air-conditioning. A smart grid would also make it easier for homeowners to postpone energy-intensive chores such as washing dishes or drying laundry until off-peak hours. More on this later.

All these advances would operate at the regional level. Although there are transmission wires running coast to coast, electricity cannot in fact travel that far. The line loss to heat and friction would be too great. Instead, the nation is divided into eleven regional "reliability councils," all of which function as giant power pools. The PJM, for example, primarily takes in Pennsylvania, New Jersey, and Maryland, while the Western Electricity Coordinating Council takes in fourteen states in and around the Rockies.

Utilities and customers within these reliability councils are well connected and can buy and sell power efficiently.

Even though we are largely linked coast to coast, the connections between the reliability councils are generally tenuous and weak. Some of them meet at only a few very vulnerable points. We do not yet really have a national grid, both because the connections have not been built and because electricity cannot travel that far over the existing system, which carries 345 kilovolts of alternating current. For very long distances it becomes more efficient to use direct current at very high voltages. Sending electricity cross-country will involve building an entirely new national grid of 745 kV DC lines, none of which are now in place. New conversion stations will also have to be built at each end. The project will be on about the same scale as rebuilding the interstate highway system and is not likely to happen soon.

What this means is that, as previously discussed, the vision of running the country on windmills on Midwestern farmland and solar collectors in Southwestern deserts is still far, far from being realized. The current electrical system cannot support it. We not only have to build a smart grid, we have also to build a much stronger grid designed to carry much heavier loads. Both of these are significant undertakings.

The world's first electric grid was created by Thomas Edison, who put a coal-fired generator in a basement in Lower Manhattan and strung wires for several blocks to deliver electric lighting to the surrounding neighborhood. Edison used direct current, which doesn't travel very far, but at the time it was the only way to drive an electric motor. As usual, Edison was looking far ahead. He imagined that every city neighborhood would be powered by its own generating station distributing electricity to users no farther than a mile or two away.

George Westinghouse had a different idea. He preferred alternating current because it could be transmitted over much longer distances—hundreds of miles in fact. He envisioned harnessing the power of resources such as Niagara Falls and distributing the electricity across the countryside. The problem was that electric motor. No electric machine could be operated by a current that switched directions sixty times a second.

Then a Serbian immigrant named Nikola Tesla came to Westinghouse's door. A scientific genius, Tesla had had a vision one day while walking the streets of Paris. He imagined an electrical current that could be delivered in "phases," so that the second phase would keep a motor turning in the same direction just as the first phase was about to reverse. That would enable alternating current to drive an electric motor. We still use Tesla's phased current today. It is the reason why every electrical device has three wires, two for the phases and one to ground the circuit.

Soon Edison and Westinghouse were locked in the "war of the currents," which raged across the country during the 1890s. Edison's supporters electrocuted dogs in public trying to convince people that AC was very dangerous. (In fact you can electrocute a dog with either one.) Westinghouse and Tesla's system had distinct advantages, however, and when they harnessed Niagara Falls to bring power to Buffalo and upstate New York, the battle was over. The march of long-distance transmission wires across the country began. (See Philip Schewe, *The Grid: A Journey Through the Heart of Our Electrified World.*)

Transmission lines connecting power plants with population centers became one of the main symbols of industrial progress during the twentieth century. Rural electrification was a principal undertaking of the New Deal. The Tennessee Valley Authority brought power to the rural South. Western dams were built to serve Portland, San Francisco, and Los Angeles. For cross-country transmission, voltage was stepped up to 345 kilovolts (350,000 volts), and then stepped down again to a nice, manageable 120 volts before it enters your home.

Like almost everything else having to do with electricity, however, all this began to run into opposition in the 1970s. People began to complain that transmission lines marred the natural landscape. Or, if they were going through populated areas, they always seemed to run near some school or church or other inviolable institution. Then the rumor got started that high-tension transmission lines cause cancer. That was disproved over and over, but the rumor still pops up today when anyone tries to build a transmission line.

And so the grid began to fall out of date. Complicating all this is that during the electrical deregulation of the 1990s, nonowners were given access to the privately owned grid. Transmission wires were designated common carriers, meaning that everybody has to have access to them. But what belongs to everybody belongs to nobody. There's no incentive to maintain equipment when you can't charge a market price for using it, and so large portions of the grid have fallen into disrepair. Moreover, jurisdictional disputes further complicate the matter if one area wants to improve the grid and someone at the other end says no. Electrical engineers now say America has first world generating capacity but a third world grid.

All this was brought home to me right after the Great Northeast Blackout of 2003. Widespread panic had engulfed the eastern seaboard. No one was sure when power would come back on or who would get it first. One state without electricity was Connecticut. As workers scrambled to restore power, Connecticut's political leaders began looking beyond their border to find other sources of power.

In the years leading up to the blackout, Connecticut's neighbor, New York, had been seeking permission to activate a power cable that had been built under Long Island Sound from Long Island to Connecticut. New Yorkers wanted to tap the power being generated by Connecticut's two nuclear reactors, Millstone 2 and 3, after deciding not to open the $6 billion Shoreham reactor on Long Island. But environmental groups contended the cable would destroy Long Island Sound's ecosystem. Connecticut officials concurred, arguing the cable was not sufficiently buried beneath the ocean floor.

All this quickly changed when the lights went out. Suddenly, I was inundated with demands from Connecticut officials to use my "emergency powers" as secretary of energy to activate the underwater cable. The same individuals who had led the opposition were now screaming that it should be immediately brought on line.

Obviously, New York officials wanted the cable turned on as well, so I quickly signed an executive order. After a few days, though, when it looked as if the blackout threat was receding, the same Connecticut officials were once again at my doorstep demanding I repeal the order. I refused. I explained that since we still did not know the cause of the blackout we were not going to take any chances. Needless to say, our friends in Connecticut were outraged, but we held our ground, keeping the transmission line open until we were absolutely certain there would be no more blackouts. The cable was not permanently activated until the following year, but the duel between the states was costly.

Transmission-siting problems are not limited to interstate situations. An example has occurred right next door to Washington, D.C., in Northern Virginia, where the information age had brought huge growth in the form of new Internet companies and server farms around Dulles Airport. More than 50% of Internet traffic now flows through this region and Dominion Virginia Power, which services the area, estimates that, by 2012, 10% of its electricity will go to serving these data centers.

Public opposition made the idea of putting a new coal or nuclear plant in this area almost impossible. So Dominion decided to bring in surplus power from its coal plants in West Virginia. That would mean building new transmission lines through the Northern Virginia countryside, which is when the fun began. Local environmentalists predictably opposed it. What was astonishing was that a number of senior officials from the technology firms joined the opposition. Amusing stories began to appear in the papers as CEOs proclaimed their opposition to the transmission plan. One corporate leader said it was important to solve power problems like these through new technology rather than transmission lines. Apparently he didn't realize that, absent the new lines, his industry would be facing power interruptions before any new technology could be developed. Server farms, after all, are extremely sensitive, and power interruptions of less than a second can destroy data.

Fortunately for the CEOs, state officials approved Dominion's plan. Transmission lines are being expanded largely along a current right-of-way. That their construction was so difficult in an area that so desperately needed electricity, however, shows how self-defeating, contrary, and confusing the arguments can be when it comes to upgrading the electrical grid.

Almost from the beginning of my term of office it became clear to me that we needed federal authority to expedite transmission line construction. After all, the federal government has control over natural gas pipelines and dams across rivers that flow state to state. Why shouldn't it have authority over interstate transmission lines as well? It is obviously interstate commerce. Lacking this authority, getting everyone to agree on a proposed route is often impossible.

Nevertheless, this reasoning cut no ice with state governments. One of my speeches as secretary of energy was before a meeting of the National Governors Association. I made a strong appeal for federal eminent domain authority in the development of transmission lines. After finishing my remarks, I was assailed by both Republican and Democratic governors from every region of the country. After absorbing twenty minutes of this, I was sent back to Washington by a bipartisan coalition.

Once I got back, I knew the idea of giving the federal government unfettered power in the siting of transmission lines was dead. After thinking it over for several weeks, however, the DOE team came up with a new approach. The idea would be to give the department authority to make long-range projections of electricity demand. Based on these analyses, the department could then designate certain transmission corridors as being in the "national interest." The federal government would have the power to site lines in these corridors if the state governments having jurisdiction in these regions failed to do so.

Ultimately, something very close to this idea was made into law in 2005. However, the states have not gone down easily. As soon as the DOE began moving forward and designated the first national corridor, various parties filed protest suits. Hopefully, federal authority will be sustained. In its absence, there is a high probability we will find ourselves facing even larger transmission problems in the future.

Amazingly, although it might seem as if a world run on renewable sources would demand less in terms of electrical transmission, the need will actually be much more. Environmentalists didn't always think so. When energy guru Amory Lovins wrote *Soft Energy Paths* in 1976, the book that inspired California's jump into renewable energy, he imagined a renewable world in which there would be no central power plants! Pointing out that two-thirds of a fuel's energy is lost in the generation of electricity, Lovins argued we could rescue this lost energy by "distributing" generation all over the countryside. "Waste" steam would be captured for industrial uses. Once this distribution system was in place, people would eventually start generating their own electricity with backyard and neighborhood windmills and solar collectors. The electrical grid would wither away.

The reality has turned out to be the exact opposite. Local wind and solar resources don't produce enough power to run households on a twenty-four-hour basis, let alone businesses or industrial plants. So the recommended solution has been to locate generation where these resources are abundant and transmit it to population centers. That means building windmills on the Great Plains and solar collectors in Southwestern deserts. But shipping electricity over those great distances isn't feasible with current technology. Electrical engineers estimate that every hundred miles of transmission loses about 3% to 8% of the power to waste heat. It turns out that the best way to avoid this loss is to go back to direct current at 765 kV, which can transmit longer distances without line loss. Maybe Thomas Edison was right after all.

Building a brand-new 765-kV cross-country grid will be like

rebuilding the Interstate Highway System to eight lanes. It won't be easy or cheap. The cost could be well over a trillion dollars, and completing the work could take twenty years or more.

Already people are formulating plans to start the process. Western states have decided to begin a whole new generation of transmission lines to access renewable energy. The Western Governors Association, together with the DOE, is mapping out geothermal resources in California and Nevada and identifying transmission lines that will be needed to bring the energy to major cities. California has started its own Renewable Energy Transmission Initiative, which has identified four major pathways, including a line that would bring wind and solar electricity from Oregon and Nevada to San Francisco. Harry Reid, the Senate majority leader and the principal opponent of Yucca Mountain, is now proposing that we consolidate authority for building transmission lines under a single federal agency to bring renewable energy to urban areas.

Clearly, these are significant project concepts, but that does not mean they will not meet environmental resistance. For instance, in 2006, California utilities proposed the Green Path North Renewable Energy Transmission Line, designed specifically to carry power generated by windmills and solar collectors from the desert east of Los Angeles. Four years later, the project has not yet broken ground. Opposing it are the Sierra Club, the Center for Biological Diversity, the California Desert Coalition, the Redlands Conservancy, Friends of Big Morongo Canyon Preserve, and just about every municipal government in its path. The bottom line is nothing aroused more opposition than the siting of long-distance transmission lines. Every community, every landowner, every state and federal agency in the pathway gets a say, and, more likely than not, some or all will object.

The fact that a new transmission line will help deliver renewable energy won't necessarily make any difference. Almost as soon as California governor Arnold Schwarzenegger announced the state's first major desert solar plant, Senator Diane Feinstein objected on the grounds that the transmission lines would run through the Mojave Preserve, Joshua Tree National Park, and even near the old Highway 66, which is now little used but defended by the Route 66 Alliance. On top of that, in one of the first announcements of the Obama administration, Jon Wellinghoff, the newly appointed chairman of the Federal Energy Regulatory Commission, said he didn't know whether the federal government should be in the business of siting power lines. I repeat, building a new grid will not be an easy task.

Although building a national grid to 765 kV may be a Herculean task, implementing a smart grid should be much easier. It will be key to helping us achieve a 10% efficiency improvement by 2030. Basically, what we have to do is install computerized devices at various points on the grid through which we can *monitor* the flow of electricity, then *change* the flow of electricity and make all sorts of real-time adjustments that are not now possible. The result will be an intelligent grid in which the flow of electricity will be appropriate to the task at hand.

There are many things that could be accomplished with a smart grid. First, service interruptions and blackouts could be reduced by isolating big dips or surges in current when and where they occur. Second, peak loads could be alleviated by shifting nonessential peak uses to other parts of the day. This could be done either voluntarily by customers or automatically through computers. Third, renewable sources could be better integrated into the grid by coordinating their intermittent output with other, steadier sources. Gas turbines could be immediately fired up if a cloud bank rolled in or the wind stopped blowing. Finally, wind and solar output throughout the grid could be leveled by automatically dumping excess output into adjoining systems. (This is done in Europe, where Denmark regularly dumps excess wind generation into neighboring Sweden and Germany.) This would make wind and solar more compatible with a balanced grid.

I talked earlier about the Puget Sound program in which

customers are offered financial rewards for shifting portions of their electrical use to different times of the day. The smart grid will be the same program on steroids. Some people have imagined consumers planning their electrical use each morning and then monitoring prices throughout the day. What is more likely is the whole thing will eventually be handled by computers. Your smart meter will be instructed to minimize your electric bill, just as programmed trading buys and sells at certain price points on the stock market.

What might these tasks be in the home? Washing and drying clothes and dishes are always mentioned. Of course, this might not be as easy as it sounds. People may want to schedule other tasks like shopping or running errands and won't necessarily be home to benefit from low prices. Some kind of automated combined washer-dryer may eventually evolve, since you don't want to leave clothes that have been washed sitting wet for too long. There is also the suggestion that people could save on air-conditioning costs by "precooling" their homes—running the air conditioner on high during morning hours and then turning it off when prices peak during midafternoon. Residential uses may not be the biggest area of savings. The real action may take place in industry, where large manufacturers can shift their production schedules to take advantage of low electrical rates.

Still, smart grid technology can only accomplish part of the efficiency objective. In 2008 the Electric Power Research Institute (EPRI) published an exhaustive study, *The Green Grid*, outlining all the possible savings that might come with a completely computerized electrical distribution system. The study went so far as to consider shaving the voltage in the residential sector from 120 V to 114 V, since most household appliances don't need the full amount. It even included the gasoline the utilities might save by not having to send out meter readers, since the whole thing would now be handled remotely. EPRI concluded that the best we can expect in energy savings from a smart grid system is that by 2025 we might reduce our anticipated consumption by 5% to 11%. This is a worthy objective. Combining those savings with efficiency improvements in buildings, appliances, and other categories, we have an excellent chance to hit our 10% efficiency goal by 2030.

So what actions will be needed to facilitate this transition to a smart grid? I think there are several clear priorities. First, we must establish strong federal authority to site critical transmission lines where needed, or else vital improvements will not be made in a timely manner. The Federal Energy Regulatory Commission (FERC) should be given a broad authority to site interstate lines so long as the mission meets a reasonable threshold of national interest.

Second, we must also give FERC the ability to mandate the implementation of smart grid deployment where state public service commissions have failed to act. The interconnectivity of the grid requires that all systems be roughly equivalent in terms of capabilities. For the country to transition to a smart grid, all states must be ready to play. Where states fail to act, the FERC should be empowered to instigate implementation. Otherwise, we may find ourselves with a crazy quilt infrastructure of smart and dumb grids.

CHAPTER 15

Making Intelligent Technology Investments

Many people in the political arena like to believe that our energy problems can be solved with one word, "technology." This is not surprising. We've all come to marvel at the advances that have taken place in recent decades, from dramatic developments in consumer electronics, computers, and information technology to amazing breakthroughs in medicine. It is almost impossible to turn on a newscast, pick up a newspaper, or get together with friends without learning of some new development that will change the world.

In this light, it is no wonder so many people believe all our energy problems will be solved with some fabulous new energy invention or discovery. Earlier we discussed the tendency to talk about a second Manhattan Project. As I stated there, I believe that talk of a new Manhattan Project is just a way of avoiding the tough decisions on energy issues. But the concept of a new Apollo or Manhattan Project reflects the faith and fascination we all still have with technology.

Part of the reason for this is the huge mystery that surrounds the world of science. Who hasn't been fascinated by gazing at stars through a telescope or thinking of man's flight into space? We find ourselves captivated by a visit to an aquarium or a documentary film about the deep oceans. In recent years we've shown a similar fascination with computer technology. Americans may not be as interested in Bill Gates as they are in the Beatles or

Johnny Depp, but he isn't far behind. The annual Consumer Electronics Show in Las Vegas is still one of the most highly reported events of the year.

Politicians are, if anything, even more fascinated with the world of technology than is the rest of the population. Like most other freshman legislators, I arrived in the United States Senate in 1995 looking for a niche, a field where I could put my skills and background to use and distinguish myself. The high-profile areas had already been claimed by long-established leaders, so I began looking at issue areas that fitted my personal interests and committee assignments. My staff and I eventually chose technology.

Remember, this was back in 1995. The Internet was in its infancy, most people still had analog television, and the iPod hadn't been invented. Silicon Valley and its counterparts around the country had not yet been discovered by Washington. But with economic growth beginning to concentrate in the tech sector, it was clear to me that the federal government might soon get involved. Issues such as Internet taxes, intellectual property rights, and Microsoft's domination of the market would soon be on everyone's plate.

So in 1996 I made my first trip to Silicon Valley. At the invitation of the American Electronics Association, I had dinner with a large number of tech company CEOs to hear about their concerns. It turned out I was one of the first senators to visit the Valley since the dot-com boom began, and I will never forget the reaction. All informed me they wanted nothing to do with Washington. "Just leave us alone," they said, "and we'll continue to invent new technologies and create wealth for America." I remember one CEO saying, "We don't have an office in Washington, we won't ever have an office in Washington, and we don't want Washington to help us on anything."

I recall thinking that this CEO's hopes were not likely to be realized. This was an underestimation. In the years that followed, technology has taken a front seat in the nation's capital. Virtually every company represented at that dinner has since opened a

Washington office and staffed it extensively. In the end, while I had a nice head start on technology issues, many congressmen and senators soon jumped on the bandwagon. Within a few years, fundraising stops in Palo Alto, Santa Clara, and Sunnyvale were the staple of every campaign.

As a result, Washington has come to expect a lot more from technology than is reasonable. At the Department of Energy, I came to recognize that almost every member of Congress knew somebody who knew a scientific genius who was right on the brink of solving the nation's energy problems. Whether it was at congressional hearings, social events, or chance encounters, almost every member of Congress I ran into over four years wanted to get me together with the technology wizard from back home.

Although I became fairly adept at sidestepping these encounters, every so often I would find myself in the secretary's conference room sitting with some virtuoso who guaranteed me that if the department would only give him $1 million, the elixir he was carrying in a nondescript bottle would soon be powering the entire U.S. motor vehicle fleet. I'm not exaggerating. If it wasn't a new potion, it was a new gadget or technology. I remember one entrepreneur who had devised a tech concept for the disposing of nuclear waste. Instead of building Yucca Mountain we would use his equipment and system to sprinkle small amounts of the stuff all over America. I guess he figured it somehow made sense to antagonize all fifty states rather than just Nevada.

After each of these meetings I would ask my staff how I ended up with the mad inventor of the day. Inevitably it turned out the meeting had been arranged by some powerful member of Congress in whose district the genius resided. Although it is possible to say no most of the time, the inventor's patron was always some key congressman or senator who controlled the department's budget or played some other key role in funding, which made it impossible to reject his or her request. After a couple of these sessions, I realized that the congressman or senator didn't really believe in the elixir, either. They just wanted to get the genius off their back.

If it wasn't a private meeting, it would be a request to earmark research funds for the local lab or start-up business back home. No matter how hard we tried to convince members that their pet projects were not one of our priorities, some individuals always insisted on diverting funds. Now I am a strong believer in investing in research—especially in the basic sciences—but it's got to be done the right way.

Instead, I found that in Washington we tended to pursue a "flavor-of-the-month" approach with no overall strategy or resistance to whatever was in vogue at the moment. As a result, important research efforts were seriously impeded because legislators were always being persuaded to divert money from the "old new thing" to the "new new thing."

For example, for many years the environmental community has been urging us to develop an alternative to the internal combustion engine run on gasoline. When I became secretary in 2001, the department had focused a significant amount of research attention on gas-electric hybrids. This is important because whatever the Department of Energy pursues is likely to be reflected in the private sector as well.

Just as we're making some progress, however, the same groups that had been encouraging us to investigate hybrids decided that clean diesel engines were actually the way to go. Pressure built on Capitol Hill, and the administration was forced to change some of its focus toward diesel. As usually happens, the private sector began to follow suit.

Just as we were getting started with diesel, the emphasis switched again, this time to hydrogen. Then hydrogen was the future of transportation. So, in his 2003 State of the Union address, President George W. Bush announced a major new hydrogen project, dubbed the "Freedom CAR," which was to run on hydrogen fuel cells.

For a while Congress backed the president's hydrogen initiative and provided funding, although even then they directed a fair amount of funds away from our research plan and toward their pet projects, which immediately threatened our strategy and time-table. But as with hybrids and clean diesel, hydrogen's day in the sun was brief. By 2004 the new new thing had become biofuels. Based on highly optimistic forecasts from the ethanol industry, strong congressional support for federal subsidies, and a lot of speculation in the scientific community, the conviction became that cellulose biofuels were just around the corner. Once again the momentum shifted.

By the middle of President Bush's second term, biofuels were all the rage. In his 2006 State of the Union address, the president made his famous statement about American being "addicted to oil" and mentioned "switch grass" as a potential source of cellulose ethanol. The research hadn't yet produced anything positive—and still hasn't—but once again we were struggling to keep up with the latest fads. No sooner had switch grass occupied center stage, however, than it found itself in competition with another new idea—plug-in hybrids. And so we were more or less back where we started in 2001. General Motors has bet much of the ailing company's fortunes on the introduction of the plug-in Volt—only a few years after it had invested heavily in the "Hy-wire," a car that ran on hydrogen fuel cells.

The point here is to highlight the difficulties we encounter in trying to set technology investment priorities in Washington. In a world where interest groups and advocates play a significant role and where politics, not sound business practices, often governs decision making, research efforts frequently get undermined. With advanced automotive systems, we have ended up partly funding a number of different projects and sending enormously confusing signals to the private sector. Consequently, none of the aforementioned projects has ever received sufficient funding.

So let's devise a few ground rules that can help us to avoid this helter-skelter approach. They will be tough to implement and require some fortitude, but they are vitally needed.

First, there should be no congressional earmarking of federal energy research funds. The Department of Energy should be free to choose funding objectives using its expert panels and advisors rather than ceding decisions to the interests of legislators.

Second, once a priority is chosen, we should stick with it. There should be no flavor-of-the-month oscillations. Research is a long-term undertaking and we should treat it as such. While it might make sense to go all out on several projects at once, we gain nothing by backing multiple programs while not providing adequate research resources to any.

Third, the private sector can play a part. This is particularly important, since private research so often follows the lead of government investment. In particular we should consider the creation of one or more strategic investment funds in which the government would team with private investors to stretch research and venture dollars.

Finally, government should stay out of the business of picking specific winners and losers. This applies to Congress as well. Nothing can lead us down the wrong road faster than government trying to promote specific choices by itself.

Now, assuming that we accept the above conditions and stick with long-term funding, there are a few major areas of research on which I think we should concentrate.

BATTERY CAPACITY AND ELECTRICITY STORAGE. In *The People's Tycoon*, a biography of Henry Ford, Steven Watts describes a posh dinner in New York City that the young Henry Ford attended as a guest of prominent Detroit business leaders. At the other end of the table sat the renowned inventor Thomas Edison. During the dinner, Edison requested that Ford describe the operating system of his motor vehicle. Afterward, Edison enthusiastically congratulated the young inventor on having designed what appeared to be a workable internal combustion engine. Edison then recounted his many failed attempts to utilize electricity to power a vehicle and his frustration that he had never been able to store enough electricity to make it work.

The problem that Edison described has never been solved. Electricity travels at the speed of light, 186,000 miles per second. It reverberates around the electrical grid through a network of wires and then is gone. There is no way to hold it in place for an hour or even a few minutes until it is needed. Instead, electricity must be stored by converting it to something else and then converting that back to electricity. That "something else" must be chemical or physical. It should be remembered that all these conversion processes *lose* energy, with a payback of only about 50%–60%. Thus, storing electricity for future use means generating *more* electricity, not less.

The most common way to store electricity chemically is with rechargeable batteries. The lead-acid battery you have in your car has long been the prevailing technology. Lead-acid batteries are, however, very heavy. Therefore it is impractical to try to replace an internal combustion engine with a lead-acid battery that would power an entire vehicle. So new technologies have been developed—nickel-cadmium, lithium-ion, and even more exotic combinations. These batteries are much lighter and can hold a bigger charge. The lithium-ion battery in the new Chevy Volt will be able to power the car for 40 miles. (The range of a gasoline engine, on the other hand, is around 400 miles.) The problem with these exotic substances is that they tend to be rare and expensive, making them impractical for mass production. The world's largest lithium reserves, for example, are in Chile and Bolivia, although the Bolivian resources are yet to be developed. If hybrids like the Volt become successful, we will become largely dependent on these imports.

The best method ever devised to store electricity using physical means is called "pumped storage." This requires two different bodies of water at different levels—usually a lake or a river and an upper mountain reservoir. Water is pumped uphill during nighttime off-peak hours and then released during periods of peak demand. There are thirty-five pumped storage plants around the country capable of storing 19,000 MW of electricity. The largest pumped storage plant in the world (2,772 MW) is in Bath County, Virginia, while the Rocky River and Candlewood Lake facility in Connecticut, built in 1929, stores only 31 MW. We might build more of these, but as we shall see in the next chapter, pumped storage has not always been favorably received.

There have been various experiments with other technologies, such as storing compressed air in underground caverns and then releasing it to generate electricity. The force of the air can drive a turbine, but the preferred technology is to use the air to enhance the combustion of natural gas. This, of course, consumes natural gas as well. Another strategy has been to build giant flywheels that can preserve rotary motion for hours afterward. This works on a small scale but has obvious limits for commercial quantities.

Thermal solar plants in the desert are now experimenting with storing heat in salts and other mineral substances so it can be used hours later to boil water to run an electric turbine. Several companies building solar plants in the California desert claim to have developed molten salts that can extend output for hours and even days after the sun has gone down or disappeared behind clouds. This technology obviously holds some promise.

Electrical storage will be the key to developing both hybrid cars and renewable energy. The Toyota Prius couples a gasoline engine with a battery that recharges during braking, getting 30 to 50 miles per gallon. The Volt uses a small gasoline engine to recharge the battery while driving and claims it will get over 100 mpg. All this may do wonders in reducing our dependence on oil. Likewise, commercial-scale electrical storage would make wind and solar energy far more practical.

This prospect is what makes storage and battery capacity such a promising area of research. If we can improve battery technology by only small amounts, hybrid plug-ins could become a game changer when it comes to replacing oil imports. In addition, if homeowners could store excess electricity derived from rooftop solar panels for after-dark use, an area where new developments are emerging, cost calculations would change dramatically. Battery and electrical storage could play an enormous role in our energy future.

USING COAL IN A LESS ENVIRONMENTALLY DAMAGING FASHION. Carbon sequestration must be another federal research priority. We already know how to separate carbon through gasification; we just don't know what to do with it afterward.

As previously noted, we have a substantial market for carbon dioxide in enhanced oil recovery. The problem is, we don't have enough oil fields to hold all the CO_2 we produce. Nor do we have a comprehensive network of pipelines to move the material to enhanced recovery sites. At the Department of Energy there has already been a fair amount of investment in advanced sequestration research. But there is more we can do. We would not only begin to solve our own problems with emissions, but we would have a technology to sell to the rest of the world.

THERE IS STILL PROMISE FOR HYDROGEN. This is my old favorite. President Bush's hydrogen initiative was one of the top technology priorities during my tenure. For reasons already partly chronicled, it soon fell out of favor. In fact, the Obama administration unsuccessfully tried to eliminate the program in 2009. Yet there is no question that hydrogen still has a future. First, it is emissions-free. Second, hydrogen can be derived from a variety of sources, including fossil fuels, nuclear, and renewable sources. Third, it can be manufactured from off-peak electricity, improving the performance of power plants. What we need to work on is a safe means of distributing hydrogen so it can be used as conveniently as gasoline today. For decades people have speculated that we were still twenty years away from developing a significant market for hydrogen. We need to bring this into the present.

Beyond these three priorities, I believe we should explore improving electrical transmission through superconductivity. This is still a far-off possibility, but it's the kind of long-range research that government should be sponsoring. We began moving down this road during the Bush administration and need to continue. Another priority should be advanced emission-control technologies. There is still room for improvement in the way sulfur dioxide, nitrogen oxide, and mercury are removed from coal exhausts. Auto exhausts could also be improved, even though we have already made spectacular progress, reducing the 1960s rates of emission by 90%. Private sector research has made some interesting discoveries, but the federal government should do more in this area.

So here's the key question: Can technological progress solve our energy problems? I believe it can play a very important role but not to the point of replacing our conventional energy sources. Technology isn't going to allow us to stop using oil and coal, at least not for a long, long time. It won't substitute for the hard work of improving energy efficiency and building out the electrical grid. It also won't allow us to walk away from the question of whether to revive nuclear power. There will be no grand slams in energy technology research, but we can keep hitting singles and doubles that keep the rally going in contending with our energy challenges such as increasing the yield of wind and solar. Perhaps someone will hit a home run somewhere down the line, but we can't sit around waiting for it. We need to go with the lineup we have now.

CHAPTER 16

"Not in My Backyard"—The NIMBY Syndrome

Perhaps nothing frustrated me more in my term as secretary of energy than watching well-conceived projects frustrated by the NIMBY syndrome—"Not in My Backyard."

Almost every new project proposed anywhere these days will run into a wall of opposition from people who claim it is the worst possible idea ever conceived and will ruin the environment and poison the planet. Some of this is understandable. If the state wants to condemn your property and run a new highway through it, naturally you are going to be upset. Someone is always going to be adversely affected by new construction anywhere.

What makes it difficult is that some groups appear to be in the business of opposing *everything*. They will tell you one day that we ought to be burning natural gas instead of coal in our electrical boilers and the next day they'll be railing against drilling for natural gas. Or they will tell you that small hydroelectric dams are renewable energy while going around the country trying to tear down such small dams. What makes it even more difficult is that the law is very much on their side these days.

Every major project built anywhere must now file an environmental impact statement, which will run to thousands of pages. Almost no one ever reads them except opposition groups intent on taking the project to court. They will comb every paragraph looking for points to challenge. How do the developers know this liquid natural gas station won't be affected by hurricanes that might occur once every hundred years? What about this new species of grasshopper that's just been discovered in the region?

It's gotten a lot easier to play defense than offense in this game. Anyone trying to build something faces an enormous burden of proof while people trying to stop things get no penalty for delay of game. Protesters can stretch these court battles out endlessly while the interest payments and construction costs continue to mount. This is what killed nuclear power in the 1980s. It simply became too expensive and time-consuming to fight through the thicket of regulatory battles and court challenges. Reactors ended up taking fifteen years to complete and coming in at six times their original estimated cost. Now the same pressure is being applied to coal plants. It's unlikely anyone will be able to put up coal plants in the near future except in certain parts of "coal country"; environmental objections will stop them.

So what's left? As previously noted, natural gas has been everyone's favorite fuel. The recent discovery of large shale formations suggests that we may have a lot more reserves than projected. But environmental groups in New York State are already objecting to drilling in the Marcellus Shale. Then there will be the problem of building pipelines. The Millennium Pipeline, which was supposed to bring much-needed natural gas from Canada to the Bronx and Manhattan by 2000, has never received permission to cross the Hudson into New York City due to environmental objections.

Wind and solar are in favor these days, but as soon as these somewhat over-the-horizon technologies come into view, opposition groups find them objectionable as well, particularly when it becomes clear how much land they will take. The Nature Conservancy has coined the phrase "energy sprawl" to describe the huge, thousand-square-mile "farms" of windmills and solar panels. As noted, when California announced plans to build a 300 MW solar facility in the Mojave Desert, Senator Diane Feinstein said she would introduce legislation to block the project because of its impact on the desert environment.

All these objections may have substance, but somewhere we have to break this everything-is-objectionable syndrome or we're going to find ourselves in the same position California was in during the winter of 2000–2001—without enough electricity to run traffic lights.

I don't mind people raising legitimate objections to projects that are poorly conceived or need reworking. But sometimes, and increasingly, it seems the opposition raises blanket objections to the whole enterprise of civilization. When *The New York Times* wrote an editorial on the need for energy conservation in 2009, one retired professor of engineering at MIT wrote a letter to the editor proposing we solve the carbon crisis by giving up air travel. Another writer said everyone should ride bicycles, and a third said we should all give up eating meat. Such dreamy attitudes may have fringe appeal, but they don't work as public policy.

Anyone who has ever run for public office knows differently. When you are in politics, you have to deal with the vast majority of people and what they want. From my experience I can assure you the vast majority does not want to bake their own bread in solar ovens or generate electricity with backyard windmills. I would question whether even a tiny minority really wants to do these things. In *Hot, Flat, and Crowded,* Thomas Friedman imagines the country taming its energy appetite by everybody working out their "personal energy plan" for the day. Anyone holding public office knows that the vast majority wants no part in such an effort. They just want to pay their electric bills at the end of the month—not too expensive, of course—and spend the rest of their time working, enjoying time with family, or lounging at the beach. Politics is the art of the possible, and persuading people to go back to living the simple life is not one of the possibilities. We are going to need more power plants, refineries, and transmission lines.

What we especially need is the recognition that all energy choices will create problems and involve compromise. Someone is always going to feel inconvenienced by a new power plant, whether it is right next door or halfway across the state. One farmer may feel satisfied collecting $3,000 from the electric company for putting a windmill on his land, but his neighbors might find the forty-story structure a blight on the rural landscape. One community may object to having high-tension transmission lines run across a nearby mountaintop, but people in a far-off city may desperately want the power. Someone is always going to be unhappy with change, but we can't let such objections determine every outcome. We have to weigh the disadvantages against the benefits a new project may bring.

One thing I've noticed about opposition groups is that they're always in favor of some new technology as long as it's over the horizon. They'll tell you we don't need to build coal plants now because something new and better is going to take their place. But when the new thing arrives, they find it's not as clean and green as they thought it was. No matter, there's something better coming along, so now we can wait for that. Or if they don't object to the new thing, someone else will. And so we end up going round and round, with each technology developing its own opposition.

One of the first great environmental battles fought in America was at Storm King Mountain, fifty miles north of New York City, in the 1960s. Con Edison was meeting more and more opposition to building coal and oil plants in New York City, so it proposed a pumped storage plant on the Hudson River. The plant would pump water to an uphill reservoir at night and then release it to meet peak demand during the day. The plant was welcomed in the Newburgh area, where it would provide jobs and taxes, but resistance came from a little band of wealthy New Yorkers who had built second homes in the mountains. They formed a group called the Scenic Hudson Preservation Committee and started a campaign to "save Storm King." As Robert F. Kennedy Jr., one of New York's leading environmentalists, would write thirty years later in *Riverkeeper*:

The committee quickly found support among the well-heeled residents of the Hudson Highlands. Many of its founding members were the children and grandchildren of the Osborns, Stallmans, and Harrimans, the robber barons who had laid out great estates amid the Highlands' spectacular scenery and whose descendants had fought fiercely since the turn of the century to preserve the views for themselves and the public.

The little group first tried mustering support in the village of Cornwall, where the plant would be located. They forced a referendum on the village board's decision to condemn the upper reservoir but lost the vote 499 to 25. Where they did find support was on the editorial page of *The New York Times,* which began a decade-long campaign, "Save Storm King." Pumped storage was new at the time, and the protesters ridiculed the idea. Why pump water uphill just to let it run down again? It was a waste of energy. (The Energy Information Administration's Annual Reports of Power Generation does indeed list pumped storage as a *negative* contributor to energy output. The important thing is it delivers electricity when it is needed.)

Searching around for an alternative, the protestors came up with a new suggestion. Why not build another nuclear plant at Indian Point? Nuclear power was in its infancy then and had an over-the-horizon appeal. Later, there were other technologies. What about mine-mouth generation, where coal would be burned at the coal mine and electricity transmitted to the cities? Then there were fuel cells. Weren't they about to become commercial? No one had thought of wind and solar yet, but the possibilities were endless. Anything made sense as long as it was not pumped storage.

So the plant was never built. A new reactor was built at Indian Point but it didn't solve peaking problems, and environmentalists quickly lost their enthusiasm for that technology as well. One of the advantages of pumped storage was that it would help prevent blackouts. If a generator failed somewhere else, the sluice gates could be opened in an instant and 2,000 megawatts would flow onto the grid at once. People scoffed at the concern, but in 1977 a generator in Queens went down, transmission lines failed to carry power from upstate New York, and the city suffered a brutal blackout. Within hours "the Bronx was burning," and rioters caused a billion dollars in damage. The Storm King plant might have prevented all this.

That might be the end of the story except that environmentalists eventually decided maybe pumped storage wasn't so bad after all. Storage is the big problem for wind and solar power, of course, and pumped storage is the only technology capable of handling commercial quantities. If there were a 2,000 MW pumped storage plant on the Hudson today, New York would be able to line the Hudson Valley with windmills and solar collectors and generate enough electricity to close the Indian Point nuclear reactor— which the state government itself is trying to do. But then somebody might find that objectionable as well.

Like Storm King, many NIMBY battles are actually fought between local people who support the project for its economic benefits and a few dissenters backed by free-floating outsiders or national groups that don't have any economic stake in the matter and oppose the technology on principle. One of the surprising things about nuclear reactors, for example, is that people who live next door to them usually love them. Public support for nuclear now stands at 60%, the highest in history. But among people who live in a community with a nuclear reactor, it is an incredible 80%. That's because people recognize the technology is not dangerous and brings huge economic benefits. When the Calvert Cliffs Reactor in Maryland went before the Nuclear Regulatory Commission for relicensing in 1998, practically the whole county showed up in support. Once one of the poorest counties in Maryland, Calvert County is now one of the wealthiest, even though its residents pay extremely low taxes. When Unit 1 of Three Mile Island (the one that didn't melt down) came up for relicensing in 2008, a poll by Susquehanna Polling and Research found 87% of the residents in surrounding counties supported the renewal.

Oppositional campaigns are always portrayed as David-versus-Goliath efforts, with a tiny group of beleaguered nature lovers pitted against the giant utility company. What people don't realize is that the battle is usually very unequal in the opposite way. Small groups now have enormous leverage, particularly when it comes to preventing things from being built. As I've said, it's much easier to play defense than offense. Meanwhile, the public good suffers.

Take the example of importing liquid natural gas. When domestic supplies ran short in 2000, oil companies proposed liquid natural gas terminals on the East and West Coasts to import foreign supplies. Natural gas, remember, can't be piped under the ocean but must be transported in tankers. In Los Angeles, the Sierra Club called the proposed terminals "frightfully dangerous" and said importing would only make us more dependent on foreign fuels. In Delaware the club opposed an isolated terminal on the Delaware River, and in New York there were complaints about a floating terminal to be built twenty-five miles at sea off Long Island. None of these projects were ever built. The Sierra Club also opposed drilling for gas offshore and on Western federal lands. Yet at the very same time it was arguing that natural gas was one of the best ways to replace coal for our base load electricity!

California serves as the perfect example of where all this is headed. The state is constantly hailed as "clean and green" and is supposedly leading the country into a world where conservation and renewable energy will take the place of fossil fuels and nuclear power. A symbol of this policy is the Rancho Seco Power Station near Sacramento, where a nuclear reactor once generated 900 MW. Stirred by antinuclear crusaders, Sacramento voters chose to close the reactor in 1989 after only fourteen years of operation. Today the site is covered by one of the largest solar electricity installations in the world. This huge solar facility generates all of 4 MW.

So where does California get its electricity? Almost half of it now comes from out-of-state plants—nuclear, coal, and hydro. This is possible only because Arizona, New Mexico, Utah, Nevada, Oregon, and Washington are willing to ship large blocks of power to the Golden State. Another 40% comes from natural gas, more than double the average for the rest of the country. The remaining 12% comes from renewable sources, half of that provided by large geothermal resources that are not available in other states.

As a result of all this, California now has the most expensive electricity west of New Jersey in the lower forty-eight states, and manufacturers have fled the state in droves. Whereas the Golden State once had eight auto manufacturing plants, it now has none. Google has moved the bulk of its servers to Oregon, and Intel put its new manufacturing plant in Phoenix. Both were searching for cheaper energy. The chemical and aerospace industries are long gone. The state economy has been the victim. In the 1980s California had a triple-A bond rating, the highest rating in the country. Today its single-A rating is lowest among the fifty states. Reckless spending for other programs has played a part in California's decline, but the real undermining of the state's economy has largely come from its failure to deal realistically with its energy needs.

California illustrates what happens when the NIMBY syndrome runs wild. For the last two decades it has been impossible to build any kind of major power plant in the state except for those using expensive natural gas. Nuclear and coal are banned altogether. Even wind farms are being built out of state because most of the unobjectionable sites have been developed. Despite all this, Governor Arnold Schwarzenegger promulgated a new and unlikely to be met mandate to raise renewable sources to 20% by 2010. Another mandate will end imports of out-of-state coal by 2010. In 2009 the state auditor issued a report warning that the reckless pursuit of renewable sources was leading the state toward another electrical shortage. A similar fate awaits the whole country if we do not curb the NIMBY syndrome and face hard choices on siting energy plants.

Here's what we need to do. First and foremost, we must recognize that access to the natural resources of the United States is vital to the entire country, not just the province of the states in or near where such resources are located. At the same time, we must also recognize that those states whose offshore territory is home to vital resources deserve satisfactory compensation in exchange for allowing such natural resources to be accessed.

What does this mean? It means that we can no longer allow either federal moratoriums or state-level objections to domestic energy development to prohibit the tapping of vital resources, like offshore oil and gas, to the point where we are undermining our energy security. In my view, we need a national entity to serve as an appeals office for decisions, either to allow critical energy development projects or to stop them.

I propose a Federal Energy Development Commission along the lines of the Defense Base Closure and Alignment Commission (BRAC) that has been used to determine military base closings. BRAC, comprised of a bipartisan group of appointees, has proven capable of putting the national interest ahead of other considerations. This new commission would serve as an adjudicatory body to determine whether or not domestic energy development off our coastlines would be permitted. I do not believe we should extinguish all states' rights to protect their coastlines from energy development. Instead, this board would have jurisdiction on all development taking place beyond the states' jurisdictional waters.

At the same time, I believe we should significantly increase the percentage of royalties (payments made by producers in exchange for offshore energy development rights) that would be returned to the state governments off whose coastlines such development occurs. By providing a much greater financial incentive for offshore development, it should be possible to somewhat ameliorate the concerns of states over the development of energy near their coasts.

With respect to energy development on federal lands, I believe we likewise need such an independent decision-making process that separates politics from energy resource decisions. Thus, issues such as those related to the Arctic National Wildlife Refuge should be looked at not from the standpoint of which interest group wields the most power in Congress, but rather the outcome that best serves the nation.

We will never convince everyone that they should give up their political or local concerns in the name of energy independence and energy security. That is simply unrealistic. But what we can do is make sure that these critical judgments are not totally left to partisan politics, pressure group politics, or a small number of wealthy but influential landowners seeking to protect their property value. Failing to take a reasonable course on these issues is a prescription for an energy security disaster.

CHAPTER 17

A Global Energy Strategy

For the most part, this book focuses on the actions we should take to protect our energy future. But America is not alone in confronting the threats of environmental degradation, supply dislocations, and geopolitical threats to the marketplace. For all these reasons, we should close by looking at the global actions necessary to meet the energy challenges of the twenty-first century.

I remember vividly my meeting with the power minister of India. As I laid out my projections for U.S. electricity growth over the next quarter century, he smiled as if to say, "This is child's play." Then he related what India faces in terms of electrical demand. Over the next few years, the country would be required to double its power capacity. After that it would have to double it again over the following decade or so. Even then, many parts of the country would remain without electricity, but at least there would be some progress. For India, meeting future energy growth is a world apart from what we face in America.

In the same vein, I recall meeting with my counterparts from China in 2003 and 2004. These meetings were aimed at assisting their government to conduct a "green" 2008 Olympiad in Beijing. Even as we discussed the technologies and programs the United States could provide, Chinese officials acknowledged that their environmental problems are overwhelming. Indeed, anyone who has traveled to China in recent years knows what relying so heavily on untreated coal can do to a nation's breathable air.

Almost every meeting I conducted with a fellow energy minister included a discussion of the geopolitics of energy. If it was a representative of an oil-importing country, the agenda always turned to the problem of supply disruptions. If it was with a nuclear energy minister, the question always turned to nuclear proliferation. And if the meeting was with one of the major oil-producing nations, the subject of production levels dominated the conversation. Inevitably, I would hear about the pressures they were receiving from Iran and Venezuela to limit production and keep prices high.

In short, every nation has its environmental threats, its geopolitical concerns, and its worries about energy security. Obviously, many of the policies outlined in this book may not apply to other nations, but I believe there are a number of actions we can take on an international basis to collectively address some of our mutual challenges.

First and foremost, I believe we should collaborate with other nations in developing energy technologies. Already, several important efforts have taken place. The Large Hadron Collider, on the French-Swiss border, is an excellent example of how a major research project can be developed on a multinational basis. The machine is an underground circular racetrack seventeen miles in diameter in which high-energy particle beams are collided as a means of investigating the nature of subatomic physics. It was built in collaboration with over ten thousand scientists and engineers from over a hundred countries and hundreds of universities and laboratories. It opened in 2008 amid the predictable alarms that colliding particle beams might blow up the universe.

Another opportunity for international research is nuclear fusion. For decades, scientists and science fiction writers have asked whether it will be possible to reproduce on earth the fusion of hydrogen atoms that powers the fires of the sun. Although a number of countries have made experimental progress, it has become clear that the costs of such an effort are beyond the financial capacity of any one nation. As a result, six entities—the United States, the European Union, Japan, South Korea, Russia, and China—have founded the International Thermonuclear Experimental Reactor Project (ITER). Even working together, it will take decades before ITER is completed. And even then, it isn't clear whether we will be able to translate the research into an energy source, but ITER is an excellent example of how the international community can work together to advance energy science.

In 2003, we launched another such collaboration, the International Partnership for the Hydrogen Economy (IPHE). This brings sixteen countries and the European Union into an alliance to work on hydrogen development. Nearly all the partner countries have now initiated or completed national strategies for hydrogen and fuel cell research and development. During my tenure as secretary, we also undertook a substantial international effort toward research in carbon sequestration via the Carbon Sequestration Leadership Forum (CSLF). Under its aegis, several major countries are now engaged in collaborative efforts to explore carbon disposition.

In my view a key part of our future energy strategy should be to develop more of these international partnerships. One technology worth pursuing on an international level is clean coal. It makes sense for countries with large coal reserves to work together to reduce its environmental impact. Other promising areas of related research are coal-to-liquid technologies and coal scrubbing.

Another obvious area of opportunity is conservation and energy efficiency. Given the increase in consumption forecast for almost every nation over the next several decades, we have to focus on curbing demand. This is an obvious area in which international collaboration can be extremely productive, particularly for improving efficiency in buildings and motor vehicles. Battery storage capacity is another promising area of research. And smart grid technology can also be taken to the international level. In this regard, the potential in Asia and other developing regions is greater because they have not yet built out their infrastructure. Just as China has virtually bypassed landlines and gone directly to cell phones, so they may be able to build their grid as "smart" from the outset.

Probably the most important area for international collaboration, however, is nuclear energy. At present, approximately thirty countries operate a total of 436 reactors producing 372,000 MW of electricity, 15% of the world's total generation. Fifty-plus countries operate over 280 smaller research reactors, and there are another 220 reactors powering submarines and navy vessels. Sixteen countries, including Japan, Slovenia, and Lithuania, actually get a higher percentage of their electricity from nuclear power than we do. Of the reactors under construction in the world right now, almost all are in Asia, with China and India starting to undertake huge efforts. None are in the United States.

Because of climate change concerns and energy demand growth, the appeal of nuclear power is likely to expand in the years ahead. With this expansion will come the issue of which countries should be allowed to manufacture their own fuel and thus have access to potential bomb material. Given the risks associated with nuclear fuel fabrication, I feel we should take a long hard look at leading the development of an international supply bank.

During my tenure as energy secretary, the Bush administration spent a great deal of time working with the International Atomic Energy Agency on this subject. Although our approach differed from the IAEA's, there was fundamental agreement that every country in the world should not be manufacturing nuclear materials. To me, this is probably the single most important area in which international cooperation will be required. Our goal should be to make nuclear energy available to all, without running the risk of nuclear proliferation.

The clandestine efforts of Pakistan's Dr. A. Q. Khan to assist other nations in making a nuclear weapon underscore the importance of establishing a strong international nuclear supplier group. Under a well-run system, countries seeking to develop nuclear energy would be provided with fuel by members of a supplier organization. The recipient country would have to follow a highly monitored system of security protocols. They would also have to commit to allowing the supplier nations to maintain control over the fuel in their reactors and to retrieve the spent rods. Such a program would probably require reexamination of the Nonproliferation Treaty (which, after the experiences of recent years, certainly needs reappraisal), but its benefits make the effort worthwhile.

Another area where more international cooperation will be required is the protection of energy infrastructure. Obviously, every nation wants to protect its own wells, pipelines, refineries, and transport networks. However, we should recognize that the disruption of energy markets anywhere in the world would have a ripple effect everywhere else. Clearly, the threat of acts of terror should be foremost in everyone's minds. Any successful attack on a major oilfield or pipeline would inflict suffering across the planet.

Thus, we face the question: Do we sit back and hope every other nation takes the necessary precautions to protect its energy assets, or should there be greater global coordination against a terrorist attack? I feel greater international cooperation is needed.

What should such an international effort look like? I believe it should start with sharing information and advanced technology. Already the United States and many other nations share intelligence in the war on terror. While we currently place some focus on the energy sector, I feel the level of intensity must be substantially upgraded. Clearly, we must be careful about providing others with proprietary or certain classified information, but protecting energy infrastructure is very important, and I believe we can collaborate on this matter without jeopardizing intellectual property or security.

Here's another area. The prospects of energy supply interruptions have been long recognized. For that reason, the United States established the Strategic Petroleum Reserve in 1979. By the time President George W. Bush took office in 2001, the SPR had been filled to 545 million barrels. Following the 9/11 attacks, however, the president decided to fill the reserve to its maximum capacity of 700 million barrels. Within a few months of the attack we began systematically adding supplies. It was a slow process. At 70,000 barrels a day, it would take us three years to reach our goal.

Nor was this effort without controversy. As energy prices rose in 2003 and 2004, members of Congress began questioning the wisdom of our policy. Then, when prices spiked, they urged us to start tapping the SPR to bring them down again. This had been done near the end of the Clinton administration. As the debate grew, I was deluged with demands that we either stop filling the SPR or release oil. I remember receiving phone calls from executives of several fuel-dependent businesses who demanded we act. These CEOs had completely bought the theory that adding oil to the SPR was the primary reason world prices were going up. (Of course, in those days, this meant prices of $30 or $40 a barrel, rather than the $130 to $140 we encountered in subsequent years.) Nothing I would say to these business leaders could persuade them any differently.

First, I would remind them that the Strategic Petroleum Reserve was designed for national security, not to manipulate oil prices. Next, I would point out that 70,000 barrels of oil per day out of worldwide consumption of 80 million barrels was a drop in the bucket. Finally, I would tell them that if the United States did succeed in driving down prices by tapping the Strategic Petroleum Reserve, OPEC could quickly reduce its production to drive them back up again.

None of these arguments was ever persuasive. I found this hard to understand. The SPR is America's most important safety net against serious supply interruptions. The total reserve only amounts to three months of our national consumption. It is foolish to start playing with it on less-than-essential occasions. Tapping it once would set a precedent for tapping it again and again, until we were relying on it for short-term supplies. Then when a real emergency occurred, there wouldn't be enough to meet the demand.

The concept of a reserve is not just important to to America's energy security, but I think we should be encouraging other countries to develop their own SPRs, as well as providing them technical help to do so. Consuming nations will all need a fallback position in the event of a serious world crisis, and this is an area where we should be working together.

In addition to devising international collaborations the United States must also work to strengthen our relationships with energy producers. Clearly, the war in Iraq strained America's relationships in the Middle East. But a change of administration offers an opportunity to redefine our interactions in the region. Of course, as long as the specter of terrorism threatens the West, there will be challenges to our relationships with some Arab countries. This should in no way prevent us from maintaining strong ties to most of the energy-producing states.

There are other opportunities to strengthen our relationships with producing nations. West Africa has become an important supplier of oil and gas. George W. Bush's efforts in Africa had a significant positive impact there, and we should build on those ties. Ultimately, this means helping as President Bush did on the AIDS crisis and trying to stabilize the region. President Obama is excellently positioned to take this to the next level. A stable West Africa has the potential to ramp up production dramatically in the coming decades.

Probably the most significant new energy market of the future will be Latin America. From Mexico to Argentina, there is huge potential for expanded energy production. Unfortunately, many of these countries have had unpleasant experiences with foreign developers, specifically American. The Mexican constitution actually prohibits foreign investment and ownership of energy assets. When Vicente Fox became president, he tried to change these laws to attract foreign investment, but was unsuccessful largely because of the impression that it would lead to U.S. exploitation.

When I first ran for United States Senate in 1994, like many other candidates I ran against Washington. Until I became secretary of energy I just assumed that running against Washington was confined to candidates for federal office in America. I soon discovered that running against Washington is a universal political strategy. In energy-rich countries throughout Latin America, candidates commonly base their campaigns on the charge that their opponent is too close to Washington. In these places one of easiest ways to court popular favor is to say your opponent is too receptive to American investment in the energy market. The result is that vast amounts of energy resources in Latin America remain untapped. The countries cannot afford to develop them on their own, but it is politically risky to accept outside capital. Hopefully, some of this resistance can be addressed in the years ahead.

Latin America's energy picture is also clouded by the unpredictable actions of Hugo Chávez, president of Venezuela. President Chávez has frequently threatened to declare an energy war against the United States. No one takes him very seriously because Venezuela is highly dependent on revenue it generates from sales to our country. In fact, Venezuela actually owns the CITGO gas station chain, which has a large share of the U.S. market, so we can assume that Venezuela will probably not place CITGO at risk by pursuing these threats. I do believe, however, that Venezuela's behind-the-scenes actions have made it much harder for foreign energy companies, especially American ones, to operate in Central and South America. A good example is the way things have unraveled in Ecuador. There a new government decided to expel Occidental Petroleum Co. from its energy operations in 2007. The government leaders appeared to be highly influenced by Venezuela.

I got a first-hand view of this undercurrent in 2004. As secretary I represented the United States at the Tobago meeting of the Western Hemispheric Energy Ministerial Conference, a loose association of energy ministers that convenes periodically. For the most part, the biggest accomplishment at these sessions is a communiqué stating our continuing interest in working together on common energy problems. The 2004 meeting looked to be the same until Venezuela arrived intent on challenging the United States over any and all issues. Since nothing of much importance was being discussed, the Venezuelan delegates decided to argue the wording of the communiqué. They repeatedly demanded changes in the document, even though it was mostly boilerplate material. Since there was nothing controversial about the document, the energy minister of Trinidad and Tobago and I, in our roles as cochairmen, agreed to their every amendment. This utterly frustrated the Venezuelan delegates, who were unable to provoke a confrontation. The meeting ended with no blows struck.

While this conference produced no real incidents, there is no question in my mind that Venezuela will continue to try to turn our Latin American neighbors against us. Therefore, it is imperative that we devote more attention to building stronger ties in the region, particularly where it relates to energy. America will benefit, but so will the world if Mexico and the Latin American nations are able to expand their energy output in the future.

A final area of importance is the Caspian region, where nations such as Kazakhstan and Azerbaijan have enormous energy potential. The United States must continue to encourage these nations to develop their resources and build the infrastructure to bring them to market. During my tenure we helped these nations launch the Baku-Tbilisi-Ceyhan pipeline, a thousand-mile-long conduit connecting the Caspian region with the Mediterranean Sea, constructed with the effort of companies from Greece, France, and the United States. The pipeline has been particularly helpful to Kazakhstan, which had been looking for a way to export its oil without transporting it through Russia. The Russians and Iranians have blocked Kazakhstan from building its own Trans-Caspian pipeline, but the Kazakhs are now shipping their oil in tankers across the Caspian Sea to connect with the pipeline at Baku. This was a major victory for U.S. policy, for it prevented the bottling up of supplies in the Caspian and Muslim states to its south. We will have to be equally alert to assure that supplies can reach the West from other corners of the globe.

U.S. energy policy involves us in global affairs whether we like it or not. While the topic of climate change has dominated discussions in recent years, it is important to remember that other energy issues require our attention as well. China and Russia are busy making friends, signing deals, and trying to lock up long-term contracts for oil throughout the world. We must be equally active. Failing to expand the scope of our international energy operations could have a very detrimental effect on both America and the rest of the world for decades.

Conclusion

I began this book by outlining some of the many myths that have corrupted serious debate about energy policy. No, the oil companies do not engage in periodic conspiracies to briefly spike the price of gasoline. No, climate change is not a gigantic hoax being foisted on the world. No, despite the scary claims, nuclear power plants are extremely safe to build and operate. Unhappily, myths like these have contributed to the stalemate that has prevented serious progress on energy policy.

While it is true that many of the frightening stories about energy are merely myths, the indubitable facts that confront us are in many ways more disturbing. The United States has become extremely dependent on foreign sources of energy. The amount of carbon we emit into the atmosphere is growing at a dramatic pace. The projected increase in energy demand over the coming two decades is enormous and will be extremely difficult to meet. All of these energy realities present us with serious challenges of a global nature. Failing to surmount them will have dire political, economic, and environmental consequences. We have two choices: sit around and wait to be caught up in various geopolitical energy crises by pursuing the failed approaches of the past, or take aggressive action to protect our security.

Unfortunately, we've spent decades avoiding the tough decisions on energy. The fault is not the province of one political party or one branch of government. There is plenty of blame to go around. Businesses, environmental groups, the media, and the public have all contributed to the impasse that has blocked action in Washington. Decision makers have failed, in part, because they've attempted to pursue policies that were inevitably contradictory. We have also erred by trying to find shortcuts to our goals. Our misguided view that we can solve all the energy problems we face by relying on one or two superfuels will not get the job done. Nor will we make much progress if we continue to defer tough decisions in the vain hope that a new Manhattan Project will somehow come along to address all our energy concerns.

What is needed are clear objectives, fortitude, and tough decisions. As a nation we need to commit to reconfiguring our power generation sector so that by the year 2030 we derive 30% of our electricity from nuclear energy, 30% from natural gas and coal gasification, and 20% from hydroelectricity and other renewable sources like wind and solar power. Finally, we must increase our energy efficiency so we reduce the growth of demand by at least 10% over the coming two decades as well.

For this to happen, we need to make a national commitment to building at least fifty new nuclear power plants over the next twenty years. To facilitate that construction the federal government needs to provide investment capital to cover up to 50% of the project financing (or assume responsibility for cost overruns) in exchange for proportionate ownership. This may seem like a formidable expenditure, but I would argue that investments like these and similar commitments to expanding our renewable energy and clean coal production are critical to American security. I believe that energy assets will increasingly become high-level terrorist targets. I also see the real possibility of political and military confrontations over access to energy taking place in the decades ahead. Therefore, if necessary, I strongly support shifting some resources from the war on terror and our other security priorities to insuring that we have a dependable, growing, domestic supply of affordable energy.

The government also needs to embark upon a serious effort to address the issue of nuclear waste. It's time to begin reprocessing our waste, just as so many other industrial countries that deploy nuclear energy already do.

At the same time, we need to pave the way for major increases in the use of renewable energy and in energy efficiency. These industries and conservation efforts require a long-term commitment of federal incentives to bring about the desired results. Instead of short-term tax breaks, we need a decade-long program whose certainty provides reassurance to investors, developers, and energy consumers.

Because the promise of improved energy efficiency is so great with respect to electricity transmission, it is critical that the federal government lay the groundwork for the modernization of our electrical grid and the introduction of intelligent transmission systems on a nationwide basis. This will mean expanding federal authority over the siting of transmission lines, despite the predictable opposition of state and local officials. It will also mean that if regional and local power authorities fail to adopt smart grid technology systems, Washington has the ability to mandate their deployment.

We also must continue our robust investment in energy research at the federal level and, if possible, take it to an even more productive level. Congressional micromanagement of federal energy research efforts must end, and short-term efforts must be replaced by long-term commitments to projects so that their promise can be fulfilled.

To speed the transition of our coal sector, we must deploy a fleet of new, clean coal-gasification power plants over the next twenty years that utilize full carbon capture and disposition. As with nuclear energy, we need federal financial support to help capitalize these ventures. We also need to develop effective carbon sequestration capabilities for these facilities, along with the ability to transport carbon from carbon-capture sites to disposition locations.

Even as we transition toward a more diverse power generation sector, America still needs to use large quantities of its own natural resources if we are to enhance our energy security. It's time we reform the process by which energy development decisions are made so that national interests are given precedent over political ones. Thus, we need to create a high-level federal commission empowered to make resource development decisions about the exploration for resources off the U.S. coasts and on federal lands.

Finally, we must remember that we are not alone in confronting an uncertain energy future. The problems we face are in most cases global ones, and a lot of the solutions to those problems will come from international energy collaboration. Whether it's protecting energy assets, developing new high-cost energy technologies, expanding the use of nuclear power in a way that minimizes the risk of nuclear proliferation, or enhancing the ability of energy-producing countries to help meet the world's needs, we must restore America's traditional role of leadership on energy in the decades ahead.

As noted in the preface to this book, I arrived at the Department of Energy in 2001 amid an energy crisis that was mercifully short in duration but regrettably substantial in terms of its consequences to the people and businesses of California. Throughout my tenure and since my departure from the department, other energy-related crises arose both here and around the world. Each time, fortunately, we found a way to avert disaster. But I believe we really are living on borrowed time.

In my opinion, our global economic future is directly linked to our ability to address the energy threats posed in this book. Will America as well as the developing world enjoy the economic growth we desire, consistent with strong environmental stewardship, or will the years ahead be marked by repeated experiences like the world economic disaster of 2008–09? To a large extent, the answer depends on whether we are able to meet our energy challenges.

Will geopolitical interests or the objectives of terrorists imperil our energy security and destabilize the global community, or will we be able to maintain sound and secure energy markets in the years to come? This, too, will depend on whether we meet our energy challenges in a strong and constructive way.

A lot is now at stake, and we must not lose more time in addressing the issues. Rather than rely any longer on the old politics of energy and the failed decision-making approaches of the past, we need action now.

During my first few days as energy secretary I remember thinking about the consequences of seeing the lights go out in California for an extended period of time. What if rolling blackouts gave way to one long extended blackout? Later, during the Great Northeast Blackout of 2003, we got a taste of what that would be like, and it wasn't very pretty. It is in this context that we have to think about the implications of continuing to ignore energy priorities. We have to imagine what would happen if our desire to play politics with energy issues postpones tough decisions too long. We have to recognize that the time for moving forward is upon us and that we have an obligation, as public policy makers and as citizens, to solve our energy problems today. This is a formidable challenge, and it will take a national commitment and a lot of hard work and sacrifice to achieve it. But it is a challenge that must be met fully, and soon, before the lights really do go out.

Campbell, C. J. *The Coming Oil Crisis*. Brentwood, Essex, England: Multiscience Publishing Company & Petroconsultants, S.A., 1988.

Cohen, Bernard. *The Nuclear Energy Option: An Alternative for the 1990s*. New York: Plenum Press, 1990.

Cravens, Gwyneth. *Power to Save the World: The Truth About Nuclear Energy*. New York: Alfred A. Knopf, 2007.

Darley, Julian. *High Noon for Natural Gas: The New Energy Crisis*. White River Junction, Vt.: Chelsea Green Publishing Company, 2004.

Deffeyes, Kenneth S. *Beyond Oil: The View From Hubbert's Peak*. New York: Hill & Wang, 2005.

Deffeyes, Kenneth S. *Hubbert's Peak: The Impending World Oil Shortage*. Princeton, N.J.: Princeton University Press, 2001.

Deutch, John M.; Lauvergeon, Anne; Prawiraatmadia, Widhyawan. *Energy Security and Climate Change: A Report to the Trilateral Commission: 61*. Triangle Papers, 2007.

Domenici, Pete V. *A Brighter Tomorrow: Fulfilling the Promise of Nuclear Energy*. Lanham, Md.: Rowman & Littlefield, 2004.

Fargione, Joseph, et. al. "Land Clearing and the Biofuel Carbon Debt," *Science* 319:1235 (2008).

Flannery, Tim. *The Weather Makers*. New York: Atlantic Monthly Press, 2005.

Ford, Daniel. *The Cult of the Atom: The Secret Papers of the Atomic Energy Commission*. New York: Simon & Schuster, 1982.

Freeman, S. David. *Winning Our Energy Independence.* Layton, Ohio: Gibbs Smith Publisher, 2007.

Freese, Barbara. *Coal: A Human History.* Cambridge, Mass.: Perseus Publishing, 2003.

Gamov, George. *Thirty Years That Shook Physics.* New York: Doubleday Anchor Books, 1966.

Goodell, Jeff. *Big Coal: The Dirty Secret Behind America's Energy Future.* Boston: Houghton Mifflin Company, 2006.

Gore, Al. *An Inconvenient Truth.* Emmaus, Pa.: Rodale Press, 2006.

Herken, Gregg. *The Brotherhood of the Bomb: The Tangled Lives and Loyalties of Robert Oppenheimer, Ernest Lawrence, and Edward Teller.* New York: Henry Holt and Company, 2002.

Horner, Christopher C. *The Politically Incorrect Guide to Global Warming and Environmentalism.* Washington, D.C.: Regnery Publishing, 2007.

Huber, Peter, and Mark P. Mills. *The Bottomless Well: The Twilight of Fuel, the Virtue of Waste, and Why We Will Never Run Out of Energy.* New York: Basic Books, 2005.

Jungk, Robert. *Brighter Than 1,000 Suns: The Moral and Political History of the Atomic Scientist.* London: Victor Gollancz Ltd., 1958.

Kemeny, John G. *The Need for Change: The Legacy of TMI; Report of the President's Commission on the Accident at Three Mile Island.* Washington, D.C.: Government Printing Office, 1979.

Klare, Michael. *Resource Wars: The New Landscape of Global Conflict.* New York: Henry Holt and Company, 2001.

Kolbert, Elizabeth. *Field Notes to a Catastrophe: Man, Nature, and Climate Change.* New York: Bloomsbury, 2006.

Krupp, Fred, with Miriam Horn. *Earth: The Sequel, The Race to Reinvent Energy and Stop Global Warming.* New York: W. W. Norton, 2008.

Lomborg, Bjorn. *The Skeptical Environmentalist: Measuring the Real State of the World.* London: Cambridge University Press, 2001.

Lovins, Amory B. *Soft Energy Paths: Toward a Durable Peace.* New York: Harper & Row, 1977.

Mahaffey, James. *Atomic Awakening: A New Look at the History and Future of Nuclear Power.* New York: Pegasus Books, 2009.

McPhee, John. *The Curve of Binding Energy.* New York: Farrar, Straus & Giroux, 1973.

———*Encounters with the Archdruid.* New York: Farrar, Straus & Giroux, 1971.

Rhodes, Richard. *The Making of the Atomic Bomb.* New York: Touchstone, 1986.

Roberts, Paul. *The End of Oil: On the Edge of a Perilous New World.* Boston: Houghton Mifflin Company, 2004.

Rockwell, Theodore. *Creating the New World: Stories and Images From the Dawn of the Atomic Age.* Bloomington, Ind.: First Books, 2004.

Romm, Joseph. *Hell and High Water.* New York: William Morrow, 2007.

Romm, Joseph. *The Hype About Hydrogen: Fact and Fiction in the Race to Save the Climate.* Washington, D.C.: Island Press, 2004.

Scheer, Herman. *The Solar Economy: Renewable Energy for a Sustainable Future.* London: Earthscan, 2002.

Schewe, Phillip F. *The Grid: A Journey Through the Heart of Our Electrified World.* Washington, D.C.: Joseph Henry Press, 2007.

Schulz, Max. *Energy and Environment: Myths and Facts.* New York: Manhattan Institute, 2007.

Searchinger, Timothy, et al. "Use of U.S. Croplands for Biofuels Increases Greenhouse Gases Through Emissions From Land-Use Change," *Science* 319:1235 (2008).

Siddiqui, O. *The Green Grid: Energy Savings and Carbon Emissions Reductions Enabled by a Smart Grid.* Electric Power Research Institute, June 2008.

Simmons, Matthew R. *Twilight in the Desert: The Coming Saudi Oil Shock and the World Economy.* Hoboken, N.J.: John Wiley & Sons, 2005.

Smil, Vaclav. *Energy at the Crossroads: Global Perspectives and Uncertainties.* Cambridge, Mass.: MIT Press, 2003.

Sweet, William. *Kicking the Carbon Habit: Global Warming and the Case for Renewable and Nuclear Energy.* New York: Columbia University Press, 2006.

Tucker, William. *Terrestrial Energy: How Nuclear Power Will Lead the Green Revolution and End America's Energy Odyssey.* Savage, Md.: Bartleby Press, 2008.

Vaitheeswaran, Vijay. *Power to the People: How the Coming Energy Revolution Will Transform an Industry, Change Our Lives, and May Even Save the Planet.* New York: Farrar, Straus & Giroux, 2003.

Von Baeyer, Hans Christian. *Warmth Disperses and Time Passes: The History of Heat.* New York: Modern Library, 1999.

Walker, J. Samuel. *Permissible Dose: A History of Radiation Protection in the Twentieth Century.* Berkeley: University of California Press, 2000.

Walker, Nikki. *Generating Wind Power.* New York: Crabtree Publishing Company, 2007.

Waltar, Alan E. *Radiation and Modern Life: Fulfilling Marie Curie's Dream.* Amherst, N.Y.: Prometheus Books, 2004.

Watts, Steven. *The People's Tycoon: Henry Ford and the American Century.* New York: Vintage Books, 2005.

Weinberg, Alvin. *The First Nuclear Era: The Life and Times of a Technological Fixer.* Woodbury, N.Y.: American Institute of Physics Press, 1994.

Whitcomb, Robert and Wendy Williams. *Cape Wind: Money, Celebrity, Energy, Class Politics, and the Battle for Our Energy Future.* New York: Public Affairs, 2007

Wilson, Jeff. *The Manhattan Project of 2009: Energy Independence NOW.* Jeff Wilson, 2009.

Yergin, Daniel. *The Prize: The Epic Quest for Oil, Money and Power.* New York: Simon & Schuster, 1991.